HOW GREAT IS OUR GOD

How GREAT is our GOD

TIMELESS DAILY READINGS
ON THE NATURE OF GOD

NavPress
Discipleship Inside Out™

NAVPRESS
Discipleship Inside Out™

NavPress is the publishing ministry of The Navigators, an international Christian organization and leader in personal spiritual development. NavPress is committed to helping people grow spiritually and enjoy lives of meaning and hope through personal and group resources that are biblically rooted, culturally relevant, and highly practical.

For a free catalog go to www.NavPress.com
or call 1.800.366.7788 in the United States or 1.800.839.4769 in Canada.

ISBN-13: 978-1-61291-078-9

Text compiled by Thomas Womack
Cover design by Studiogearbox
Cover image by istockphoto

Printed in the United States of America

1 2 3 4 5 6 7 8 / 16 15 14 13 12 11

Foreword

The collection you hold in your hands is a gathering in one place of some of the best writing of our time — as well as of earlier days — on the nature of God. These are stunning and memorable words that have deeply influenced generations in the movement of discipleship to Jesus. The best books are timeless, and most often they cross cultural barriers. Created by a dozen outstanding authors, the selections in this book have stood the test of time and have shown the power to touch a new generation of disciples in many settings around the world.

Jesus said, "Every teacher of the law who has been instructed about the kingdom of heaven is like the owner of a house who brings out of his storeroom new treasures as well as old" (Matthew 13:52, NIV). At NavPress, we are conscious of both the old and the new, and we treasure both. We live in a world of profound change in publishing, and NavPress is at the forefront of keeping up with the new media. But we are also looking to our faith's heritage for classic writing that never lets us forget where we have come from and to pass along those timeless messages that have proven to change lives. That's the kind of writing you hold in your hands — some of the greatest selections on the nature of our God.

The ministry of The Navigators began in the 1930s through the call of God to Dawson Trotman. Trotman's vision was to teach others, one-to-one, the biblical principles of discipleship he found beneficial in his own life. He began to teach high school students and local Sunday school classes. In 1933, he and his friends extended their work to reach out to sailors in the U.S. Navy. From there, Trotman met and established a partnership with the then up-and-coming evangelist Billy Graham.

One of the men Trotman chose to lead the work with Billy Graham was Lorne Sanny. Sanny went on to become Trotman's successor and served The Navigators for thirty years as its president. This book contains writing that is what Lorne Sanny used to call "life-borne" messages. These are messages that grow out of a life steeped in the Scriptures and lived out in passionate love and obedience to God. They are tested in real life, and they have a practical authenticity that prompts genuine transformation.

Over the years, I personally have been touched by all the messages in this collection. Each one is part of the fabric of my own discipleship. Now I'm convinced that you, too, will find in them an abundance of godly stimulation and transformative guidance for your own walk with God.

DR. MICHAEL D. MILLER
president, NavPress
chief business officer, The Navigators

God's Invitation

Those who know your name put their trust in you, for you, O Lord, have not forsaken those who seek you.

(Psalm 9:10, esv)

God is not a concept or a doctrine. He is a Person who seeks a close, one-on-one relationship with you and me. God does not want us to merely believe in Him, He wants to relate to us on a personal level. He does not just want to hear us recite prayers. He wants to converse with us. God's plan is not to abandon Christians once we are born again, leaving us to build the best life we can. He does not intend that we simply use our wits to "get by," to bravely "survive" until we are finally ushered into heaven. God wants to be actively involved in our lives each day.

God knows what your life can become. Only He understands your full potential as His child. He does not want you to miss out on anything He has for you. I believe that within the heart of every Christian is an innate desire to know God and to do His will.

When you became a Christian, you were immediately adopted as a child of the heavenly King. The King's business became your business. And now, as your Savior and Lord, Christ wants to bring your life into the middle of His activity, which offers salvation to every person on earth. God Himself will give you the desire to serve and obey Him. The Holy Spirit will create within you a longing to know the Father's will and to become involved in what God is doing around you.

Yet God has far more in store for your life than merely giving you an assignment to accomplish for Him. He wants you to have an intimate love relationship with Him that is real and personal. Jesus said: "This is eternal life: that they may know You, the only true God, and the One You have sent — Jesus Christ" (John 17:3, hcsb).

Henry Blackaby and Richard Blackaby, in *Experiencing God*

Meeting Our Greatest Need

God shows his love for us in that while we were still sinners, Christ died for us.

(Romans 5:8, ESV)

In times of prolonged adversity, we can begin to entertain thoughts that essentially assert that we're more concerned about goodness than God is.

Even righteous Job came to the place where he questioned the goodness of God. He said, "I am in the right, and God has taken away my right," and "It profits a man nothing that he should take delight in God" (Job 34:5,9, ESV).

If God is perfect in His love and abundant in His goodness, how do we take a stand against our own doubts and the temptations of Satan to question the goodness of God? What truths about God do we need to store up in our hearts to use as weapons against temptations to doubt His love?

There's no doubt that the most convincing evidence of God's love in all of Scripture is His giving His Son to die for our sins. "This is how God showed his love among us: He sent his one and only Son into the world that we might live through him. This is love: not that we loved God, but that he loved us and sent his Son as an atoning sacrifice for our sins" (1 John 4:9-10, NIV).

Our greatest need is not freedom from adversity. No calamity in this life could in any way be compared with the absolute calamity of eternal separation from God. In like manner, Jesus said no earthly joy could compare with the eternal joy of our names written in heaven (see Luke 10:20).

God showed His love by meeting our greatest need—a need so great that no other can come close to it in comparison. If we want proof of God's love for us, then we must look first at the Cross where God offered up His Son as a sacrifice for our sins. Calvary is the one objective, absolute, irrefutable proof of God's love for us.

Jerry Bridges, in *Trusting God*

FOLLOWING HARD AFTER GOD

My soul clings to you; your right hand upholds me.
(PSALM 63:8, NIV)

Christian theology teaches the doctrine of prevenient grace, which briefly stated means this, that before a man can seek God, God must first have sought the man.

Before a sinful man can think a right thought of God, there must have been a work of enlightenment done within him; imperfect it may be, but a true work nonetheless, and the secret cause of all desiring and seeking and praying which may follow.

We pursue God because, and only because, He has first put an urge within us that spurs us to the pursuit. "No man can come to me," said our Lord, "except the Father which hath sent me draw him" (John 6:44, KJV), and it is by this very prevenient drawing that God takes from us every vestige of credit for the act of coming. The impulse to pursue God originates with God, but the outworking of that impulse is our following hard after Him; and all the time we are pursuing Him we are already in His hand: "Thy right hand upholdeth me" (Psalm 63:8, KJV).

In this divine "upholding" and human "following" there is no contradiction. All is of God, for as Baron von Hügel teaches, God is always previous. In practice, however, (that is, where God's previous working meets man's present response) man must pursue God. On our part there must be positive reciprocation if this secret drawing of God is to eventuate in identifiable experience of the Divine. In the warm language of personal feeling this is stated in the forty-second Psalm: "As the hart panteth after the water brooks, so panteth my soul after thee, O God. My soul thirsteth for God, for the living God: when shall I come and appear before God?" (KJV). This is deep calling unto deep, and the longing heart will understand it.

A. W. TOZER, IN *THE PURSUIT OF GOD*

Can You Trust God?

Do not boast about tomorrow,
for you do not know what a day may bring.
(Proverbs 27:1, esv)

For most of us, life is filled with frustrations, anxieties, and disappointments that tempt us to fret, fume, and worry. One author has aptly captured the flavor of this in a devotional book for high schoolers entitled, *If God Loves Me, Why Can't I Get My Locker Open?* We may smile a little at that, but the fact is, this is the plane of adversity on which many of us live each day. And it is in the crucible of even this minor level of adversity that we are tempted to wonder, "Can I trust God?"

Even when life seems to be going our way and our daily path seems pleasant and smooth, we do not know what the future holds. Someone has described life as like having a thick curtain hung across one's path, a curtain that recedes before us as we advance, but only step by step. None of us can tell what is beyond that curtain; none of us can tell what events a single day or hour may bring into our lives. Sometimes the receding curtain reveals events much as we had expected them; often it reveals events most unexpected and frequently most undesired, filling us with anxiety, frustration, heartache, and grief.

God's people are not immune from such pain. In fact it often seems as if theirs is more severe, more frequent, more unexplainable, and more deeply felt than that of the unbeliever. The problem of pain is as old as the history of man and just as universal. Even creation itself, Paul tells us, has been subjected to frustration and groans as in the pain of childbirth (see Romans 8:20-22).

So the question naturally arises, "Where is God in all of this?" Can you really trust God when adversity strikes and fills your life with pain? Does He indeed come to the rescue of those who seek Him?

Can you trust God?

Jerry Bridges, in *Trusting God*

ALWAYS THIS WAY

Obey my voice, and I will be your God, and you shall be my people.

(JEREMIAH 7:23, ESV)

What God wants from His people is obedience, no matter the circumstances, no matter how unknown the outcome.

It has always been this way — God calling His people to obedience and giving them at best a glimpse of the outcome of their effort.

Most of the great figures of the Old Testament died without seeing the fulfillment of the promise they relied upon. Paul expended himself building the early church, but as his life drew to a close he could see only a string of tiny outposts along the Mediterranean, many weakened by fleshly indulgence or divided over doctrinal disputes.

In more recent times, the great colonial pastor Cotton Mather prayed for revival several hours each day for twenty years; the Great Awakening began the year he died. The British Empire finally abolished slavery as the Christian parliamentarian and abolitionist leader William Wilberforce lay on his deathbed, exhausted from his nearly fifty-year campaign against the practice of human bondage. Few were the converts during Hudson Taylor's lifelong mission work in the Orient; but today millions of Chinese embrace the faith he so patiently implanted and tended.

Some might think this divine pattern cruel, but I am convinced there is a sovereign wisdom to it. Knowing how susceptible we are to success's siren call, God does not allow us to see, and therefore glory in, what is done through us. The very nature of the obedience He demands is that it be given without regard to circumstances or results. The centurion in Luke 7:5-13 rightly perceived Jesus' authority as that of a military commander to whom one gives unquestioning allegiance.

The Bible makes clear that unquestioning acceptance of and obedience to Jesus' authority is the foundation of the Christian life. Everything else rests upon this.

CHARLES COLSON, IN *LOVING GOD*

Blessed Dependence

For God alone my soul waits in silence; from him comes my salvation.
(Psalm 62:1, esv)

If salvation indeed comes from God and is entirely His work, just as creation was, it follows as a matter of course that our first and highest duty is to wait on Him to do the work that pleases Him. Waiting becomes then the only way to the experience of a full salvation, the only way, truly, to know God as the God of our salvation.

All the difficulties that are brought forward as keeping us back from full salvation have their cause in this one thing: the defective knowledge and practice of waiting upon God. All that the church and its members need for the manifestation of the mighty power of God in the world, is the return to our true place, the place that belongs to us, both in creation and redemption — the place of absolute and unceasing dependence upon God. Let us strive to see what the elements are that make up this most blessed and needful waiting upon God: it may help us to discover the reasons why this grace is so little cultivated and to feel how infinitely desirable it is that the church, that we ourselves, should at any price learn its blessed secret.

The deep need for this waiting on God lies equally in the nature of man and the nature of God. God, as Creator, formed man to be a vessel in which He could show forth His power and goodness. Man was not to have in himself a fountain of life, or strength, or happiness: the ever-living and only living One was each moment to be the Communicator to him of all that he needed. Man's glory and blessedness was not to be independent, or dependent upon himself, but dependent on a God of such infinite riches and love. Man was to have the joy of receiving every moment out of the fullness of God. This was his blessedness as an unfallen creature.

Andrew Murray, in *Waiting on God*

Consent to Dependence

Our eyes look to the Lord our God, till he has mercy upon us.
(Psalm 123:2, esv)

When man fell from God, he was even more absolutely dependent on Him. There was not the slightest hope of his recovery out of his state of death, except in God, His power and mercy. It is God alone who began the work of redemption; it is God alone who continues and carries it on each moment in each individual believer. Even in the regenerate man there is no power of goodness in himself: he has and can have nothing that he does not each moment receive; and waiting on God is just as indispensable, and must be just as continuous and unbroken, as the breathing that maintains his natural life.

It is because Christians do not know their relation to God of absolute poverty and helplessness that they have no sense of the need of absolute and unceasing dependence, or the unspeakable blessedness of continual waiting on God. But when a believer begins to see it, and consent to it — that he by the Holy Spirit must each moment receive what God each moment works — waiting on God becomes his brightest hope and joy. As he apprehends how God — as God, as Infinite Love — delights to impart His own nature to His child as fully as He can, how God is not weary of each moment keeping charge of his life and strength, he wonders that he ever thought otherwise of God than as a God to be waited on all the day. God unceasingly giving and working, His child unceasingly waiting and receiving: this is the blessed life.

"Truly my soul waiteth upon God: from him cometh my salvation" (Psalm 62:1, kjv). Waiting on God is the ascribing to Him the glory of being All; it is the experiencing that He is All to us.

Andrew Murray, in *Waiting on God*

A Response of Wonder

As one trespass led to condemnation for all men, so one act of righteousness leads to justification and life for all men.
(Romans 5:18, esv)

The doctrine of justification by faith — a biblical truth, and a blessed relief from sterile legalism and unavailing self-effort — has in our time fallen into evil company and been interpreted by many in such manner as actually to bar men from the knowledge of God. The whole transaction of religious conversion has been made mechanical and spiritless. Faith may now be exercised without a jar to the moral life and without embarrassment to the Adamic ego. Christ may be "received" without creating any special love for Him in the soul of the receiver. The man is "saved," but he is not hungry nor thirsty after God. In fact he is specifically taught to be satisfied and encouraged to be content with little.

The modern scientist has lost God amid the wonders of His world; we Christians are in real danger of losing God amid the wonders of His Word. We have almost forgotten that God is a Person and, as such, can be cultivated as any person can. It is inherent in personality to be able to know other personalities, but full knowledge of one personality by another cannot be achieved in one encounter. It is only after long and loving mental intercourse that the full possibilities of both can be explored.

All social intercourse between human beings is a response of personality to personality, grading upward from the most casual brush between man and man to the fullest, most intimate communion of which the human soul is capable. Religion, so far as it is genuine, is in essence the response of created personalities to the Creating Personality, God.

"This is life eternal, that they might know thee the only true God, and Jesus Christ, whom thou hast sent" (John 17:3, kjv).

A. W. Tozer, in *The Pursuit of God*

Eternal Life — Now

I came that they may have life and have it abundantly.
(John 10:10, esv)

The essence of eternal life is for you to personally know God the Father and Jesus Christ, His Son. Knowing God does not come through a program, a study, or a method. It is the result of a vibrant, growing, one-on-one relationship with God. Within this intimate connection, God will reveal Himself, His purposes, and His ways so you can know Him in deeper and profound dimensions. As you relate to Him, God will invite you to join in His activity where He is already at work. When you obey what God tells you, He will accomplish through you things only He can do. As the Lord works in and through your life, you will come to know Him ever more closely.

Jesus said, "I have come that they may have life and have it in abundance" (John 10:10, hcsb). Would you like to experience life in its fullest and richest dimensions? You may, if you are willing to respond to God's invitation to enjoy an intimate love relationship with Him.

Anything of spiritual significance that happens in your life will be a result of God's activity in you. He is infinitely more concerned with your life and your relationship with Him than you or I could possibly be. Let God's Spirit bring you into an intimate relationship with the Lord of the universe "who is able to do above and beyond all that we ask or think — according to the power that works in you" (Ephesians 3:20, hcsb). *Would you pray and surrender your life to God so He may guide and instruct you in any way He pleases?* As you prepare to obey Him, trust that God who has already begun a good work in you will complete it in His time (see Philippians 1:6).

Henry Blackaby and Richard Blackaby, in *Experiencing God*

The Keynote of Life

When the Lord restores the fortunes of his people,
let Jacob rejoice, let Israel be glad.
(Psalm 14:7, ESV)

"I have waited for thy salvation, O Lord!" (Genesis 49:18, KJV). It is not easy to say exactly in what sense Jacob used these words, in the midst of his prophecies in regard to the future of his sons. But they do certainly dictate that both for himself and for them his expectation was from God alone. It was God's salvation he waited for; a salvation that God had promised and that God alone could work out. He knew himself and his sons to be under God's charge. Jehovah the Everlasting God would show in them what His saving power is and does.

The words point forward to that wonderful history of redemption, which is not yet finished, and to the glorious future in eternity whither it is leading. They suggest to us how there is no salvation but God's salvation, and how waiting on God for that, whether for our personal experience, or in wider circles, is our first duty, our true blessedness.

God cannot part with His grace, or goodness, or strength, as an external thing that He gives us, as He gives the raindrops from heaven. No; He can only give it, and we can only enjoy it, as He works it Himself directly and unceasingly. And the only reason that He does not work it more effectually and continuously is that we do not let Him. We hinder Him either by our indifference or by our self-effort so that He cannot do what He would.

What He asks of us, in the way of surrender, and obedience, and desire, and trust, is all comprised in this one word: waiting on Him, waiting for His salvation. It combines the deep sense of our entire helplessness of ourselves to work what is divinely good, and our perfect confidence that our God will work it all in His divine power.

Andrew Murray, in *Waiting on God*

SURVEYING A GREAT MOUNTAIN

And many peoples shall come, and say:
"Come, let us go up to the mountain of the LORD."
(ISAIAH 2:3, ESV)

Recognizing that the study of God is worthwhile, we prepare to start. But where shall we start from? How do we plot our course?

Five basic truths, five foundation-principles of the knowledge about God that Christians have, will determine our course throughout:

1. God has spoken to man, and the Bible is His Word, given to us to make us wise unto salvation.
2. God is Lord and King over His world; He rules all things for His own glory, displaying His perfections in all that He does, in order that men and angels may worship and adore Him.
3. God is Savior, active in sovereign love through the Lord Jesus Christ to rescue believers from the guilt and power of sin, to adopt them as His sons, and to bless them accordingly.
4. God is Triune; there are within the Godhead three persons, the Father, the Son, and the Holy Ghost; and the work of salvation is one in which all three act together, the Father purposing redemption, the Son securing it, and the Spirit applying it.
5. Godliness means responding to God's revelation in trust and obedience, faith and worship, prayer and praise, submission and service. Life must be seen and lived in the light of God's Word.

In light of these general and basic truths, we examine in detail what the Bible shows us of the nature and character of the God of whom we have been speaking.

We are in the position of travelers who, after surveying a great mountain from afar, traveling round it, and observing how it dominates the landscape and determines the features of the surrounding countryside, now approach it directly with the intention of climbing it.

J. I. PACKER, IN *KNOWING GOD*

Personal and Conscious

Let him who boasts boast in this, that he understands and knows me.

(Jeremiah 9:24, esv)

God is a Person, and in the deep of His mighty nature He thinks, wills, enjoys, feels, loves, desires, and suffers as any other person may. In making Himself known to us He stays by the familiar pattern of personality. He communicates with us through the avenues of our minds, our wills, and our emotions. The continuous and unembarrassed interchange of love and thought between God and the soul of the redeemed man is the throbbing heart of New Testament religion.

This intercourse between God and the soul is known to us in conscious personal awareness. It is personal: that is, it does not come through the body of believers, as such, but is known to the individual, and to the body through the individuals who compose it. And it is conscious: that is, it does not stay below the threshold of consciousness and work there unknown to the soul (as, for instance, infant baptism is thought by some to do), but comes within the field of awareness where the man can "know" it as he knows any other fact of experience.

You and I are in little (our sins excepted) what God is in large. Being made in His image we have within us the capacity to know Him. In our sins we lack only the power. The moment the Spirit has quickened us to life in regeneration our whole being senses its kinship to God and leaps up in joyous recognition. That is the heavenly birth without which we cannot see the kingdom of God. It is, however, not an end but an inception, for now begins the glorious pursuit, the heart's happy exploration of the infinite riches of the Godhead.

That is where we begin, I say, but where we stop no man has yet discovered, for there is in the awful and mysterious depths of the Triune God neither limit nor end.

A. W. Tozer, in *The Pursuit of God*

Moving Forward with God

The Helper, the Holy Spirit, whom the Father will send in my name, he will teach you all things.
(John 14:26, ESV)

I have found that God always has a fresh and deeper truth He wants us to learn about Him. So once He has taught you one thing, get ready for the *next* marvelous truth God will soon introduce!

God's Holy Spirit is your personal teacher. He will draw you into a closer walk with God as He reveals God's purposes and ways to you. Jesus said, "If anyone wants to do His will, he will understand whether the teaching is from God or if I am speaking on My own" (John 7:17, HCSB).

The Holy Spirit, who resides within you, will always confirm in your heart the truth of Scripture. You can depend on the Holy Spirit to affirm whether any teaching comes from God or not. Always ask the Holy Spirit to verify—through Scripture—what others teach. Be sure to nurture your relationship with God through prayer, meditation, and Bible study so you will be able to receive and obey everything God tells you.

I urge you to allow the Holy Spirit to take your life to a new, higher, dynamic level in your walk with God. You may be presently enjoying a vibrant Christian life. But I can assure you, there is still much more God wants you to experience of Him, for He is an infinite being. You may have been disappointed in the past. Perhaps you made attempts to grow spiritually, but your enthusiasm eventually waned and your growth fizzled. I encourage you: Don't let any previous failure or disappointment stop you from confidently moving forward with God. No matter where we are, why would any of us ever become satisfied with the current status of our walk with God when there is so much He wants to do in and through our lives?

Henry Blackaby and Richard Blackaby, in *Experiencing God*

ONE DEEP BLESSED CRY

The salvation of the righteous is from the LORD;
he is their stronghold in the time of trouble.
(PSALM 37:39, ESV)

Our heart is the scene of a divine operation more wonderful than Creation. We can do as little toward the work as toward creating the world, except as God works in us to will and to do. God only asks of us to yield, to consent, to wait upon Him, and He will do it all.

Let us meditate and be still, until we see how right and blessed it is that God alone do all, and our soul will of itself sink down in deep humility to say (with Jacob): "I have waited for thy salvation, O LORD" (Genesis 49:18, KJV). And the deep blessed background of all our praying and working will be: "Truly my soul waiteth upon God" (Psalm 62:1, KJV).

There can be no good but what God works; to wait upon God, and have the heart filled with faith in His working, and in that faith to pray for His mighty power to come down, is our only wisdom.

Our private and public prayer is our chief expression of our relation to God: it is in them chiefly that our waiting upon God must be exercised. If our waiting begins by quieting the activities of nature and being still before God; if it bows and seeks to see God in His universal and almighty operation, alone able and always ready to work all good; if it yields itself to Him in the assurance that He is working and will work in us; if it maintains the place of humility and stillness, and surrenders until God's Spirit has quickened the faith that He will perfect His work: it will indeed become the strength and the joy of the soul. Life will become one deep blessed cry: "I have waited for thy salvation, O LORD."

ANDREW MURRAY, IN *WAITING ON GOD*

Christian Hedonism

Delight yourself in the Lord, and he will give you the desires of your heart.

(Psalm 37:4, esv)

Many objections rise in people's minds when they hear me talk of Christian Hedonism. Perhaps I can defuse some of the resistance by making a few brief, clarifying comments.

First, Christian Hedonism as I use the term does not mean God becomes a means to help us get worldly pleasures. The pleasure Christian Hedonism seeks is the pleasure that is in God Himself. He is the end of our search, not the means to some further end. Our exceeding joy is He, the Lord — not the streets of gold or the reunion with relatives or any blessing of heaven.

Second, Christian Hedonism does not make a god out of pleasure. It says that one has already made a god out of whatever he finds most pleasure in. The goal of Christian Hedonism is to find most pleasure in the one and only God and thus avoid the sin of covetousness, that is, idolatry (see Colossians 3:5).

Third, Christian Hedonism does not put us above God when we seek Him out of self-interest. A patient is not greater than his physician.

Fourth, Christian Hedonism is not a "general theory of *moral justification*." In other words, nowhere do I say: An act is right because it brings pleasure. My aim is not to decide what is right by using joy as a moral criterion. My aim is to own up to the amazing, and largely neglected, fact that some dimension of joy is a moral duty in all true worship and all virtuous acts.

Fifth, I do not say that the relationship between love and happiness is this: "True happiness requires love." This is an oversimplification that misses the crucial and defining point. The distinguishing feature of Christian Hedonism is not that pleasure seeking demands virtue, but that virtue consists essentially, though not only, in pleasure seeking.

John Piper, in *Desiring God*

The Ease of Mistrust

Take care, brothers, lest there be in any of you an evil, unbelieving heart, leading you to fall away from the living God.

(Hebrews 3:12, esv)

I sympathize with those who find it difficult to trust God in adversity. I've been there often enough myself to know something of the distress, despair, and darkness that fills our soul's when we wonder if God truly cares about our plight. I have spent a good portion of my adult life encouraging people to pursue holiness, to obey God. Yet, I acknowledge it often seems more difficult to trust God than to obey Him.

God's moral will given to us in the Bible is rational and reasonable; the circumstances in which we must trust God often appear irrational and inexplicable. God's law is readily recognized to be good for us, even when we don't want to obey it; the circumstances of our lives frequently appear dreadful and grim, perhaps even calamitous and tragic. Obeying God is worked out within well-defined boundaries of God's revealed will; trusting God is worked out in an arena that has no boundaries, where we're always coping with the unknown.

Yet it is just as important to trust God as it is to obey Him. When we disobey God we defy His authority and despise His holiness. But when we fail to trust God we doubt His sovereignty and question His goodness. In both cases we cast aspersions upon His majesty and His character. God views our distrust of Him as seriously as He views our disobedience.

When the people of Israel were hungry, "they spoke against God, saying, 'Can God spread a table in the wilderness? . . . Can he also give bread or provide meat for his people?'" The next two verses tell us, "When the Lord heard, he was full of wrath . . . because they did not believe in God and did not trust his saving power" (Psalm 78:19-22, esv).

In order to trust God, we must always view our adverse circumstances through the eyes of faith, not of sense.

Jerry Bridges, in *Trusting God*

All the Sweeter

Who is this King of glory? The Lord of hosts, he is the King of glory!
(Psalm 24:10, esv)

To have found God and still to pursue Him is the soul's paradox of love, scorned indeed by the too-easily-satisfied religionist, but justified in happy experience by the children of the burning heart.

Saint Bernard stated this holy paradox in a musical quatrain that will be instantly understood by every worshipping soul: "We taste Thee, O Thou Living Bread, and long to feast upon Thee still: we drink of Thee, the Fountainhead and thirst our souls from Thee to fill."

Come near to the holy men and women of the past, and you will soon feel the heat of their desire after God. They mourned for Him, they prayed and wrestled and sought for Him day and night, in season and out, and when they had found Him the finding was all the sweeter for the long seeking.

Moses used the fact that he knew God as an argument for knowing Him better. "Now therefore, I pray thee, if I have found grace in thy sight, shew me now thy way, that I may know thee, that I may find grace in thy sight"; and from there he rose to make the daring request, "I beseech thee, shew me thy glory" (Exodus 33:13,18, kjv). God was frankly pleased by this display of ardor, and the next day called Moses into the mount, and there in solemn procession made all His glory pass before him.

David's life was a torrent of spiritual desire, and his psalms ring with the cry of the seeker and the glad shout of the finder. Paul confessed the mainspring of his life to be his burning desire after Christ. "That I may know Him," was the goal of his heart, and to this he sacrificed everything. "Yea doubtless, and I count all things but loss for the excellency of the knowledge of Christ Jesus my Lord: for whom I have suffered the loss of all things, and do count them but dung, that I may win Christ" (Philippians 3:8-10, kjv).

A. W. Tozer, in *The Pursuit of God*

Foundation of Happiness

Our God is in the heavens; he does all that he pleases.
(Psalm 115:3, esv)

If God is sovereign and can do anything He pleases, then none of His purposes can be frustrated (see Psalm 33:10-11), and He must be the happiest of all beings. This infinite, divine happiness is the fountain from which the Christian Hedonist drinks and longs to drink more deeply.

Can you imagine what it would be like if God were given to grumbling and pouting and depression? What if God were frustrated and despondent and gloomy and dismal and discontented and dejected? Could we join David and say, "O God, you are my God; earnestly I seek you; my soul thirsts for you; my flesh faints for you, as in a dry and weary land where there is no water" (Psalm 63:1, esv)?

I don't think so. We would all relate to God like little children who have a frustrated, gloomy, dismal, discontented father. They can't enjoy him. They can only try not to bother him, or maybe try to work for him to earn some little favor.

Therefore if God is not a happy God, Christian Hedonism has no foundation. For the aim of the Christian Hedonist is to be happy in God, to delight in God, to cherish and enjoy His fellowship and favor. But children cannot enjoy the fellowship of their Father if He is unhappy. Therefore the foundation of Christian Hedonism is the happiness of God.

But the foundation of the happiness of God is the sovereignty of God. If God were not sovereign, if the world He made were out of control, frustrating His design again and again, God would not be happy.

Just as our joy is based on the promise that God is strong enough and wise enough to make all things work together for our good, so God's joy is based on that same sovereign control: He makes all things work together for His glory.

John Piper, in *Desiring God*

OUR ORIGINAL DESTINY

These all look to you, to give them their food in due season.
(PSALM 104:27, ESV)

Psalm 104, in praise of the Creator, speaks of the birds and the beasts of the forest; of the young lions, and man going forth to his work; of the great sea, wherein are things creeping innumerable, both small and great beasts. And it sums up the whole relation of all creation to its Creator, and its continuous and universal dependence upon Him in the one word: "These wait all upon thee" (Psalm 104:27, KJV). Just as much as it was God's work to create, it is His work to maintain. The whole creation is ruled by the one unalterable law of — waiting upon God!

The one object for which God gave life to creatures was that in them He might prove and show forth His wisdom, power, and goodness, in His being each moment their life and happiness, and pouring forth unto them, according to their capacity, the riches of His goodness and power. And just as this is the very place and nature of God, to be unceasingly the supplier of every want in the creature, so the very place and nature of the creature is nothing but this — to wait upon God and receive from Him what He alone can give, what He delights to give.

If we are at all to apprehend what waiting on God is to be to the believer, to practice it and to experience its blessedness, it is of consequence that we begin at the very beginning and see the deep reasonableness of the call that comes to us. We shall understand how the duty is no arbitrary command. We shall see how it is not only rendered necessary by our sin and helplessness. It is simply and truly our restoration to our original destiny and our highest nobility, to our true place and glory as creatures blessedly dependent on the All-Glorious God.

ANDREW MURRAY, IN *WAITING ON GOD*

HEARING GOD

Let me hear what God the LORD will speak.
(PSALM 85:8, ESV)

Hearing God? A daring idea, some would say—presumptuous and even dangerous. But what if we are made for it? What if the human system simply will not function properly without it? There are good reasons to think it will not. The fine texture as well as the grand movements of life show the need. Is it not, in fact, more presumptuous and dangerous to undertake human existence *without* hearing God?

Among our loneliest moments, no doubt, is the time of decision. There the weight of our future life clamps down upon our hearts. Whatever comes from our choice will be our responsibility, our fault. Good things we have set our hearts on become real only as we choose them. But those things, or those as yet undreamed of, may also be irretrievably lost if our choices are misguided. We may find ourselves stuck with failures and dreadful consequences that must be endured for a lifetime.

Then quickly there follows the time of second thoughts—and third, and fourth: Did I do the good and wise thing? Is it what God wanted? Is it even what *I* wanted? Can I live with the consequences? Will others think I am a fool? Is God still with me? Will He be with me even if it becomes clear that I made the wrong choice?

While we are young, we just do what we have to do or whatever turns us on. How simple it is! After collecting a few disasters, however, and learning that actions are forever, that opportunities seldom return and that consequences are relentless, we hungrily cry, "Thy will be done on earth as it is in heaven!" More than reflecting a mere general concern for world affairs to conform to His will, our prayer expresses the burning need for God to be a constant guiding presence in our individual lives.

DALLAS WILLARD, IN *HEARING GOD*

Only Through Experience

O righteous Father, even though the world does not know you, I know you.

(John 17:25, ESV)

Scripture is filled with descriptions of God's character. You can read these accounts and believe them to be true about God. Yet God does not merely want you to read *about* Him, He wants you to *know* Him.

For the Greeks, to know something meant you understood a concept in your mind. It was an academic process. In contrast, for a Hebrew person — like Jesus — knowing something entailed experiencing it. In fact, you could not truly say you knew something unless you had dealt with it personally. So it is significant that, when Jesus spoke about knowing God, He was speaking as a Hebrew.

When Jesus said eternal life is knowing God — including God the Son, Jesus Christ — He did not mean that eternal life is knowing *about* God. He was not referring to someone who has read many books and attended numerous seminars about God. He was talking about a firsthand, experiential knowledge. We come to truly know God as we experience Him in and around our lives.

Many people have grown up attending church and hearing about God all their lives, but they do not have a personal, dynamic, growing relationship with God. They never hear His voice. They have no idea what God's will is. They do not encounter His love firsthand. They have no sense of divine purpose for their lives. They may know a lot about God, but they don't really know Him.

Merely knowing about God will leave you unsatisfied. Truly knowing God comes only through experience as He reveals Himself to you through His word and as you relate to Him. Throughout the Bible we can see that God took the initiative to disclose Himself to people through their life events.

Henry Blackaby and Richard Blackaby, in *Experiencing God*

The Great Mystery

For we walk by faith, not by sight.
(2 Corinthians 5:7, esv)

Obedience to Jesus' authority provides the key to understanding what is for many the great mystery of Christianity: faith.

Saving faith — that by which we are justified, made right with God — is a gift of God; and yes, it involves a rational process as well because it comes from hearing the Word of God. "All right," the struggling Christian may say, "but practically speaking, how does my faith become real? How do I get that vibrant, strong faith of Christian maturity?"

That's where obedience comes in. For maturing faith — faith that deepens and grows as we live our Christian life — is not just knowledge, but knowledge acted upon. It is not just belief, but belief lived out — practiced. James said we are to be doers of the Word, not just hearers. Dietrich Bonhoeffer, the German pastor martyred in a Nazi concentration camp, succinctly stated this crucial interrelationship: "Only he who believes is obedient; only he who is obedient believes." This may sound like a circular proposition, but many things are — in truth and in practice. Faith is a state of mind that grows out of our actions, just as it also governs them.

So obedience is the key to real faith — the unshakable kind of faith so powerfully illustrated by Job's life. Job clung to the assurance that *God is who He is.* Job confirmed his obedience with those classic words of faith: "Though he slay me, I will hope in him" (Job 13:15, esv).

This is real faith: believing and acting obediently regardless of circumstances or contrary evidence. After all, if faith depended on visible evidence, it wouldn't be faith.

It is absurd for Christians to constantly seek new demonstrations of God's power, to expect a miraculous answer to every need. True faith, as Job understood, rests on the assurance that *God is who He is.* Indeed, on that we must be willing to stake our very lives.

Charles Colson, in *Loving God*

Measuring His Love

Our bones are dried up, and our hope is lost.
(Ezekiel 37:11, esv)

The extent of God's love at Calvary is seen in both the infinite cost to Him of giving His one and only Son and in the wretched and miserable condition of those He loved. God could not remove our sins without an infinite cost to both Himself and His Son. And because of their great love for us, both were willing to pay that great cost — the Father in giving His one and only Son, and the Son in laying down His life for us. One of the essential characteristics of love is the element of self-sacrifice, and this was demonstrated for us to its ultimate in God's love at Calvary.

Consider also the miserable and wretched condition of those God loved. Paul said, "God shows his love for us in that *while we were still sinners*, Christ died for us" (Romans 5:8, esv, emphasis added). It's sometimes difficult for those of us who grew up in morally upright or Christian homes to appreciate the force of that statement. Because we were generally upright and morally decent people in the eyes of society around us and in our own eyes, it's difficult for us to see ourselves as God saw us — as wretched, miserable, rebellious sinners, spiritually dead in our transgressions and sins (see Ephesians 2:1). Ezekiel's vision of Israel as a valley of thoroughly dry bones (see Ezekiel 37) would be an apt description of all of us before our salvation.

One day a friend and I were marveling about the conversion of one of the more notorious white-collar criminals of our time. I said to my friend, "How dead is dead? Weren't *we* just as spiritually dead before our salvation as he was?" Regardless of how morally upright we appeared in our unsaved state, to God we were like the house of Israel, nothing more than a pile of dry and brittle bones.

Jerry Bridges, in *Trusting God*

The Necessity of Waiting

When you open your hand, they are filled with good things.
(Psalm 104:28, esv)

If once our eyes are opened to the precious truth that the whole creation is ruled by the unalterable law of waiting upon God, all Nature will become a preacher, reminding us of the relationship which, founded in creation, is now taken in grace.

As we read Psalm 104 and learn to look upon all life in Nature as continually maintained by God Himself, waiting on God will be seen to be the very necessity of our being. As we think of the young lions and the ravens crying to Him, of the birds and the fishes and every insect waiting on Him, till He gives them their meat in due season, we shall see that it is the very nature and glory of God that He is a God who is to be waited on. Every thought of what Nature is, and what God is, will give new force to the call: "Wait thou only upon God" (Psalm 62:5, kjv).

It is God who giveth all: let this faith enter deeply into our hearts. Before we fully understand all that is implied in our waiting upon God, and before we have even been able to cultivate the habit, let the truth enter our souls: waiting on God, unceasing and entire dependence upon Him, is the one only true religion in heaven and earth, the one unalterable and all-comprehensive expression for the true relationship to the ever-blessed one in whom we live.

Let us resolve at once that it shall be the one characteristic of our life and worship, a continual, humble, truthful waiting upon God. We may rest assured that He who made us for Himself, that He might give Himself to us and in us, that He will never disappoint us. In waiting on Him we shall find rest and joy and strength, and the supply of every need.

Andrew Murray, in *Waiting on God*

New Themes to Explore

For the Lord is a great God, and a great King above all gods.
(Psalm 95:3, esv)

In our study to know God, what is the ascent going to involve? What are the themes that will occupy us?

We shall have to deal with the *Godhead* of God, the qualities of Deity that set God apart from men and mark the difference and distance between the Creator and His creatures: such qualities as His self-existence, His infinity, His eternity, His unchangeableness. We shall have to deal with the *powers* of God: His almightiness, His omniscience, His omnipresence. We shall have to deal with the *perfections* of God, the aspects of His moral character which are manifested in His words and deeds — His holiness, His love and mercy, His truthfulness, His faithfulness, His goodness, His patience, His justice. We shall have to take note of what pleases Him, what offends Him, what awakens His wrath, what affords Him satisfaction and joy.

For many of us, these are comparatively unfamiliar themes. They were not always so to the people of God. There was a time when the subject of God's attributes was thought so important as to be included in the catechism which all children in the churches were taught and all adult members were expected to know. Thus, to the fourth question in the Westminster Shorter Catechism, "What is God?" the answer reads as follows: "God is a Spirit, infinite, eternal, and unchangeable in His being, wisdom, power, holiness, justice, goodness, and truth" — a statement which the great Charles Hodge described as "probably the best definition of God ever penned by man."

Few children today, however, are brought up on the Westminster Shorter Catechism, and few modern worshippers will ever have read anything simple and straightforward on the subject of the nature of God. We can expect, therefore, that an exploration of the themes mentioned above will give us much that is new to think about, and many fresh ideas to ponder and digest.

J. I. Packer, in *Knowing God*

Good and Bad

I know that you can do all things,
and that no purpose of yours can be thwarted.
(Job 42:2, esv)

Are the evil and calamitous events in the world also part of God's sovereign design? Jeremiah looks over the carnage of Jerusalem after its destruction and weeps (see Lamentations 2:11). But when he looked to God, he could not deny the truth: "Is it not from the mouth of the Most High that good and bad come?" (3:38, esv).

If God reigns as sovereign over the world, then the evil of the world is not outside His design. This was the reverent saying of God's servant Job when he was afflicted with boils: "Shall we receive good from God, and shall we not receive evil?" (Job 2:10, esv). He said this even though the text says plainly that "Satan went out from the presence of the Lord and struck Job with loathsome sores" (2:7, esv). Was Job wrong to attribute to God what came from Satan? No, because the writer tells us immediately after Job's words: "In all this Job did not sin with his lips" (2:10, esv).

The evil Satan causes is only by the permission of God. It would be unbiblical and irreverent to attribute to Satan (or to sinful man) the power to frustrate the designs of God.

When God looks at a painful or wicked event through His narrow lens, He sees the tragedy of the sin for what it is in itself, and He is angered and grieved: "I have no pleasure in the death of anyone, declares the Lord God" (Ezekiel 18:32, esv).

But when God looks at a painful or wicked event through His wide-angle lens, He sees the tragedy of the sin in relation to everything leading up to it and everything flowing out from it. He sees it in relation to all the connections and effects that form a pattern, or mosaic, stretching into eternity. This mosaic in all its parts — good and evil — brings Him delight.

John Piper, in *Desiring God*

THE MIGHTY LONGING

And we all, with unveiled face, beholding the glory of the Lord.
(2 CORINTHIANS 3:18, ESV)

Hymnody is sweet with the longing after God, the God whom, while the singer seeks, he knows he has already found. "His track I see and I'll pursue," sang our fathers only a short generation ago, but that song is heard no more in the great congregation. How tragic that we in this dark day have had our seeking done for us by our teachers. Everything is made to center upon the initial act of "accepting" Christ (a term, incidentally, which is not found in the Bible), and we are not expected thereafter to crave any further revelation of God to our souls. We have been snared in the coils of a spurious logic which insists that if we have found Him we need no more seek Him. This is set before us as the last word in orthodoxy, and it is taken for granted that no Bible-taught Christian ever believed otherwise. Thus the whole testimony of the worshipping, seeking, singing church on that subject is crisply set aside. The experiential heart-theology of a grand army of fragrant saints is rejected in favor of a smug interpretation of Scripture which would certainly have sounded strange to an Augustine, a Rutherford, or a Brainerd.

In the midst of this great chill there are some, I rejoice to acknowledge, who will not be content with shallow logic. They will admit the force of the argument, and then turn away with tears to hunt some lonely place and pray, "O God, show me thy glory." They want to taste, to touch with their hearts, to see with their inner eyes the wonder that is God.

I want deliberately to encourage this mighty longing after God. Complacency is a deadly foe of all spiritual growth. Acute desire must be present or there will be no manifestation of Christ to His people. He waits to be wanted. Too bad that with many of us He waits so long, so very long, in vain.

A. W. TOZER, IN *THE PURSUIT OF GOD*

A HIGHER SOURCE OF COMFORT

Is it not from the mouth of the Most High that good and bad come?
(LAMENTATIONS 3:38, ESV)

Lamentations 3:37-38 is a Scripture passage that offends many people. They find it difficult to accept that both calamities and good things come from God. People often ask the question, "If God is a God of love, how could He allow such a calamity?" But Jesus Himself affirmed God's sovereignty in calamity when Pilate said to Him, "Do you not know that I have authority to release you and authority to crucify you?" Jesus replied, "You would have no authority over me at all unless it had been given you from above" (John 19:10-11, ESV). Jesus acknowledged God's sovereign control over His life.

Because God's sacrifice of His Son for our sins is such an amazing act of love toward us, we tend to overlook that it was for Jesus an excruciating experience beyond all we can imagine. It was for Jesus in His humanity a calamity sufficient to cause Him to pray, "My Father, if it be possible, let this cup pass from me," but He did not waver in His assertion of God's sovereign control as He prayed, "not as I will, but as you will" (Matthew 26:39, ESV).

Rather than being offended over the Bible's assertion of God's sovereignty in both good and calamity, believers should be comforted by it. Whatever our particular calamity or adversity may be, we may be sure that our Father has a loving purpose in it. As King Hezekiah said, "Behold, it was for my welfare that I had great bitterness" (Isaiah 38:17, ESV). God does not exercise His sovereignty capriciously but only in such a way as His infinite love deems best for us. Jeremiah wrote, "Though he cause grief, he will have compassion according to the abundance of his steadfast love; for he does not willingly afflict or grieve the children of men" (Lamentations 3:32-33, ESV).

JERRY BRIDGES, IN *TRUSTING GOD*

Waiting for Supplies

The eyes of all look to you, and you give them their food in due season.
(Psalm 145:15, esv)

Psalm 145 is a Psalm of the Kingdom, and "The eyes of all wait upon thee" (kjv) appears specially to point to the needs of God's saints, of all that fall and them that be bowed down. What the universe and the animal creation do unconsciously, God's people are to do intelligently and voluntarily. Man is to be the interpreter of Nature. He is to prove that there is nothing more noble or more blessed in the exercise of our free will than to use it in waiting upon God.

If an army has been sent out to march into an enemy's country, and tidings are received that it is not advancing, the question is at once asked, what may be the cause of delay. The answer will very often be: "Waiting for supplies." All the stores of provisions or clothing or ammunition have not arrived; without these it dare not proceed.

It is not otherwise in the Christian life: day by day, at every step, we need our supplies from above. And there is nothing so needful as to cultivate that spirit of dependence on God and of confidence in Him, which refuses to go on without the needed supply of grace and strength.

Is this anything different from what we do when we pray? There may be much praying with only very little waiting on God. In praying we are often occupied with ourselves, with our own needs, and our own efforts in the presentation of them.

In waiting upon God, the first thought is of the God upon whom we wait. We enter His presence and feel our need to be quiet, so that He, as God, can overshadow us with Himself. God longs to reveal Himself, to fill us with Himself. Waiting on God gives Him time in His own way and divine power to come to us.

Andrew Murray, in *Waiting on God*

THE LORD WILL PROVIDE

Abraham called the name of that place, "The LORD will provide"; as it is said to this day, "On the mount of the LORD it shall be provided."
(GENESIS 22:14, ESV)

Genesis 22 tells us that God put Abraham's faith and obedience to the test by asking him to sacrifice his only son, Isaac. The command seemingly contradicts everything we know about God. However, in Abraham's day, people sometimes would sacrifice children on altars dedicated to their idols. Nowhere else does the Bible record God ever asking someone to sacrifice a child to Him. Clearly, God was testing Abraham to see if he was as devoted to the true God as his neighbors were committed to their false gods.

Obeying such a command required Abraham to trust God at a new and deeper level of faith. On the way to the place of sacrifice, Isaac asked him, "Where is the lamb for the burnt offering?" (Genesis 22:7, HCSB). Can you imagine how sobering this moment was for Abraham? "Abraham answered, 'God Himself will provide the lamb for the burnt offering, my son'" (22:8, HCSB). We don't know all Abraham was thinking, but clearly he trusted God to provide everything he needed for the imminent sacrifice. He acted on his belief that God was his Provider. He did what God told him to do.

When God saw that Abraham did not merely claim to have faith in Him but was willing to act out his trust through obedience in this excruciating task, He stopped Abraham and provided a ram for the sacrifice. Abraham named that place after the characteristic of God he had just come to know by experience—*Jehovah Jireh*, meaning "The Lord Will Provide." Abraham came to an intimate knowledge of God that day through the experience of God as his Provider.

This is how we, too, grow to know God. As we experience God firsthand, we come to know Him in new and increasingly deeper dimensions. We can learn that God provides as we read this story about Abraham's walk, but we really know God as Provider once we experience Him providing something specifically for us.

HENRY BLACKABY AND RICHARD BLACKABY, IN *EXPERIENCING GOD*

Stripping Down to Essentials

For God alone, O my soul, wait in silence, for my hope is from him.
(Psalm 62:5, esv)

Every age has its own characteristics. Right now we are in an age of religious complexity. The simplicity that is in Christ is rarely found among us. In its stead are programs, methods, organizations, and a world of nervous activities that occupy time and attention but can never satisfy the longing of the heart. The shallowness of our inner experience, the hollowness of our worship, and the servile imitation of the world which marks our promotional methods all testify that we, in this day, know God only imperfectly, and the peace of God scarcely at all.

If we would find God amid all the religious externals we must first determine to find Him, and then proceed in the way of simplicity. Now as always God discovers Himself to "babes" and hides Himself in thick darkness from the wise and the prudent.

We must simplify our approach to Him. We must strip down to essentials (and they will be found to be blessedly few). We must put away all effort to impress and come with the guileless candor of childhood. If we do this, without doubt God will quickly respond.

When religion has said its last word, there is little that we need other than God Himself. The evil habit of seeking *God-and* effectively prevents us from finding God in full revelation. In the "and" lies our great woe. If we omit the "and," we shall soon find God, and in Him we shall find that for which we have all our lives been secretly longing.

We need not fear that in seeking God only we may narrow our lives or restrict the motions of our expanding hearts. The opposite is true. We can well afford to make God our All, to concentrate, to sacrifice the many for the One.

A. W. Tozer, in *The Pursuit of God*

Waiting for the Living One

The Lord upholds all who are falling and raises up all who are bowed down.
(Psalm 145:14, esv)

It is specially at the time of prayer that we ought to set ourselves to cultivate a spirit of quiet waiting.

Before you pray, bow quietly before God, just to remember and realize who He is, how near He is, how certainly He can and will help. Just be still before Him, and allow His Holy Spirit to waken and stir up in your soul the childlike disposition of absolute dependence and confident expectation. Wait upon God as a Living Being, as the Living God, who notices you, and is just longing to fill you with His salvation. Wait on God till you know you have met Him; prayer will then become so different.

And when you are praying, let there be intervals of silence, reverent stillness of soul, in which you yield yourself to God, in case He may have anything He wishes to teach you or to work in you. Waiting on Him will become the most blessed part of prayer, and the blessing thus obtained will be doubly precious as the fruit of such fellowship with the Holy One. God has so ordained it, in harmony with His holy nature, and with ours, that waiting on Him should be the honor we give Him. Let us bring Him the service gladly and truthfully; He will reward it abundantly.

"The eyes of all wait upon thee; and thou givest them their meat in due season" (Psalm 145:15, kjv). Dear soul, God provides in Nature for the creatures He has made; how much more will He provide in Grace for those He has redeemed. Learn to say of every want, and every failure, and every lack of needful grace: I have waited too little upon God, or He would have given me in due season all I needed. And say then too, "My soul, wait thou only upon God" (Psalm 62:5, kjv).

Andrew Murray, in *Waiting on God*

It Was Fitting

For it was fitting that he, . . . in bringing many sons to glory, should make the founder of their salvation perfect through suffering.

(Hebrews 2:10, ESV)

The death of Christ was the will and work of God the Father. Isaiah writes, "We esteemed him stricken, smitten by God. . . . It was the will of the Lord to crush him; he has put him to grief" (53:4,10, ESV). Yet surely, as God the Father saw the agony of His beloved Son and the wickedness that brought Him to the cross, He did not delight in those things in themselves (viewed through the narrow lens). Sin in itself, and the suffering of the innocent, is abhorrent to God.

Nevertheless, according to Hebrews 2:10, God the Father thought it was fitting to perfect the Pioneer of our salvation through suffering. God willed what He abhorred. He abhorred it in the narrow-lens view, but not in the wide-angle view of eternity. When the universality of things was considered, the death of the Son of God was seen by the Father as a magnificent way to demonstrate His righteousness (see Romans 3:25-26) and bring His people to glory (see Hebrews 2:10) and keep the angels praising Him forever and ever (see Revelation 5:9-13).

Therefore, when I say that the sovereignty of God is the foundation of His happiness, I do not ignore or minimize the anger and grief God can express against evil. But neither do I infer from this wrath and sorrow that God is a frustrated God who cannot keep His creation under control. He has designed from all eternity, and is infallibly forming with every event, a magnificent mosaic of redemptive history. The contemplation of this mosaic (with both its dark and bright tiles) fills His heart with joy.

And if our Father's heart is full of deep and unshakable happiness, we may be sure that when we seek our happiness in Him, we will find a Father whose heart is so full of joy that it spills over onto all those (Christian Hedonists) who are thirsty.

John Piper, in *Desiring God*

FOR INSTRUCTION

Make me to know your ways, O LORD; teach me your paths.
(PSALM 25:4, ESV)

The reason for delay in an army's advance might be the wait for supplies, but might also be a waiting for instructions, or waiting for orders. If the last dispatch has not been received with final orders of the commander-in-chief, the army dare not move. Even so in the Christian life is our deep need of waiting for instructions.

See how beautiful this comes out in Psalm 25. The writer knew and loved God's law exceedingly, and meditated in that law day and night. But he knew that this was not enough. He knew that for the right spiritual apprehension of the truth, and for the right personal application of it to his own peculiar circumstances, he needed a direct divine teaching.

The psalm has at all times been a very peculiar one, because of its reiterated expression of the felt need of the divine teaching and of the child-like confidence that this teaching would be given. Study the psalm until your heart is filled with these two thoughts—the absolute need, and the absolute certainty of divine guidance.

The Father in heaven is so interested in His child, and so longs to have his life at every step in His will and His love, that He is willing to keep his guidance entirely in His own hand. He knows so well that we are unable to do what is really holy and heavenly, except as He works it in us, that He means His very demands to become promises of what He will do, in watching over and leading us all the day. Not only in special difficulties and times of perplexity, but in the common course of everyday life, we may count upon Him to teach us His war and show us His path.

ANDREW MURRAY, IN *WAITING ON GOD*

The Heart of True Understanding

The fear of the Lord is the beginning of wisdom,
and the knowledge of the Holy One is insight.
(Proverbs 9:10, esv)

What is the most important thing in the world to every Christian? It is to grow in the knowledge of God.

The knowledge of God is the heart of salvation and of all true spiritual experience. Knowing Him is what we were created for. It will occupy us throughout all eternity. In Scripture, it is almost equivalent to salvation. Jesus said that eternal life, or salvation, means knowledge of God: "And this is eternal life, that they know you the only true God, and Jesus Christ whom you have sent" (John 17:3, esv). To be a Christian is not a *mindless* experience, but involves knowledge and understanding. It means a personal relationship and personal acquaintance with the Lord.

Behind what Jesus says in John's Gospel lies the promise that God gave centuries before in the prophecy of the new covenant: "I will give them a heart to know that I am the Lord" (Jeremiah 24:7, esv). The fulfillment of that prophecy would mean, Jeremiah added, "No longer shall each one teach his neighbor and each his brother, saying, 'Know the Lord,' for they shall all know me, from the least of them to the greatest" (31:34, esv). Isaiah similarly tells us that this knowledge of God is what would mark the reign of the promised Messiah, Jesus Christ: "The earth shall be full of the knowledge of the Lord as the waters cover the sea" (Isaiah 11:9, esv). What a vision! Yet it summarizes what Scripture tells us Christ came to do: to bring us the knowledge of God.

Such knowledge of God is really the heart of all true understanding in the Christian life. A man or woman may be a Christian and remain ignorant of many things. But we cannot be Christians and remain ignorant of God. In the final analysis, says the wise man in Proverbs, "knowledge of the Holy One is understanding" (9:10, niv).

Sinclair Ferguson, in *A Heart for God*

All the Day Long

Lead me in your truth and teach me, for you are the God of my salvation; for you I wait all the day long.
(Psalm 25:5, esv)

Waiting for guidance, waiting for instruction "all the day," is a very blessed part of waiting upon God.

We want in our times of prayer to give clear expression to our sense of need, and our faith in His help. We want definitely to become conscious of our ignorance as to what God's war may be, and the need of the divine light shining within us, if our way is to be as of the sun, shining more and more unto the perfect day. And we want to wait quietly before God in prayer, until the deep, restful assurance fills us: It will be given — "the meek will He guide in the way."

"On Thee do I wait all the day." The special surrender to the divine guidance in our seasons of prayer must cultivate, and be followed up by, the habitual looking upward "all the day." As simple as it is, to one who has eyes, to walk all the day in the light of the sun, so simple and delightful can it become to a soul practiced in waiting on God, to walk all the day in the enjoyment of God's light and leading. What is needed to help us to such a life is just one thing: the real knowledge and faith of God as the one only source of wisdom and goodness, as ever ready, and longing much to be to us all that we can possibly require — yes! this is the one thing we need. If we but saw our God in His love, if we but believed that He waits to be gracious, that He waits to be our life and to work all in us — how this waiting on God would become our highest joy, the natural and spontaneous response of our hearts to His great love and glory!

Andrew Murray, in *Waiting on God*

Having God for Our Treasure

The Lord is his inheritance, as the Lord your God said to him.

(Deuteronomy 10:9, ESV)

The anonymous author of the quaint old English classic *The Cloud of Unknowing* teaches us how to make God our all. "Lift up thine heart unto God with a meek stirring of love; and mean Himself, and none of His goods. And thereto, look thee loath to think on aught but God Himself. So that nought work in thy wit, nor in thy will, but only God Himself. This is the work of the soul that most pleaseth God."

Again, he recommends that in prayer we practice a further stripping down of everything, even of our theology. "For it sufficeth enough, a naked intent direct unto God without any other cause than Himself." Yet underneath all his thinking lay the broad foundation of New Testament truth, for he explains that by "Himself" he means "God that made thee, and bought thee, and that graciously called thee to thy degree." And he is all for simplicity: If we would have religion "lapped and folden in one word, for that thou shouldst have better hold thereupon, take thee but a little word of one syllable: for so it is better than of two, for even the shorter it is the better it accordeth with the work of the Spirit. And such a word is this word God or this word love."

The man who has God for his treasure has all things in One. Many ordinary treasures may be denied him, or if he is allowed to have them, the enjoyment of them will be so tempered that they will never be necessary to his happiness. Or if he must see them go, one after one, he will scarcely feel a sense of loss, for having the Source of all things he has in One all satisfaction, all pleasure, all delight. Whatever he may lose he has actually lost nothing, for he now has it all in One, and he has it purely, legitimately and forever.

A. W. Tozer, in *The Pursuit of God*

The Framework for Hearing God

And they shall know that I am the Lord their God.

(Exodus 29:46, ESV)

God has created us for intimate friendship with Himself—both now and forever. This is the Christian viewpoint. It is made clear throughout the Bible, especially in such passages as Exodus 29:43-46, Exodus 33:11, Psalm 23, Isaiah 41:8, John 15:14, and Hebrews 13:5-6. As with all close personal relationships, we can surely count on God to speak to each of us when and as it is appropriate. But what does this really mean? And how does it work in practice?

There is no avoiding the fact that we live at the mercy of our ideas. This is never more true than with our ideas about God. Meaning well is not enough. Those who operate on the wrong information are likely never to know the reality of God's presence in the decisions that shape their lives and will miss the constant divine companionship for which their souls were made.

The subject of hearing God cannot be successfully treated by thinking only in terms of what God wants us to do if that automatically excludes — as is usually assumed — what *we* want to do and even what *we* want *God* to do. *Hearing God is but one dimension of a richly interactive relationship, and obtaining guidance is but one facet of hearing God.*

It may seem strange, but being in the will of God is very far removed from just doing what God wants us to do — so far removed, in fact, that we can be solidly in the will of God, and be aware that we are, without knowing God's preference with regard to various details of our lives. We can be in His will as we do certain things without our knowing that He prefers these actions to certain other possibilities. Hearing God makes sense only in the framework of living in the will of God.

Dallas Willard, in *Hearing God*

God Sustains All Things

And he is before all things, and in him all things hold together.
(Colossians 1:17, esv)

The Bible teaches that God not only created the universe but that He upholds and sustains it day by day, hour by hour. Scripture says that Christ, the Son of God, "upholds the universe by the word of his power" (Hebrews 1:3, esv). As theologian A. H. Strong said, "Christ is the originator and upholder of the universe. . . . In him it consists, or holds together, from hour to hour. The steady will of Christ constitutes the law of the universe and makes it a cosmos instead of a chaos, just as his will brought it into being in the beginning."[1]

All things are indebted for their existence to the continuous sustaining action of God exercised through His Son. Nothing exists of its own inherent power of being. Nothing in all creation stands or acts independently of the Lord's will. The so-called laws of nature are nothing more than the physical expression of the steady will of Christ. The law of gravity operates with unceasing certainty because Christ continuously wills it to operate. The chair I am sitting on while I write these words holds together because the atoms and molecules in the wood are held in place by His active will.

The stars continue in their courses because He keeps them there. Scripture says that it is God "who brings out their host by number, calling them all by name, by the greatness of his might, and because he is strong in power not one is missing" (Isaiah 40:26, esv).

God's sustaining action in Christ goes beyond the inanimate creation. The Bible says that He gives life to everything: "He prepares rain for the earth; he makes grass grow on the hills. He gives to the beasts their food, and to the young ravens that cry" (Psalm 147:8-9, esv; see also Nehemiah 9:6).

God did not simply create and then walk away. He constantly sustains that which He created.

Jerry Bridges, in *Trusting God*

For All Saints

Indeed, none who wait for you shall be put to shame.
(Psalm 25:3, ESV)

Let us now think of the great company of God, saints throughout the world, who are all with us waiting on Him. And let us all join in the fervent prayer for each other, "Let none that wait on thee be ashamed" (Psalm 25:3, KJV).

Just think for a moment of the multitude of waiting ones who need that prayer; how many there are, sick and weary and solitary, to whom it is as if their prayers are not answered, and who sometimes begin to fear that their hope will be put to shame. And then, how many servants of God, ministers or missionaries, teachers or workers, of various name, whose hopes in their work have been disappointed, and whose longing for power and blessing remains unsatisfied. And then, too, how many, who have heard of a life of rest and perfect peace, of abiding light and fellowship, of strength and victory, and who cannot find the path.

With all these, they have not yet learned the secret of full waiting upon God. They need what we all need—the living assurance that waiting on God can never be in vain.

Let us remember all who are in danger of fainting or being weary, and all unite in the cry, "Let none that wait on thee be ashamed!" If this intercession for all who wait on God becomes part of our waiting on Him for ourselves, we shall help to bear each other's burdens, and so fulfill the law of Christ.

There will be introduced into our waiting on God that element of unselfishness and love, which is the path to the highest blessing, and the fullest communion with God. Love to the brethren and love to God are inseparably linked. In God, the love to His Son and to us are one: "That the love wherewith thou hast loved me may be in them" (John 17:26, KJV).

Andrew Murray, in *Waiting on God*

THINGS

And God saw everything that he had made, and behold, it was very good.
(GENESIS 1:31, ESV)

Before the Lord God made man upon the earth He first prepared for him by creating a world of useful and pleasant things for his sustenance and delight. They were made for man's uses, but they were meant always to be external to the man and subservient to him. In the deep heart of the man was a shrine where none but God was worthy to come. Within him was God; without, a thousand gifts which God had showered upon him.

But sin has introduced complications and has made those very gifts of God a potential source of ruin to the soul.

Our woes began when God was forced out of His central shrine and "things" were allowed to enter. Within the human heart, "things" have taken over. Men have now by nature no peace within their hearts, for God is crowned there no longer, but there in the moral dusk, stubborn and aggressive usurpers fight among themselves for first place on the throne.

This is not a mere metaphor, but an accurate analysis of our real spiritual trouble. There is within the human heart a tough fibrous root of fallen life whose nature is to possess, always to possess. It covets "things" with a deep and fierce passion. The pronouns "my" and "mine" look innocent enough in print, but their constant and universal use is significant. They express the real nature of the old Adamic man better than a thousand volumes of theology could do. They are verbal symptoms of our deep disease. The roots of our hearts have grown down into things, and we dare not pull up one rootlet lest we die. Things have become necessary to us, a development never originally intended. God's gifts now take the place of God, and the whole course of nature is upset by the monstrous substitution.

A. W. TOZER, IN *THE PURSUIT OF GOD*

The Lord Is Your Banner

And Moses built an altar and called the name of it,
The Lord Is My Banner.
(Exodus 17:15, esv)

The Bible is filled with examples of God helping His people come to know the reality of who He is through their experiences. As Joshua and the Israelites were fighting their relentless enemies, the Amalekites, Moses oversaw the battle from a nearby mountain. While he held his hands up to God, the Israelites were victorious, but whenever he lowered his weary arms, the Israelites began to lose.

God gave Israel victory over the Amalekites that day, and Moses built an altar to commemorate the occasion. He named it "The Lord Is My Banner." A banner was a standard or flag that armies, tribes, or nations carried in their front ranks as they marched into battle. It could be difficult at times to recognize an army as it marched through dusty fields. But when you saw its banner held high, you could immediately discern if the army was a friend or foe, and you could gain a sense of its strength by understanding which king or nation it represented. The title "The Lord Is My Banner" indicated that the Israelites belonged to God and that to oppose them was to battle against the power of God.

Moses' uplifted hands gave constant glory to God, indicating the battle was His and that the people of Israel belonged to Him. Israel came to understand God in a fresh and powerful way that day, realizing anew that they were God's people and He was their defender (see Exodus 17:8-15).

God's names in Scripture reveal something of His nature, activity, or character. You come to know God by experience — at His initiative — as He allows you to learn something new about Him. You grow to know Him more intimately and personally. As you grow, you will naturally want to express your praise, gratitude, and worship to Him. One of the ways to worship Him is to praise and honor Him by acknowledging His names.

Henry Blackaby and Richard Blackaby, in *Experiencing God*

A Clear Choice

Man does not live by bread alone, but man lives by every word that comes from the mouth of the Lord.

(Deuteronomy 8:3, ESV)

"Your word is truth," Jesus said to His Father (John 17:17, NIV). Nothing less than knowledge of that truth is demanded of Christ's disciples. That knowledge comes only from fervent study of truth — study of His Word. This is indispensable to genuine discipleship. *It is indispensable to loving God.*

Perhaps the real reason we do not pursue the radical discipleship rooted in the Word of God is that we have not recognized the clear choice before us. That choice is most clearly illustrated for us in the sharp contrasts of two biblical accounts: Eve in the Garden of Eden (see Genesis 3) and Christ in the wilderness of Judea (see Matthew 4). Consider the responses of each when confronted with Satan's challenge regarding the Word of God.

Eve knew what God said, but when put to the test, she disobeyed His Word. Her disobedience caused the fall of humanity.

Jesus also knew what God said. Put to the test, He obeyed and trusted His whole life to the Word. His obedience — even unto the death on the cross — is the way of our redemption from the Fall.

If presented with the choice to be like Eve or be like Jesus, most of us would hasten to line up with Christ. We Christians are usually quick to say we want to "be like Jesus." But if we are honest about what those familiar Sunday school words really mean, we'll see they compel us to adopt His attitudes; and that means belief *in,* and submission to, the Scriptures. Instead, we find a thousand ways to resist their truth, to rationalize their calling on our lives. For deep inside we know that obedience to the Scriptures without concern for consequences is penetrating and painful. It requires us to die to self and follow Christ. It demands that we recognize the sin in our lives and that we acknowledge and repent of this sin.

Charles Colson, in *Loving God*

Love's Depths

That in the coming ages he might show the immeasurable riches of his grace in kindness toward us in Christ Jesus.
(Ephesians 2:7, esv)

In Ephesians 2, Paul vividly describes our wretched condition apart from Christ. Besides being "dead in the trespasses and sins" (verse 1, esv) in which we lived, Paul says we followed the ways of this world (see verse 2) —that is, of the ungodly society around us. We even followed the devil, whom Paul calls "the prince of the power of the air" (verse 2, esv). Perhaps it was not by a conscious, deliberate choice that we followed the devil, but we did so because we were under his power and dominion (see Acts 26:18; Colossians 1:13). We were actually servants of the archenemy of God.

Further, Paul says we spent our days gratifying the cravings of our sinful nature, following its desires and thoughts (see Ephesians 2:3). We lived for ourselves—our ambitions, our desires, our pleasures.

Paul concludes this description of our unsaved state by saying we were "by nature" objects of God's wrath (verse 3, esv). We must not lose sight of the fact that God's wrath is very real and very justified. We've all sinned incessantly against a holy, righteous God. We have rebelled willfully against His commands, defied His moral law, and acted in total defiance of His known will for us. Because of these actions, we were justly objects of His wrath.

Why dwell so extensively upon our sinful condition? In order to help us see the depths of God's love! For in giving His Son to die for such people as Paul has described us to be, God bestows what is otherwise inconceivable: "But God, being rich in mercy, because of *the great love with which he loved us*, even when we were dead in our trespasses, made us alive together with Christ—by grace you have been saved—and raised us up with him and seated us with him in the heavenly places in Christ Jesus" (verses 4-6, esv, emphasis added).

Jerry Bridges, in *Trusting God*

OUR BEST HELP FOR OTHERS

Everyone helps his neighbor and says to his brother, "Be strong!"

(ISAIAH 41:6, ESV)

All the love of God, and of Christ, are inseparably linked with love to the brethren. And day by day we can prove and cultivate this love by daily praying for each other: "Let none that wait on thee be ashamed" (Psalm 25:3, KJV).

Take the message to all God's tried and weary ones, that there are more praying for them than they know. Let it stir them and us in our waiting to make a point of forgetting ourselves, and to enlarge our hearts; let it inspire us all with new courage — for who is there who is not at times ready to faint and be weary?

"Let none that wait on thee be ashamed" is a promise in a prayer: "They that wait on Thee *shall not* be ashamed!" From many and many a witness the cry comes to everyone who needs the help, brother, sister, tried one, "Wait on the LORD: be of good courage, and he shall strengthen thine heart: wait, I say, on the LORD" (Psalm 27:14, KJV). "Be of good courage, and he shall strengthen your heart, all ye that hope in the LORD" (31:24, KJV).

Blessed Father! We humbly beseech Thee, Let none that wait on Thee be ashamed; no, not one. Some are weary, and the time of waiting appears long. And some are feeble, and scarcely know how to wait. And some are so entangled in the effort of their prayers and their work, they think that they can find no time to wait continually.

Father, teach us all how to wait. Teach us to think of each other, and pray for each other. Teach us to think of Thee, the God of all waiting ones. Father!

"Let none that wait on thee be ashamed." For Jesus' sake. Amen.

ANDREW MURRAY, IN *WAITING ON GOD*

WHY THIS QUEST?

For if anyone thinks he is something,
when he is nothing, he deceives himself.
(GALATIANS 6:3, ESV)

Before we start to ascend the mountain in our study to know God, we need to stop and ask ourselves a very fundamental question — a question, indeed, that we always ought to put to ourselves whenever we embark on any line of study in God's Holy Book. The question concerns our own motives and intentions as students. We need to ask ourselves: what is my ultimate aim and object in occupying my mind with these things? What do I intend to *do* with my knowledge about God, once I have got it?

The fact we have to face is this: that if we pursue theological knowledge for its own sake, it is bound to go bad on us. It will make us proud and conceited. The very greatness of the subject matter will intoxicate us, and we shall come to think of ourselves as a cut above other Christians because of our interest in it and grasp of it; and we shall look down on those whose theological ideas seem to us crude and inadequate, and dismiss them as very poor specimens.

For, as Paul told the conceited Corinthians, "'Knowledge' puffs up. . . . If anyone imagines that he knows something, he does not yet know as he ought to know" (1 Corinthians 8:1-2, ESV). To be preoccupied with getting theological knowledge as an end in itself, to approach Bible study with no higher motive than a desire to know all the answers, is the direct route to a state of self-satisfied self-deception.

We need to guard our hearts against such an attitude, and pray to be kept from it. There can be no spiritual health without doctrinal knowledge; but it is equally true that there can be no spiritual health with it if it is sought for the wrong purpose and valued by the wrong standard. In this way, doctrinal study really can become a danger to spiritual life, and we today, no less than the Corinthians of old, need to be on our guard here.

J. I. PACKER, IN *KNOWING GOD*

Winning Our Praise

It is good to sing praises to our God;
for it is pleasant, and a song of praise is fitting.
(Psalm 147:1, ESV)

We praise what we enjoy because the delight is incomplete until it is expressed in praise. If we were not allowed to speak of what we value and celebrate what we love and praise what we admire, our joy would not be full. So if God loves us enough to make our joy full, He must not only give us Himself; He must also win from us the praise of our hearts — not because He needs to shore up some weakness in Himself or compensate for some deficiency, but because He loves us and seeks the fullness of our joy that can be found only in knowing and praising Him, the most magnificent of all Beings. If He is truly for us, He must be for Himself!

God is the one Being in all the universe for whom seeking His own praise is the ultimate loving act. For Him, self-exaltation is the highest virtue. When He does all things for the praise of His glory, He preserves for us and offers to us the only thing in all the world that can satisfy our longings. God is for us! And the foundation of this love is that God has been, is now, and always will be for Himself.

God is an unshakably happy God. He does everything He does to preserve and display that glory, for in this His soul rejoices.

All the works of God culminate in the praises of His redeemed people. The climax of His happiness is the delight He takes in the echoes of His excellence in the praises of the saints. This praise is the consummation of our own joy in God. Therefore, God's pursuit of praise from us and our pursuit of pleasure in Him are the same pursuit. This is the great gospel! This is the foundation of Christian Hedonism.

John Piper, in *Desiring God*

Possessing All Things

Blessed are the poor in spirit, for theirs is the kingdom of heaven.

(Matthew 5:3, ESV)

Our Lord referred to the tyranny of things when He said to His disciples, "If any man will come after me, let him deny himself, and take up his cross, and follow me. For whosoever will save his life shall lose it: and whosoever will lose his life for my sake shall find it" (Matthew 16:24-25, KJV).

Breaking this truth into fragments for our better understanding, it would seem that there is within each of us an enemy which we tolerate at our peril. Jesus called it "life" and "self," or as we would say, the self-life. Its chief characteristic is its possessiveness: the words "gain" and "profit" suggest this. To allow this enemy to live is in the end to lose everything. To repudiate it and give up all for Christ's sake is to lose nothing at last, but to preserve everything unto life eternal. And possibly also a hint is given here as to the only effective way to destroy this foe: it is by the Cross: "Let him . . . take up his cross and follow me."

The way to deeper knowledge of God is through the lonely valleys of soul-poverty and abnegation of all things. The blessed ones who possess the kingdom are they who have repudiated every external thing and have rooted from their hearts all sense of possessing. They are "poor in spirit." They have reached an inward state paralleling the outward circumstances of the common beggar in the streets of Jerusalem; that is what the word "poor" as Christ used it actually means.

These blessed poor are no longer slaves to the tyranny of things. They have broken the yoke of the oppressor; and this they have done not by fighting but by surrendering. Though free from all sense of possessing, they yet possess all things.

"Theirs is the kingdom of heaven."

A. W. Tozer, in *The Pursuit of God*

Integrity Before God

May integrity and uprightness preserve me, for I wait for you.
(Psalm 25:21, esv)

It is a great thing for a soul not only to wait upon God but to be filled with such a consciousness that its whole spirit and position is that of a waiting one — that it can, in childlike confidence, say, *Lord! Thou knowest I wait on Thee.* It will prove a mighty plea in prayer, giving ever-increasing boldness of expectation to claim the promise, "They that wait on Me shall not be ashamed!"

If we draw nigh to God, it must be with a true heart. There must be perfect integrity, wholeheartedness, in our dealing with God. As we read in Psalm 26, "Judge me, O Lord; for I have walked in mine integrity. . . . As for me, I walk in mine integrity" (verses 1,11, kjv) — there must be perfect uprightness or single-heartedness before God. The soul must know that it allows nothing sinful, nothing doubtful. If we are indeed to meet the Holy One and receive His full blessing, it must be with a heart wholly and singly given up to His will.

The whole spirit that animates us in the waiting must be, "Let integrity and uprightness" — Thou seest that I desire to come so to Thee, Thou knowest I am looking to Thee to work them perfectly in me — let them "preserve me, for I wait on Thee."

And if, as we attempt truly to live the life of fully and always waiting on God, we begin to discover how much that perfect integrity is wanting, this will just be one of the blessings which the waiting was meant to work. A soul cannot seek close fellowship with God, or attain the abiding consciousness of waiting on Him all the day, without a very honest and entire surrender to all His will.

Andrew Murray, in *Waiting on God*

God Sustains You and Me

The rain and the snow come . . . water the earth, making it bring forth and sprout, giving seed to the sower and bread to the eater.

(Isaiah 55:10, esv)

The Bible teaches that God not only sustains the universe around us, but also sustains you and me. "He himself gives to all mankind life and breath and everything. . . . For 'In him we live and move and have our being'" (Acts 17:25,28, esv). He supplies our daily food (see 2 Corinthians 9:10). Our times are in His hands (see Psalm 31:15).

Every breath we breathe is a gift from God; every bite of food we eat is given to us from His hand; every day we live is determined by Him. He has not left us to our own devices or the whims of nature or the malevolent acts of other people. No! He constantly sustains, provides for, and cares for us every moment of every day. Did your car break down when you could least afford the repairs? Did you miss an important meeting because the plane you were to fly in developed mechanical problems? The God who controls the stars in their courses also controls nuts and bolts and everything on your car and on that plane you were to fly in.

When I was an infant I had a bad case of measles. The virus apparently settled in my eyes and in my right ear, leaving me with monocular vision and deafness in that ear. Was God in control of that virus, or was I simply a victim of a chance childhood disease? God's moment-by-moment sustaining of His universe and everything in it leaves me no choice but to accept that the virus was indeed under His controlling hand. God was not looking the other way when that virus settled in the nerve endings of my ear and the muscles of my eyes. If we are to trust God, we must learn to see that He is continuously at work in every aspect and every moment of our lives.

Jerry Bridges, in *Trusting God*

WAITING FOR WHAT?

O LORD, be gracious to us; we wait for you.
(ISAIAH 33:2, ESV)

Our waiting for God may be waiting for Him in our times of prayer to take His place as God, and to work in us the sense of *His* holy presence and nearness. It may be a special petition, to which we are expecting an answer. It may be our whole inner life, in which we are on the lookout for God's putting forth of His power. It may be the whole state of His Church and saints, or some part of His work, for which our eyes are ever toward Him.

It is good that we sometimes count up to ourselves exactly what the things are we are waiting for, and we shall be emboldened to say, "On Thee do I wait."

On Whom we are waiting? Not an idol, but the living God, such as He really is in His great glory, His infinite holiness, His power, wisdom, and goodness, in His love and nearness. It is the presence of a master that wakens up the whole attention of the servant who waits on Him. It is the presence of God, as He can in Christ by His Holy Spirit make Himself known, and keep the soul under its covering and shadow, that will waken and strengthen the true waiting spirit.

This waiting on God has hardly yet been acknowledged as the only true Christianity. And yet, if it be true that God alone is goodness and joy and love; if it be true that our highest blessedness is in having as much of God as we can; if it be true that Christ has redeemed us wholly for God, and made a life of continual abiding in His presence possible, nothing less ought to satisfy than to be ever breathing this blessed atmosphere, "I wait on Thee."

ANDREW MURRAY, IN *WAITING ON GOD*

Everything You Need

Blessed are the people . . . who walk, O Lord, in the light of your face, who exult in your name all the day.

(Psalm 89:15-16, esv)

When Moses encountered God in a burning bush, he asked, "If I go to the Israelites and say to them: The God of your fathers has sent me to you, and they ask me, 'What is His name?' what should I tell them?" (Exodus 3:13, hcsb).

"God replied to Moses, 'I AM WHO I AM. This is what you are to say to the Israelites: I AM has sent me to you'" (3:14, hcsb). By this God was declaring, "I am the eternal One. I will be what I will be." In essence this declaration held a promise: "Whatever you need Me to be in your life, that is what I will be. I am everything you will need." During the next forty years, Moses came to experience God as *Yahweh*, the Great I AM. God was everything Moses and Israel needed Him to be.

Whenever God reveals His nature in a new way, *it is always for a purpose.* He created you for a love relationship with Him. When He encounters you, He is allowing you to know Him by experience. Encounters with God are always an expression of God's love for you. Jesus said: "The one who has My commands and keeps them is the one who loves Me. And the one who loves Me will be loved by My Father. I also will love him and will reveal Myself to him" (John 14:21, hcsb).

If you have a love relationship with God, you will experience Him actively working in and through your life. For instance, you could not truly know God as the "Comforter in sorrow" unless you experienced His compassion during a time of grief or sadness.

The various names of God found in Scripture can become our call to worship. Acknowledging God's name amounts to recognizing who God is. Calling on His name indicates we are seeking His presence. To praise His name is to exalt Him. God's name is majestic and worthy of our praise.

Henry Blackaby and Richard Blackaby, in *Experiencing God*

Strength and Courage

Be strong, and let your heart take courage; wait for the Lord!
(Psalm 27:14, esv)

The psalmist had just said, "I had fainted, unless I had believed to see the goodness of the Lord in the land of the living" (Psalm 27:14, kjv). If it had not been for his faith in God, his heart had fainted. But in the confident assurance in God which faith gives, he urges himself and us to remember one thing above all — to wait upon God. "Wait on the Lord: be of good courage . . . wait, I say, on the Lord" (Psalm 27:14, kjv).

One of the chief needs in our waiting upon God, one of the deepest secrets of its blessedness and blessing, is a quiet, confident persuasion that it is not in vain. It is courage to believe that God will hear and help; that we are waiting on a God who never could disappoint His people.

"Be strong and of good courage." These words are frequently found in Scripture in connection with some great and difficult enterprise, in prospect of the combat with the power of strong enemies, and the utter insufficiency of all human strength. Is waiting on God a work so difficult that, for this too, such words are needed — "Be strong, and let your heart take courage"? Yes, indeed.

Our souls are so little accustomed to hold fellowship with God; the God on whom we wait so often appears to hide Himself. We who have to wait are often tempted to fear that we do not wait aright, that our faith is too feeble, that our desire is not as upright or as earnest as it should be, that our surrender is not complete.

Amid all these causes of fear or doubt, how blessed to hear the voice of God, "Be strong, and let thine heart take courage!" Let nothing in heaven or earth or hell — let nothing keep you from waiting on your God in full assurance that it cannot be in vain.

Andrew Murray, in *Waiting on God*

A Glorious Duty

Whatever you do, do all to the glory of God.
(1 Corinthians 10:31, esv)

It is the duty of every person to live for the glory of God. If God made us for His glory, it is clear that we should live for His glory. Our duty comes from God's design.

What does it mean to glorify God?

It does not mean to make Him more glorious. It means to acknowledge His glory, to value it above all things, and to make it known. It implies heartfelt gratitude: "The one who offers thanksgiving as his sacrifice glorifies me" (Psalm 50:23, esv). It also implies trust: Abraham "grew strong in his faith as he gave glory to God" (Romans 4:20, esv).

Glorifying God is the duty not only of those who have heard the preaching of the gospel, but also of people who have only the witness of nature and their own conscience: "For his invisible attributes, namely, his eternal power and divine nature, have been clearly perceived, ever since the creation of the world, in the things that have been made. So they are without excuse. For although they knew God, they did not honor him as God or give thanks to him, but they became futile in their thinking, and their foolish hearts were darkened" (Romans 1:20-21, esv).

God will not judge anyone for failing to perform a duty if the person had no access to the knowledge of that duty. But even without the Bible, all people have access to the knowledge that we are created by God and therefore are dependent on Him for everything, thus owing Him the gratitude and trust of our hearts. Deep within us we all know that it is our duty to glorify our Maker by thanking Him for all we have, trusting Him for all we need, and obeying all His revealed will.

John Piper, in *Desiring God*

More Than Doing

Behold, my servants shall sing for gladness of heart.
(Isaiah 65:14, esv)

Generally speaking, we are in God's will whenever we are leading the kind of life He wants for us. And that leaves a lot of room for initiative on our part, which is essential: our individual initiatives are central to His will for us.

Of course, we cannot fail to do what He directs us to do and yet still be in His will. And quite apart from any specific directions He may give us, there are many ways of living and being that are clearly not in His will. The Ten Commandments given to Moses are so deep and powerful on these matters that if humanity followed them, daily life would be transformed beyond recognition, and large segments of the public media would collapse for lack of material. Consider a daily newspaper or television newscast and eliminate from it every report that presupposes a breaking of one of the Ten Commandments. Very little will be left.

But one who inquires seriously after God's guidance must never forget that even if one were to do all the particular things God wants and explicitly commands us to do, one might still not be the person God would have one to be. It is always true that "the letter kills, but the Spirit gives life" (2 Corinthians 3:6, esv). An obsession merely with *doing* all God commands may be the very thing that rules out *being* the kind of person that He calls us to be.

What God wants us to do is very important, of course, and we must be careful to learn how to know it and do it, but it is never enough by itself to allow us to understand and enter the radiant life before the shining face of God that is offered to us in the grace of the gospel — a life pleasing to him, in view of which He can say, "This is my beloved child, in whom I am well pleased."

Dallas Willard, in *Hearing God*

The Surrender Tested

For whoever would save his life will lose it,
but whoever loses his life for my sake will find it.
(Matthew 16:25, esv)

"Blessed are the poor in spirit: for theirs is the kingdom of heaven" (Matthew 5:3, kjv). Let me exhort you to take seriously this surrendering, this freedom from all sense of possessing. It is not to be understood as mere Bible teaching to be stored away in the mind along with an inert mass of other doctrines. It is a marker on the road to greener pastures, a path chiseled against the steep sides of the mount of God. We dare not try to bypass it if we would follow on in this holy pursuit. We must ascend a step at a time. If we refuse one step we bring our progress to an end.

As is frequently true, this New Testament principle of spiritual life finds its best illustration in the Old Testament. In the story of Abraham and Isaac we have a dramatic picture of the surrendered life as well as an excellent commentary on the first Beatitude.

Abraham was old when Isaac was born, and the child became at once the delight and idol of his heart, till at last the relationship bordered upon the perilous. God stepped in to save both father and son from the consequences of an uncleansed love.

"Take now thy son," said God to Abraham, "thine only son Isaac, whom thou lovest, and get thee into the land of Moriah; and offer him there for a burnt offering upon one of the mountains which I will tell thee of" (Genesis 22:2, kjv).

This was Abraham's trial by fire, and he did not fail in the crucible. He would offer his son as God had directed him to do, and then trust God to raise him from the dead. It is beautiful to see that, while he erred as to God's method, he had correctly sensed the secret of His great heart. And the solution accords well with the New Testament Scripture, "Whosoever will lose . . . for my sake shall find" (Matthew 16:25, kjv).

A. W. Tozer, in *The Pursuit of God*

The Blessedness of Possessing Nothing

Then Abraham reached out his hand and took the knife to slaughter his son.
(Genesis 22:10, ESV)

God let Abraham go through with it up to the point where He knew there would be no retreat, then forbade him to lay a hand upon the boy. The old man lifted his head to respond to the Voice and stood there on the mount strong and pure and grand, a man marked out by the Lord for special treatment, a friend and favorite of the Most High. Now he was wholly surrendered, utterly obedient, a man who possessed nothing. He had concentrated his all in the person of his dear son, and God had taken it from him.

God could have begun out on the margin of Abraham's life and worked inward to the center; He chose rather to cut quickly to the heart and have it over in one sharp act of separation. In dealing thus, He practiced an economy of means and time. It hurt cruelly, but it was effective.

I have said that Abraham possessed nothing. Yet was not this poor man rich? Everything he owned before was still his to enjoy: sheep, camels, herds, goods of every sort. He had also his wife and friends, and best of all he had Isaac safe by his side. He had everything, but he possessed nothing. There is the spiritual secret. There is the sweet theology of the heart which can be learned only in the school of renunciation. The books on systematic theology overlook this, but the wise will understand.

After that bitter and blessed experience I think the words "my" and "mine" never had again the same meaning for Abraham. The sense of possession which they connote was gone from his heart. *Things* had been cast out forever. They had now become external to the man. His inner heart was free from them. The world said, "Abraham is rich," but he knew that he owned nothing, that his real treasures were inward and eternal.

A. W. Tozer, in *The Pursuit of God*

Coming in Confidence

For you, O Lord, are my hope, my trust, O Lord, from my youth.
(Psalm 71:5, esv)

Above everything, when you wait on God, do so in the spirit of abounding hopefulness. It is God — in His glory, in His power, in His love longing to bless you — that you are waiting on.

If you say you are afraid of deceiving yourself with vain hope, because you do not see or feel any warrant in your present state for such special expectations, my answer is: *God* is the warrant for your expecting great things. You are not going to wait on *yourself* to see what you feel and what changes come to you. You are going to *wait on God* — to know first *what He is*, and then, after that, what He will do.

The whole duty and blessedness of waiting on God has its root in this, that He is such a blessed Being — full to overflowing of goodness and power and life and joy — that we, however wretched, cannot for any time come into contact with Him without that life and power secretly, silently beginning to enter into us and blessing us.

God is Love! That is the one, only, and all-sufficient warrant of your expectation. Love seeketh out its own: God's love is just His delight to impart Himself and His blessedness to His children.

Come, and however feeble you feel, just wait in His presence. As a feeble, sickly invalid is brought out into the sunshine to let its warmth go through him, come with all that is dark and cold in you into the sunshine of God's holy, omnipotent love, and sit and wait there, with the one thought: Here I am, in the sunshine of His love. As the sun does its work in the weak one who seeks its rays, God will do His work in you.

Oh, do trust Him fully!

Andrew Murray, in *Waiting on God*

WHAT GOD HAS DONE

The saying is trustworthy and deserving of full acceptance, that Christ Jesus came into the world to save sinners.
(1 TIMOTHY 1:15, ESV)

In His great mercy, God sent forth His Son, Jesus Christ, to save sinners by dying in their place on the cross and rising bodily from the dead. Over against the terrifying news that we have fallen under the condemnation of our Creator and that He is bound by His own righteous character to preserve the worth of His glory by pouring out eternal wrath on our sin, there is the wonderful news of the gospel. This is a truth no one can ever learn from nature. It has to be told to neighbors and preached in churches and carried by missionaries.

The good news is that God Himself has decreed a way to satisfy the demands of His justice without condemning the whole human race. Hell is one way to settle accounts with sinners and uphold His justice. But there is another way. The wisdom of God has ordained a way for the love of God to deliver us from the wrath of God without compromising the justice of God.

And what is this wisdom? The death of the Son of God for sinners! The death of Christ is the wisdom of God (see 1 Corinthians 1:23-24) by which the love of God saves sinners from the wrath of God, all the while upholding and demonstrating the righteousness of God in Christ. Romans 3:25-26 may be the most important verses in the Bible: "God put [Christ] forward as a propitiation by his blood, to be received by faith. This was to show God's righteousness, because in his divine forbearance he had passed over former sins. It was to show his righteousness at the present time, so that he might be just and the justifier of the one who has faith in Jesus" (ESV).

Not either/or! Both! God is wholly just! *And* He justifies the ungodly! He acquits the guilty, but is not guilty in doing so. This is the greatest news in the world!

JOHN PIPER, IN *DESIRING GOD*

A Line, Not a Circle

I press on to make it my own,
because Christ Jesus has made me his own.
(Philippians 3:12, esv)

The Christian life is not futile. It does not follow the pattern of the circle. The image of the Christian life is a line. It has a beginning, a middle, and an end. There is an end goal of glory. The God who started all things in the beginning has a goal for His people. We reach ahead for the day when we hear Christ say, "Come, My beloved, enter the kingdom which My Father has prepared for you."

With the apostle Paul we say, "Forgetting what lies behind and reaching forward to what lies ahead, I press on toward the goal for the prize of the upward call of God in Christ Jesus" (Philippians 3:13-14, nasb). In the Christian life there is an *upward call*. One does not move upward in a circle. We are on a line that is going somewhere. It is moving forward. In a word, there is *progress* to the Christian life.

All Christians make progress. Progress is made certain by the indwelling Holy Spirit who refuses to allow us to stand still. Oh, we try to stand still. We even regress. Like the disciples, we hide in our upper rooms, huddled in fear. But Jesus will not allow us to stay there.

The Lord is intensely interested in our welfare and our maturing. He wants us to learn more and more about God and how to please God. He wants us to find joy in pleasing God. He wants us to change, like the healed blind man, so that our vision clears, so that we grow in how we perceive the world and how we act in it. Growth and change in such perception means learning more and more about what pleases the Holy God. The growth in pleasing God is sanctification.

R. C. Sproul, in *Pleasing God*

CONFIDENCE IN GOD'S SOVEREIGNTY

Our God is in the heavens; he does all that he pleases.

(PSALM 115:3, ESV)

Confidence in God's sovereignty in all that affects us is crucial to our trusting Him. If there's a single event in all the universe that can occur outside of God's control, then we cannot trust Him. His love may be infinite, but if His power is limited and His purpose can be thwarted, we cannot trust Him. You may entrust to me your most valuable possessions; I may love you, and my aim to honor your trust may be sincere. But if I don't have the power or ability to guard your valuables, you cannot truly entrust them to me.

Paul, however, said we can entrust our most valuable possession to the Lord: "I know whom I have believed, and am convinced that he is able to guard what I have entrusted to him for that day" (2 Timothy 1:12, NIV). "But," someone says, "Paul is speaking there of eternal life. It's our problems in this life that make me wonder about God's sovereignty."

It should be evident, however, that God's sovereignty does not begin at death. His sovereign direction in our lives even precedes our births. God rules as surely on earth as He does in heaven. He permits, for reasons known only to Himself, people to act contrary to and in defiance of His revealed will. But He never permits them to act contrary to His sovereign will.

Our plans can succeed only when they are consistent with God's purpose, and no plan can succeed against Him (see Proverbs 16:9; 19:21; 21:30). No one can straighten what He makes crooked or make crooked what He has made straight (see Ecclesiastes 7:13). No one can say, "I'll do this or that," and have it happen if it is not part of God's sovereign will (see James 4:15).

JERRY BRIDGES, IN *TRUSTING GOD*

THE HEART'S WAITING

Be strong, and let your heart take courage,
all you who wait for the LORD!
(PSALM 31:24, ESV)

It is with the heart we must wait upon God. "Let your heart take courage!"

All our waiting depends upon the state of the heart. As a man's heart is, so is he before God. We can advance no further or deeper into the holy place of God's presence to wait on Him there, than our heart is prepared for it by the Holy Spirit. The message is, "Let your heart take courage, all ye that wait on the Lord."

The truth appears so simple that some may ask, Do not all admit this? Where is the need of insisting on it so specially?

Because very many Christians have no sense of the great difference between the religion of the mind and the religion of the heart, and the former is far more diligently cultivated than the latter. They know not how infinitely greater the heart is than the mind. It is in this that one of the chief causes must be sought of the feebleness of our Christian life, and it is only as this is understood that waiting on God will bring its full blessing.

Present your heart before Him as that wonderful part of your spiritual nature in which God reveals Himself, and by which you can know Him. Cultivate the greatest confidence that, though you cannot see into your heart, God is working there by His Holy Spirit. Let the heart wait at times in perfect silence and quiet; in its hidden depths God will work.

Be sure of this, and just wait on Him. Give your whole heart, with its secret workings, into God's hands continually. He wants the heart, and takes it, and as God dwells in it. "Be strong, and let your heart take courage, all ye that wait on the Lord."

ANDREW MURRAY, IN *WAITING ON GOD*

Giving Up "Things"

For who sees anything different in you?
What do you have that you did not receive?
(1 Corinthians 4:7, esv)

We are often hindered from giving up our treasures to the Lord out of fear for their safety; this is especially true when those treasures are loved relatives and friends. But we need have no such fears. Our Lord came not to destroy but to save. Everything is safe which we commit to Him, and nothing is really safe which is not so committed.

Our gifts and talents should also be turned over to Him. They should be recognized for what they are, God's loan to us, and should never be considered in any sense our own. We have no more right to claim credit for special abilities than for blue eyes or strong muscles.

The Christian who is alive enough to know himself even slightly will recognize the symptoms of this possession malady and will grieve to find them in his own heart. If the longing after God is strong enough within him, he will want to do something about the matter. Now, what should he do?

First he should put away all defense and make no attempt to excuse himself either in his own eyes or before the Lord. Let him come defenseless before the Lord and he will have for his defender no less than God Himself. Let the inquiring Christian trample under foot every slippery trick of his deceitful heart and insist upon frank and open relations with the Lord.

Then he should remember that this is holy business. No careless or casual dealings will suffice. Let him come to God in full determination to be heard. Let him insist that God accept his all, that He take *things* out of his heart and Himself reign there in power. It may be he will need to become specific, to name things and people by their names one by one.

A. W. Tozer, in *The Pursuit of God*

A Love We Can Trust

By this we know love, that he laid down his life for us.

(1 John 3:16, esv)

According to 1 John 4:16, "God is love." This does not say that God loves, though He does love perfectly and unconditionally. The Scripture says that God's essential nature is love. God will never act contrary to His nature. You will never experience God expressing His will except in a demonstration of perfect love. God's kind of love always seeks His best for each person. If we reject His best, He will discipline us. However, the discipline will come from a heavenly Father who loves us and who will do whatever is necessary to bring us to a place in our lives where we can receive what He wants to give us (see Hebrews 12:5-11).

God does bring discipline, judgment, and wrath on those who continue to live in sin and rebellion against Him. Even this discipline, though, is based on love. "For the Lord disciplines the one He loves, and punishes every son whom He receives" (Hebrews 12:6, hcsb). Because His nature is love, I'm confident that however He expresses His love to me is always best.

Your confidence in the love nature of God is crucial. This has been a powerful influence in my life. I always view my circumstances against the backdrop of the cross, where God clearly demonstrated once and for all His deep love for me. I may not always understand my current situation or how things will eventually turn out, but I can trust in the love Christ proved to me when He laid down His life for me on the cross. In the death and resurrection of Jesus Christ, God forever convinced me that He loves me. I choose to base my trust in God on what I know — His love for me — and I choose to trust that in time He will help me understand the confusing circumstances I may be experiencing.

Henry Blackaby and Richard Blackaby, in *Experiencing God*

ULTIMATE SURRENDER

Remember, then, what you received and heard. Keep it, and repent.

(REVELATION 3:3, ESV)

Repentance is much more than regret, more than deep sorrow for past sins. The biblical word for repentance literally means "a change of mind." One church scholar describes it as "that mighty change in mind, heart, and life, wrought by the Spirit of God."[2]

Thus, repentance is replete with radical implications, for a fundamental change of mind not only turns us from the sinful past, but transforms our life plan, values, ethics, and actions as we begin to see the world through God's eyes rather than ours. That kind of transformation requires the ultimate surrender of self.

The call to repentance—individual and corporate—is one of the most consistent themes of Scripture. The demand for repentance is clear in God's command to Moses (see Leviticus 26:40-41), and its brokenhearted reality and passion flows through David's eloquent prayer of contrition in Psalm 51. It is the consistent refrain of the prophets.

Repentance is the keynote of the New Testament as well. It is John the Baptist's single message: "Repent, for the kingdom of heaven is at hand (Matthew 3:2, ESV). And according to Mark's Gospel, "Repent and believe in the gospel" (1.15, ESV) were among Jesus' first public words. And His last earthly instructions to His disciples included the directive "that repentance and forgiveness of sins should be proclaimed in his name to all nations" (Luke 24:47, ESV).

Repentance is an indispensable part of the conversion process that takes place under the convicting power of the Holy Spirit. But repentance is also a continuing state of mind. Believers are told, for example, to "prove their repentance by their deeds" (Acts 26:20, NIV).

Without a continuing repentant attitude—a persistent desire to turn away from our own nature and seek God's nature—Christian growth is impossible; loving God is impossible.

CHARLES COLSON, IN *LOVING GOD*

A Loaded Question

Behold, God is my salvation; I will trust, and will not be afraid.

(Isaiah 12:2, esv)

The question "Can you trust God?" has various possible meanings. Can you *trust* God? In other words, is He dependable in times of adversity? But a second meaning is also critical: Can *you* trust God? Do you have such a relationship with God, such a confidence in Him, that you believe He is with you in your adversity even though you do not see any evidence of His presence and His power?

It isn't easy to trust God in times of adversity. No one enjoys pain, and when it comes, we want it relieved as quickly as possible. Even the apostle Paul pleaded with God three times to take away the thorn in his flesh before he finally found God's grace to be sufficient (see 2 Corinthians 12:7-10). Joseph pleaded with Pharaoh's cupbearer to get him out of prison (see Genesis 40:14). And the writer of Hebrews very honestly states, "For the moment all discipline seems painful rather than pleasant" (Hebrews 12:11, esv).

While writing this, I experienced one of those periods of adversity when I found it difficult to trust God. Mine happened to be a physical ailment that exacerbated a lifelong infirmity. It came at a very inconvenient time and for several weeks would not respond to any medical treatment.

During those weeks, as I continually prayed to God for relief, I was reminded of Solomon's words: "Consider what God has done: Who can straighten what he has made crooked?" (Ecclesiastes 7:13, niv).

God had brought a "crooked" event into my life, and I became acutely aware that only He could straighten it. Could I trust God whether or not He straightened my "crook" and relieved my distress? Did I really believe that a God who loved me and knew what was best for me was in control of my situation? Could I trust Him even if I didn't understand? That's a question for us all.

Jerry Bridges, in *Trusting God*

Mind and Heart

Trust in the Lord with all your heart,
and do not lean on your own understanding.
(Proverbs 3:5, esv)

People imagine that if their mind is occupied with the truth, the spiritual life will as a matter of course be strengthened. This is by no means the case. The understanding deals with conceptions and images of divine things, but it cannot reach the real life of the soul. Hence the command, "Trust in the Lord *with all thine heart*; and lean not unto thine own understanding" (kjv, emphasis added). It is with the heart man believeth and comes into touch with God. It is in the heart God has given His Spirit, to be there to us the presence and the power of God working in us.

It is the heart that must trust and love and worship and obey. My mind is utterly impotent in creating or maintaining the spiritual life within me: the heart must wait on God for Him to work it in me.

Reason may tell me what God's word says, but it can do nothing to the feeding of the soul on the bread of life — this the heart alone can do by its faith and trust in God. The Christian needs ever, when he has studied or heard God's word, to cease from his thoughts, to put no trust in them, and to waken up his heart to open itself before God, and seek the living fellowship with Him.

This is the blessedness of waiting upon God, that I confess the impotence of all my thoughts and efforts, and set myself still to bow my heart before Him in holy silence, and to trust Him to renew and strengthen His own work in me.

Remember the difference between knowing with the mind and believing with the heart. Beware of the temptation of leaning upon your understanding, with its clear strong thoughts. They only help you to know what the heart must get from God: in themselves they are only images and shadows.

Andrew Murray, in *Waiting on God*

The Ultimate Concern

Blessed is everyone who fears the Lord, who walks in his ways!
(Psalm 128:1, esv)

Is it not a fact that a love for God's revealed truth, and a desire to know as much of it as one can, is natural to every person who has been born again? Look at Psalm 119 — "Teach me your statutes!"; "Open my eyes, that I may behold wondrous things out of your law"; "Oh how I love your law!"; "How sweet are your words to my taste, sweeter than honey to my mouth!"; "Give me understanding, that I may know your testimonies!" (verses 12,18,97, 103,125, esv). Does not every child of God long, with the psalmist, to know just as much about his heavenly Father as he can learn? Is this not indeed one proof that he has been born again? And is it not right that he should seek to satisfy this God-given desire to the full?

Yes, of course it is. But if you look back to Psalm 119 again, you will see that the psalmist's concern to get knowledge about God was not a theoretical, but a practical concern. His supreme desire was to know and enjoy God Himself, and he valued knowledge about God simply as a means to this end. He wanted to understand God's truth in order that his heart might respond to it and his life be conformed to it.

Observe the emphasis of the psalm's opening verses. "Blessed are those whose way is blameless, who *walk in the law of the Lord!* Blessed are those who keep his testimonies, who *seek him with their whole heart. . . .* Oh that *my ways may be steadfast in keeping your statutes!*" (verses 1,2,5, esv, emphasis added). He was interested in truth and orthodoxy, in biblical teaching and theology, not as ends in themselves, but as means to the further ends of life and godliness. His ultimate concern was with the knowledge and service of the great God whose truth he sought to understand.

J. I. Packer, in *Knowing God*

Making Faith Possible

And I will put my Spirit within you, and cause you to walk in my statutes and be careful to obey my rules.

(Ezekiel 36:27, esv)

Repentance and faith are our work. But we will not repent and believe unless God does His work to overcome our hard and rebellious hearts. This divine work is called *regeneration.* Our work is called *conversion.*

Conversion does indeed include an act of will by which we renounce sin and submit ourselves to the authority of Christ and put our hope and trust in Him. We are responsible to do this and will be condemned if we don't. But just as clearly, the Bible teaches that, owing to our hard heart and willful blindness and spiritual insensitivity, we cannot do this.

We must first experience the regenerating work of the Holy Spirit. The Scriptures promised long ago that God would devote Himself to this work in order to create for Himself a faithful people: "The Lord your God will circumcise your heart and the heart of your offspring, so that you will love the Lord your God with all your heart and with all your soul, that you may live" (Deuteronomy 30:6, esv). "I will give them a heart to know that I am the Lord, and they shall be my people and I will be their God, for they shall return to me with their whole heart" (Jeremiah 24:7, esv). "And I will give them one heart, and a new spirit I will put within them. I will remove the heart of stone from their flesh and give them a heart of flesh. . . . And they shall be my people, and I will be their God" (Ezekiel 11:19-20, esv).

These great promises from the Old Testament describe a work of God that changes a heart of stone into a heart of flesh and causes people to "know" and "love" and "obey" God. Without this spiritual heart transplant, people will not know and love and obey God. This prior work of God is what we mean by regeneration.

John Piper, in *Desiring God*

Our Testing Time

God tested Abraham and said to him, "Abraham!"
And he said, "Here am I."
(Genesis 22:1, ESV)

Let us never forget that the truth of "the blessedness of possessing nothing," and all such truths, cannot be learned by rote as one would learn the facts of physical science. They must be experienced before we can really know them. We must in our hearts live through Abraham's harsh and bitter experiences if we would know the blessedness which follows them.

The ancient curse will not go out painlessly; the tough old miser within us will not lie down and die obedient to our command. He must be torn out of our heart like a plant from the soil; he must be extracted in agony and blood like a tooth from the jaw. He must be expelled from our soul by violence as Christ expelled the money changers from the temple. And we shall need to steel ourselves against his piteous begging, and to recognize it as springing out of self-pity, one of the most reprehensible sins of the human heart.

If we would indeed know God in growing intimacy we must go this way of renunciation. And if we are set upon the pursuit of God, He will sooner or later bring us to this test. Abraham's testing (see Genesis 22) was, at the time, not known to him as such, yet if he had taken some course other than the one he did, the whole history of the Old Testament would have been different. God would have found His man, no doubt, but the loss to Abraham would have been tragic beyond the telling.

So we will be brought one by one to the testing place, and we may never know when we are there. At that testing place there will be no dozen possible choices for us; just one and an alternative—but our whole future will be conditioned by the choice we make.

A. W. Tozer, in *The Pursuit of God*

Every Detail Under His Control

Many are the plans in the mind of a man,
but it is the purpose of the Lord that will stand.
(Proverbs 19:21, esv)

Not only are the willful malevolent acts of other people under God's sovereign control, so also are the mistakes and failures of other people. Did another driver go through a red light, strike your car, and send you to the hospital with multiple fractures? Did a physician fail to detect your cancer in its early stages, when it would have been treatable? Did you end up with an incompetent instructor in an important course in college, or an inept supervisor who blocked your career in business? All these circumstances are under God's controlling hand, as He works them out in our lives for our good.

Neither the willful malicious acts nor the unintended mistakes of people can thwart God's purpose for us. "No wisdom, no understanding, no counsel can avail against the Lord" (Proverbs 21:30, esv). The Roman governor Felix unjustly left Paul in prison for over two years because he wanted to grant a favor to the Jews (see Acts 24:27); Joseph was left in prison for two years because Pharaoh's cupbearer forgot him (see Genesis 40:14,23; 41:1). These two godly men were left to languish in prison — one because of deliberate injustice and the other because of inexcusable forgetfulness — but both their predicaments were under the sovereign control of an infinitely wise and loving God.

Nothing is so small or trivial as to escape the attention of God's sovereign control; nothing is so great as to be beyond His power to control it. The insignificant sparrow cannot fall to the ground without His will; the mighty Roman empire cannot crucify Jesus unless that power is given it by God (see Matthew 10:29; John 19:10-11). And what is true for the sparrow and for Jesus is true for you and me. No detail of life is too insignificant for our heavenly Father's attention; no circumstance is so big that He cannot control it.

Jerry Bridges, in *Trusting God*

Fear and Hope

Behold, the eye of the Lord is on those who fear him,
on those who hope in his steadfast love.
(Psalm 33:18-22, esv)

God's eye is upon His people; their eye is upon Him. In waiting upon God, our eye, looking up to Him meets His looking down upon us. This is the blessedness of waiting upon God, that it takes our eyes and thoughts away from ourselves, even our needs and desires, and occupies us with our God. We worship Him in His glory and love, with His all-seeing eye watching over us, that He may supply our every need.

Let us consider this wonderful meeting between God and His people, and mark well what we are taught here of them on whom God's eye rests, and of Him on whom our eye rests.

"The eye of the Lord is upon them that *fear* him, upon them that *hope* in his mercy" (Psalm 33:18, kjv, emphasis added). Fear and hope are generally thought to be in conflict with each other; in the presence and worship of God they are found side by side in perfect and beautiful harmony. In God Himself, all apparent contradictions are reconciled. Righteousness and peace, judgment and mercy, holiness and love, infinite power and infinite gentleness, a majesty that is exalted above all heaven, and a condescension that bows very low, meet and kiss each other.

There is indeed a fear that hath torment, that is cast out entirely by perfect love. But there is a fear that is found in the very heavens.

The deeper we bow before His holiness in holy fear and adoring awe, in deep reverence and humble self-abasement, even as the angels veil their faces before the throne, the more will His holiness rest upon us, and the soul be filled to have God reveal Himself; the deeper we enter into the truth "that no flesh should glory in his presence" (1 Corinthians 1:29, kjv) will it be given us to see His glory.

Andrew Murray, in *Waiting on God*

The First Step Home

We have confidence to enter the holy places by the blood of Jesus.

(Hebrews 10:19, esv)

God formed us for His pleasure, and so formed us that we as well as He can in divine communion enjoy the sweet and mysterious mingling of kindred personalities. He meant us to see Him and live with Him and draw our life from His smile. But we have been guilty of that "foul revolt" of which John Milton speaks when describing the rebellion of Satan and his hosts. We have broken with God. We have ceased to obey Him or love Him and in guilt and fear have fled as far as possible from His manifest Presence. We have fled, like Adam, to hide among the trees of the garden, or like Peter to shrink away crying, "Depart from me; for I am a sinful man, O Lord" (Luke 5:8, kjv).

So the life of man upon the earth is a life away from the Presence, wrenched loose from that "blissful center" which is our right and proper dwelling place, our first estate which we kept not, the loss of which is the cause of our unceasing restlessness.

The whole work of God in redemption is to undo the tragic effects of that foul revolt, and to bring us back again into right and eternal relationship with Himself. This requires that our sins be disposed of satisfactorily, that a full reconciliation be effected and the way opened for us to return again into conscious communion with God and to live again in the Presence as before. Then by His prevenient working within us He moves us to return.

This first comes to our notice when our restless hearts feel a yearning for the Presence of God and we say within ourselves, "I will arise and go to my Father." That is the first step, and as the Chinese sage Lao-tze has said, "The journey of a thousand miles begins with a first step."

A. W. Tozer, in *The Pursuit of God*

What God Wants to Tell Us

There is no faithfulness or steadfast love,
and no knowledge of God in the land.
(Hosea 4:1, ESV)

While man has never had so much knowledge about the world as he possesses today, perhaps he has never had so little knowledge of God. That is why our times are marked by a singular lack of understanding, appreciation, and genuine insight into the need of the hour.

When people truly know God and are growing in a genuine relationship with Him, their lives are marked by integrity and reliability. They do not treat dishonesty of the heart or of the lips indifferently. They are, in a word, *holy.* But our age is frightened of holiness. It is all the more tragic, therefore, that the church has also become frightened of holiness. It likes nothing less than to be different. The same may be true of us individually. Why? Because we do not know God as we should. If we really knew Him, it would show in the character of our lives.

The knowledge of God is essential to Christian growth. In the opening section of Peter's second letter, he draws attention to this crucial fact. He urges his friends to grow spiritually, wishing them grace and peace "in the knowledge of God" (1:2, ESV). He tells them that God's power has given us everything we need to live the Christian life "through the knowledge of him who called us to his own glory and excellence" (verses 2-3, ESV). Similarly, when Paul expresses his desire for the Christians at Colossae to grow spiritually, the same theme recurs: Growth is particularly accompanied by "increasing in the knowledge of God" (Colossians 1:10, ESV).

Our mistake has been to compose our *own* ground rules for the Christian life — how presumptuous can we be? — instead of listening to what God Himself wants to say to us, namely: "If you want to grow as a Christian, you must first of all grow in the knowledge of me."

Sinclair Ferguson, in *A Heart for God*

Hope in the Midst of Danger

Let your steadfast love, O Lord, be upon us, even as we hope in you.
(Psalm 33:22, esv)

"The eye of the Lord is upon them . . . to deliver their soul from *death,* and to keep them alive in *famine*" (Psalm 33:18-19, kjv, emphasis added). Not to prevent the danger of death and famine — this is often needed to stir the waiting on Him — but to deliver and to keep alive. For the dangers are often very real and dark; the situation, whether in the temporal or spiritual life, may appear to be utterly hopeless. There is always one hope: God's eye is on them.

That eye sees the danger, and sees in tender love His trembling waiting child, and sees the moment when the heart is ripe for the blessing, and sees the way in which it is to come. This living, mighty God — oh, let us fear Him and hope in His mercy!

Oh, the blessedness of waiting on such a God! He is a very present help in every time of trouble; a shield and defense against every danger. Children of God! Will you not learn to sink down in entire helplessness and impotence and in stillness to wait and see the salvation of God?

In the utmost spiritual famine, and when death appears to prevail, oh, wait on God! He *does* deliver, He *does* keep alive. Say it not only in solitude, but say it to each other — this psalm speaks not of one but of God's people — "*Our* soul waiteth for the Lord: he is *our* help and *our* shield. For *our* heart shall rejoice in him, because *we* have trusted in his holy name" (33:20-21, kjv, emphasis added).

Strengthen and encourage each other in the holy exercise of waiting, that each may not only say of it himself, but of his brethren, "We have waited for him, we will be glad and rejoice in his salvation" (Isaiah 25:9, kjv).

Andrew Murray, in *Waiting on God*

Behind the Veil

We have this as a sure and steadfast anchor of the soul,
a hope that enters into the inner place behind the curtain.
(Hebrews 6:19, esv)

The interior journey of the soul from the wilds of sin into the enjoyed Presence of God is beautifully illustrated in the Old Testament tabernacle.

The returning sinner first entered the outer court where he offered a blood sacrifice on the brazen altar and washed himself in the laver that stood near it. Then through a veil he passed into the holy place where no natural light could come, but the golden candlestick, which spoke of Jesus the Light of the World, threw its soft glow over all. There also was the shew-bread to tell of Jesus, the Bread of Life, and the altar of incense, a figure of unceasing prayer.

Though the worshipper had enjoyed so much, still he had not yet entered the Presence of God.

Another veil separated from the Holy of Holies where above the mercy seat dwelt the very God Himself in awful and glorious manifestation. While the tabernacle stood, only the high priest could enter there, and that but once a year, with blood that he offered for his sins and the sins of the people. It was this last veil which was rent when our Lord gave up the ghost on Calvary, and the sacred writer explains that this rending of the veil opened the way for every worshipper in the world to come by the new and living way straight into the divine Presence.

Everything in the New Testament accords with this Old Testament picture. Ransomed men need no longer pause in fear to enter the Holy of Holies.

God wills that we should push on into His presence and live our whole life there. This is to be known to us in conscious experience. It is more than a doctrine to be held, it is a life to be enjoyed every moment of every day.

A. W. Tozer, in *The Pursuit of God*

Expecting to Hear God

This is God, our God forever and ever. He will guide us forever.
(Psalm 48:14, esv)

People are meant to live in an ongoing conversation with God, speaking and being spoken to. Rightly understood, this can be abundantly verified in experience. God's visits to Adam and Eve in the Garden, Enoch's walks with God, and the face-to-face conversations between Moses and Jehovah are all commonly regarded as highly exceptional moments in the religious history of humankind. Aside from their obviously unique historical role, however, they are not meant to be exceptional at all. Rather they are examples of the normal human life God intended for us: God's indwelling His people through personal presence and fellowship. Given who we are by basic nature, we live — really live — only through God's regular speaking in our souls, and thus "by every word that comes from the mouth of God" (Matthew 4:4, esv).

Should we expect anything else, given the words of the scriptural record and the heritage of the Christian church? As Christians we stand in a millennia-long tradition of humans who have been addressed by God. The ancient Israelites heard the voice of their God speaking to them out of the midst of fire (see Deuteronomy 4:33). A regular place of communion and conversational interchange between the high priest and God was established in the mercy seat over the ark of God (see Exodus 25:22; Luke 1:11-21).

But the *individual* with faith among the Israelites also cried out expectantly to be taught by God: "Teach me to do your will, for you are my God! Let your good Spirit lead me on level ground!" (Psalm 143:10, esv). Israel's experience led the prophet Isaiah — who also had firsthand experience of conversing with God (see Isaiah 6) — to describe conditions of the faithful this way: "Then you shall call, and the Lord will answer; you shall cry, and he will say, 'Here I am.' . . . And the Lord will guide you continually" (Isaiah 58:9,11, esv).

Dallas Willard, in *Hearing God*

What Is God Doing?

My food is to do the will of him who sent me and to accomplish his work.

(John 4:34, esv)

Jesus considered God's will to be His highest priority (see John 4:32-34). Following God's will is also important for you. Often when people want to know God's will, they will ask, "What is God's will for my life?" As one of my seminary professors used to say, "If you ask the wrong question, you are going to get the wrong answer."

"What is God's will for my life?" is not the best question to ask. The better inquiry is, "What is God's will?" Because people are naturally self-centered, we tend to view the whole world — even God's activity — in terms of our own lives. Of course, we want to know what we should do and how events will affect us. But that is actually an inverted life-perspective. Once I know God's will, then my life gains its proper perspective, and I can adjust my life to Him and to His purposes. In other words, what is it that God is purposing to accomplish where I am? Once I know what God is doing, then I see what I should do. My focus needs to be outward on God and His purposes, not inward on my life.

Now, that does not mean God has no plans for your life. He certainly does. He created you, and He knows how your life can reach its maximum potential. The Bible says He wants you to live an abundant life and to be filled with divine joy. But the plans He has for your life are based on what He is doing in the world around you. He has a larger purpose in mind for all humanity. His desire is for you to become involved in what He is doing to bring salvation to others. Discovering God's greater plan helps you know what He wants to do through you.

Henry Blackaby and Richard Blackaby, in *Experiencing God*

Waiting Patiently on God

Be still before the Lord and wait patiently for him.
(Psalm 37:7, esv)

"In your patience possess ye your souls" (Luke 21:19, kjv). "Ye have need of patience" (Hebrews 10:36, kjv). "Let patience have her perfect work, that ye may be perfect and entire" (James 1:4, kjv). Such words of the Holy Spirit show us what an important element in the Christian life and character patience is. And nowhere is there a better place for cultivating or displaying it than in waiting on God. There we discover how impatient we are, and what our impatience means.

We confess at times that we are impatient with men, with circumstances that hinder us, or with ourselves and our slow progress in the Christian life. If we truly set ourselves to wait upon God, we shall find that it is with Him we are impatient, because He does not at once, or as soon as we could wish, do our bidding. It is in waiting upon God that our eyes are opened to believe in His wise and sovereign will, and to see that the sooner and the more completely we yield absolutely to it, the more surely His blessing can come to us.

All the exercises of the spiritual life, our reading and praying, our willing and doing, have their very great value. But they can go no further than this, that they point the way and prepare us in humility to look to and to depend alone upon God Himself, and in patience to wait His good time and mercy. The waiting is to teach us our absolute dependence upon God's mighty working, and to make us in perfect patience place ourselves at His disposal. They that wait on the Lord shall inherit the land; the promised land and its blessing. The heirs must wait; they can afford to wait.

Andrew Murray, in *Waiting on God*

A New Taste

Without faith it is impossible to please him, for whoever would draw near to God must believe that he exists and that he rewards those who seek him.

(Hebrews 11:6, esv)

The faith that pleases God is a confidence that God will reward us when we come to Him. The reward we long for is the glory of God Himself and the perfected companionship of Christ. We will sell everything to have the treasure of Christ Himself.

So the faith that pleases God is the assurance that when we turn to Him, we will find the all-satisfying Treasure. We will find our heart's eternal delight. But this implies that something has happened in our hearts *before* the act of faith. It implies that beneath and behind the act of faith that pleases God, a new taste has been created — a taste for the glory of God and the beauty of Christ. Behold, a joy has been born!

Once we had no delight in God, and Christ was just a vague historical figure. We enjoyed many things . . . but not God. He was an idea — even a good one — and a topic for discussion; but He was not a treasure of delight.

Then something miraculous happened. It was like the opening of the eyes of the blind during the golden dawn. First the stunned silence before the unspeakable beauty of holiness. Then the shock and terror that we had actually loved the darkness. Then the settling stillness of joy that this is the soul's end. The quest is over. We would give anything if we might be granted to live in the presence of this glory forever and ever.

And then, faith — the confidence that Christ has made a way for me, a sinner, to live in His glorious fellowship forever, the confidence that if I come to God through Christ, He will give me the desire of my heart to share His holiness and behold His glory.

But before the confidence comes the craving. Before the decision comes the delight. Before the trust comes the discovery of Treasure.

John Piper, in *Desiring God*

Waiting to Show Himself

That they should seek God, in the hope that they might feel their way toward him and find him.
(Acts 17:27, esv)

In the tabernacle's Holy of Holies, the Flame of the Presence was the beating heart of the Levitical order. Without it all the appointments of the tabernacle were characters of some unknown language; they had no meaning for Israel or for us.

The greatest fact of the tabernacle was that *Jehovah was there*; a Presence was waiting within the veil. Similarly the Presence of God is the central fact of Christianity. At the heart of the Christian message is God Himself waiting for His redeemed children to push in to conscious awareness of His Presence.

Who is this within the veil who dwells in fiery manifestations? It is none other than God Himself, "One God the Father Almighty, Maker of heaven and earth, and of all things visible and invisible," and "One Lord Jesus Christ, the only begotten Son of God; begotten of His Father before all worlds, God of God, Light of Light, Very God of Very God; begotten, not made; being of one substance with the Father," and "the Holy Ghost, the Lord and Giver of life, Who proceedeth from the Father and the Son, Who with the Father and the Son together is worshiped and glorified." Yet this holy Trinity is One God, for "we worship one God in Trinity, and Trinity in Unity; neither confounding the Persons, nor dividing the Substance. For there is one Person of the Father, another of the Son, and another of the Holy Ghost. But the Godhead of the Father, of the Son, and of the Holy Ghost, is all one: the glory equal and the majesty co-eternal." So in part run the ancient creeds, and so the inspired Word declares.

Behind the veil is God. He has discovered Himself to some extent in nature, but more perfectly in the Incarnation; now He waits to show Himself in ravishing fullness to the humble of soul and the pure in heart.

A. W. Tozer, in *The Pursuit of God*

Easy Patience

In returning and rest you shall be saved;
in quietness and in trust shall be your strength.
(Isaiah 30:15, esv)

It is resting in the Lord, in His will, His promise, His faithfulness, and His love, that makes patience easy. And the resting in Him is nothing but being silent unto Him, still before Him. Having our thoughts and wishes, our fears and hopes, hushed into calm and quiet in that great peace of God which passeth all understanding. That peace keeps the heart and mind when we are anxious for anything, because we have made our request known to Him. The rest, the silence, the stillness, and the patient waiting—all find their strength and joy in God Himself.

The need for patience, and the reasonableness, and the blessedness of patience will be opened up to the waiting soul. Our patience will be seen to be the counterpart of God's patience. He longs far more to bless us fully than we can desire it. But, as the husbandman has long patience till the fruit be ripe, so God bows Himself to our slowness and bears long with us. Let us remember this, and wait patiently: of each promise and every answer to prayer the word is true: "I the Lord will hasten it in his time" (Isaiah 60:22, kjv).

"Rest in the Lord, and wait patiently for him" (Psalm 37:7, kjv). Yes, for *Him*. Seek not only the help, the gift, thou needest; seek *Himself*; wait for *Him*. Give God His glory by resting in Him, by trusting Him fully, by waiting patiently for Him. This patience honors Him greatly; it leaves Him as God on the throne to do His work; it yields self wholly into His hands. It lets God be God.

Whether it be in the shorter specific periods of waiting or as the continuous habit of the souls, rest in the Lord—be still before the Lord, and wait patiently.

Andrew Murray, in *Waiting on God*

HIS WISE, LOVING, SOVEREIGN PLAN

He does according to his will . . . and none can stay his hand.
(DANIEL 4:35, ESV)

God does as He pleases, only as He pleases; He works out every event to bring about the accomplishment of His will. Such a bare unqualified statement of the sovereignty of God would terrify us if that were all we knew about God. But God is not only sovereign, He is perfect in love and infinite in wisdom. God exercises His sovereignty for His glory and the good of His people.

But how is this any more than merely an abstract statement about God to be debated by the theologians, a statement that has little relevance to our day-to-day lives? The answer is that God does have a purpose and a plan for you, and He has the power to carry out that plan. It's one thing to know that no person or circumstance can touch us outside of God's sovereign control; it's still another to realize that no person or circumstances can frustrate God's purpose for our lives.

God has an overarching purpose for all believers: to conform us to the likeness of His Son, Jesus Christ (see Romans 8:29). He also has a specific purpose for each of us that is His unique, tailor-made plan for our individual life (see Ephesians 2:10). And God will fulfill that purpose. As Psalm 138:8 says, "The LORD will fulfill his purpose for me" (ESV). Because we know God is directing our lives to an ultimate end and because we know He is sovereignly able to orchestrate the events of our lives toward that end, we can trust Him. We can commit to Him not only the ultimate outcome of our lives, but also all the intermediate events and circumstances that will bring us to that outcome.

JERRY BRIDGES, IN *TRUSTING GOD*

Finding Him in His Ways

Wait for the Lord and keep his way,
and he will exalt you to inherit the land.
(Psalm 37:34, esv)

When waiting on God, be careful to keep His ways; outside these, we never can expect to find Him. "Thou meetest him that rejoiceth and worketh righteousness, those that remember thee in thy ways" (Isaiah 64:5, kjv). We may be sure God is never and nowhere to be found but in His ways—where He is always most surely to be found by the soul who seeks and patiently waits.

See the close connection between the two parts of the injunction in Psalm 37:34: "Wait on the Lord"—in our worship and disposition; "and keep his way"—in our walk and work (kjv). The outer life must be in harmony with the inner; the inner must be the inspiration and the strength for the outer.

Our God has made known His ways in His Word for our conduct, and He invites our confidence for His grace and help in our heart. If we do not keep His ways, our waiting on Him can bring no blessing. The surrender to full obedience to all His will is the secret of full access to all the blessings of His fellowship.

Psalm 37 speaks of the evildoer who prospers in his way, and it calls on the believer not to fret himself. When we see men around us prosperous and happy while they forsake God's ways, and ourselves left in difficulty or suffering, we are in danger of first fretting at what appears so strange, and then gradually yielding to seek our prosperity in their path.

The psalm says, "Trust in the Lord, and do good. . . . Depart from evil, and do good. . . . The Lord . . . forsaketh not his saints. . . . The righteous shall inherit the land. . . . The law of his God is in his heart; none of his steps shall slide" (verses 3,27-31, kjv).

Do what God asks you to do; God will do more than you can ask Him to do.

Andrew Murray, in *Waiting on God*

The Fire

And the angel of the Lord *appeared to him in a flame of fire out of the midst of a bush.*
(Exodus 3:2, esv)

What a broad world to roam in, what a sea to swim in is this God and Father of our Lord Jesus Christ.

He is *eternal*, which means He antedates time and is wholly independent of it. To it He pays no tribute and from it He suffers no change. He is *immutable*, which means He has never changed and can never change in any smallest measure. He is *omniscient*, which means He knows in one free and effortless act all matter, all spirit, all relationships, all events. He has no past and no future. He *is*, and none of the limiting and qualifying terms used of creatures can apply to Him. *Love* and *mercy* and *righteousness* are His, and *holiness* so ineffable that no comparisons or figures will avail to express it.

Only fire can give even a remote conception of it. In fire He appeared at the burning bush; in the pillar of fire He dwelt through all the long wilderness journey. The fire that glowed between the wings of the cherubim in the holy place was called the *shekinah*, the Presence, through the years of Israel's glory, and when the Old had given place to the New, He came at Pentecost as a fiery flame and rested upon each disciple.

The world is perishing for lack of the knowledge of God, and the church is famishing for want of His Presence. The instant cure of most of our religious ills would be to enter the Presence in spiritual experience, to become suddenly aware that we are in God and that God is in us. This would lift us out of our pitiful narrowness and cause our hearts to be enlarged. This would burn away the impurities from our lives as the bugs and fungi were burned away by the fire that dwelt in the bush.

A. W. Tozer, in *The Pursuit of God*

A Different Kind of Serving

If anyone serves me, he must follow me;
and where I am, there will my servant be also.
(John 12:26, esv)

To participate in God's work you must be a servant. As God's servant, Jesus came to earth to accomplish God's will in redeeming humanity; Paul described His humble attitude and commended it to us: "Make your own attitude that of Christ Jesus, who . . . emptied Himself by assuming the form of a slave. . . . He humbled Himself by becoming obedient to the point of death" (Philippians 2:5-8, hcsb).

We are to develop the servant attitude of Christ that requires humility and obedience. In His instructions to His disciples about servanthood, Jesus described His own role: "Whoever wants to be first among you must be your slave; just as the Son of Man did not come to be served, but to serve, and to give His life — a ransom for many" (Matthew 20:27-28, hcsb).

Jesus also explained our relationship to Him: "As the Father has sent Me, I also send you" (John 20:21, hcsb). When you respond to God's invitation to salvation, you join Him in His mission of world redemption. The salvation God offers comes with a corresponding summons to be on mission with Him. In this new relationship you move into a servant role with God as your Lord and Master.

The common understanding of a servant is someone who approaches the master and says, "Master, what do you want me to do?" The master tells him, and the servant goes off and does it. But that is not the biblical picture of a servant of God. Being God's servant is quite different from working for a human master. While an ordinary servant labors for his master, God works *through* His servants.

The biblical portray of God's servant is more like a potter and clay (see Jeremiah 18:1-6). To be useful, clay has to be pliable. And once it is made into a vessel, its usefulness is still subject to the discretion of the potter.

Henry Blackaby and Richard Blackaby, in *Experiencing God*

Facing Up to Repentance

God's kindness is meant to lead you to repentance.

(Romans 2:4, esv)

Why is repentance so seldom preached and so little understood? I believe there are three reasons.

Church historian J. Edwin Orr sums up the first: *The appeal of modern evangelism is "not for repentance but for enlistment."*[3] Repentance can be a threatening message — rightly so. The gospel must be the bad news of the conviction of sin before it can be the good news of redemption. Because that message is unpalatable for many middle-class congregations preoccupied with protecting their affluent lifestyles, many pastors tiptoe warily around the subject.

The result is a watered-down message that, in large part, accounts for today's easy believism, Christianity without cost, or "cheap grace" as German martyr Dietrich Bonhoeffer aptly labeled it a generation ago — grace in which "no contrition is required, still less any real desire to be delivered from sin . . . a denial of the living word of God, in fact, a denial of the incarnation."[4]

The second reason repentance is ignored or misunderstood comes much closer to home, as I have discovered: *Often we are simply unwilling or unable to accept the reality of personal sin and therefore to accept our need for repentance.* In our fallen state we have an infinite capacity for justifying whatever acts we commit. Psychologists call this the "self-serving bias" and confirm the truth of William Saroyan's opening words in one of his novels, "Every man is a good man in a bad world . . . as he himself knows."[5]

And this leads to the third reason for our shallow understanding of repentance: *Our culture has written sin out of existence.* Even Christians who should understand the basic truth that *all* are heirs of Adam's fall and thus *all* are sinners influenced, often blinded, by humanist values.

Whatever became of sin? The answer lies within each of us, but to find it we must come face to face with who we really are.

Charles Colson, in *Loving God*

Intimacy Leads to Trust

Because he holds fast to me in love, I will deliver him;
I will protect him, because he knows my name.

(Psalm 91:14, esv)

Just as the faith of salvation comes through hearing the message of the gospel (see Romans 10:17), so the faith to trust God in adversity comes through the Word of God alone. Only in the Scriptures will we find an adequate view of God's relationship to and involvement in our painful circumstances. Only from the Scriptures, applied to our hearts by the Holy Spirit, will we receive the grace to trust God in adversity.

In the arena of adversity, the Scriptures teach us three essential truths about God: (1) God is completely sovereign; (2) God is infinite in wisdom; (3) God is perfect in love. Someone has expressed these three truths as they relate to us in this way: "God in His love always wills what is best for us. In His wisdom He always knows what is best, and in His sovereignty He has the power to bring it about."

As we become so convinced of these scriptural truths that we appropriate them in our daily circumstances, we learn to trust God in the midst of our pain, whatever form it may take. It doesn't matter whether our pain is trivial or traumatic, temporary or interminable. Regardless of the nature of the circumstances, we must learn to trust God if we would glorify God in them.

In order to trust in God's sovereignty, love, and wisdom, we must know Him in an intimate, personal way. David said in Psalm 9:10, "Those who know your name put their trust in you, for you, O Lord, have not forsaken those who seek you" (esv). To know God's name means coming into a deeper personal relationship with Him as a result of seeking Him in the midst of our personal pain and discovering Him to be trustworthy. It's only as we know God in this personal way that we come to trust Him.

Jerry Bridges, in *Trusting God*

Keeping His Ways

So you shall keep the commandments of the Lord your God by walking in his ways and by fearing him.
(Deuteronomy 8:6, esv)

"Wait on the Lord, and keep his way" (Psalm 37:34, kjv). It may be that the consciousness of shortcoming and sin makes those words look more like a hindrance than a help in waiting on God. Let it not be so.

It is true you have not the strength yet to keep all God's ways. But keep carefully those for which you have received strength already. Surrender yourself willingly and trustingly to keep all God's ways, in the strength which will come in waiting on Him, without reserve and without doubt. He will work in you that which is pleasing in His sight through Jesus Christ.

Keep His ways, as you know them in the Word. Keep His ways, as nature teaches them, in always doing what appears right. Keep His ways, as Providence points them out. Keep His ways, as the Holy Spirit suggests. However weak you feel, only be willing, and He who has worked to will, will work to do by His power.

Come with everything evil you feel in yourself, every memory of unwillingness, unwatchfulness, unfaithfulness, and all that causes such unceasing self-condemnation. Put your power in God's omnipotence, and find in waiting on God your deliverance.

Your failure has been owing to only one thing: you sought to conquer and obey in your own strength. Come and bow before God until you learn that He alone is good, and He alone can work any good thing. Believe that there is no true power in you, and in all that nature can do.

Be content to receive from God each moment the inworking of His mighty grace and life, and waiting on God will become the renewal of your strength to run in His ways and not be weary, to walk in His paths and never faint.

Andrew Murray, in *Waiting on God*

BEFORE GOD

From the end of the earth I call to you. . . .
Lead me to the rock that is higher than I.
(PSALM 61:2, ESV)

Our aim in studying the Godhead must be to know God Himself the better. Our concern must be to enlarge our acquaintance, not simply with the doctrine of God's attributes, but with the living God whose attributes they are. We must seek, in studying God, to be led to God. It was for this purpose that revelation was given, and it is to this use that we must put it.

How are we to do this? How can we turn our knowledge *about* God into knowledge *of* God? The rule for doing this is demanding, but simple. It is that we turn each truth that we learn *about* God into matter for meditation *before* God, leading to prayer and praise *to* God.

We have some idea, perhaps, what prayer is, but what is meditation? Meditation is the activity of calling to mind, and thinking over, and dwelling on, and applying to oneself, the various things that one knows about the works and ways and purposes and promises of God. It is an activity of holy thought, consciously performed in the presence of God, under the eye of God, by the help of God, as a means of communion with God. Its purpose is to clear one's mental and spiritual vision of God, and to let His truth make its full and proper impact on one's mind and heart. It is a matter of talking to oneself about God and oneself; it is, indeed, often a matter of arguing with oneself, reasoning oneself out of moods of doubt and unbelief into a clear apprehension of God's power and grace. Its effect is ever to humble us, as we contemplate God's greatness and glory, and our own littleness and sinfulness, and to encourage and reassure us as we contemplate the unsearchable riches of divine mercy displayed in the Lord Jesus Christ.

J. I. PACKER, IN *KNOWING GOD*

Loving the Light

The light has come into the world, and people loved the darkness rather than the light because their works were evil.

(John 3:19, ESV)

The reason people do not come to the light is because they do not love it. "For everyone who does wicked things hates the light and does not come to the light, lest his works should be exposed" (John 3:20, ESV).

Love for the light is not caused by coming to the light. We come because we love it. Otherwise, our coming is no honor to the light. Could there be any holy motivation to believe in Christ where there is no taste for the beauty of Christ?

To be sure, we could be motivated by the desire to escape hell or the desire to have material riches or the desire to rejoin a departed loved one. But how does it honor the light when the only reason we come to the light is to find those things that we loved in the dark? Is this saving faith?

Saving faith is the cry of a new creature in Christ. And the newness of the new creature is that it has a new taste. What was once distasteful or bland is now craved. Christ Himself has become a Treasure Chest of holy joy. The tree of faith grows only in the heart that craves the supreme gift that Christ died to give: not health, not wealth, not prestige — but God! Test yourself here. There are many professing Christians who delight in God's gifts, but not God. Would you want to go to heaven if God were not there, only His gifts?

"Christ . . . suffered once for sins . . . that he might bring us to *God*" (1 Peter 3:18, ESV, emphasis added). "Through him we . . . have access in one Spirit to *the Father*" (Ephesians 2:18, ESV, emphasis added). "Through him we have . . . obtained access by faith into this grace . . . and we rejoice in hope of the glory of *God*. . . . We . . . rejoice in *God* through our Lord Jesus Christ" (Romans 5:2,11, ESV, emphasis added).

John Piper, in *Desiring God*

OUR GOAL

Seek first the kingdom of God and his righteousness.
(MATTHEW 6:33, ESV)

In learning to please God, the Christian must have a clear idea of what his goal is. Though the Bible makes that goal clear, it is one that is easily forgotten.

Jesus stated the goal in Matthew 6:33. First, Jesus said we must *seek*. To seek something requires effort. It involves a diligent search. Seeking is not accomplished by taking a nap. It involves persistent work. We do not sit back and wait for God to drop it in our laps.

We are to seek *the kingdom of God* and God's *righteousness.* Jesus says we are to seek these things *first.* The New Testament word used here for *first* carries the force of *priority.* A more accurate translation of the concept would be, "Seek first, *above all else,* the kingdom of God and His righteousness." Seek the kingdom. Seek righteousness. These are the priorities of the Christian life.

There is much confusion about spiritual seeking in the Christian world. We frequently hear this comment: "My friend is not a Christian, but he's seeking."

What is the non-Christian seeking? One thing we know he is not seeking. He is not seeking God. Paul declares, "There is none who seeks after God" (Romans 3:11, NKJV). The unbeliever never, never, never seeks God. The unbeliever is a fugitive from God. In his sinful state he may look for answers to life's puzzles, but he does not seek God. Unbelievers are seeking happiness, peace of mind, relief from guilt, a meaningful life, and a host of other things that we know only God can give them. But they are not seeking God. They are seeking the *benefits* of God. Natural man's sin is precisely this: He wants the benefits of God without God Himself.

I belabor this point for this reason: Seeking after God is a Christian enterprise. The seeking of God *begins* at conversion.

R. C. SPROUL, IN *PLEASING GOD*

A Burning Love for Jesus

As a deer pants for flowing streams, so pants my soul for you, O God.
(Psalm 42:1, esv)

Fredrick Faber was one of those saints whose soul panted after God as the doe pants after the water brook, and the measure in which God revealed Himself to his seeking heart set the good man's whole life afire with a burning adoration rivaling that of the seraphim before the throne. His love for God extended to the three Persons of the Godhead equally, yet he seemed to feel for each One a special kind of love reserved for Him alone.

His love for the Person of Christ was so intense that it threatened to consume him; it burned within him as a sweet and holy madness and flowed from his lips like molten gold. In one of his sermons he said, "Wherever we turn in the church of God, there is Jesus. He is the beginning, middle, and end of everything to us. . . . There is nothing good, nothing holy, nothing beautiful, nothing joyous which He is not to His servants. No one need be poor, because if he chooses he can have Jesus for his own property and possession. No one need be downcast, for Jesus is the joy of heaven, and it is His joy to enter into sorrowful hearts. . . .

"We can never exaggerate . . . the compassionate abundance of the love of Jesus to us. All our lives long we might talk of Jesus, and yet we should never come to an end of the sweet things that might be said of Him. Eternity will not be long enough to learn all He is, or to praise Him for all He has done, but then, that matters not; for we shall be always with Him, and we desire nothing more."

And addressing our Lord directly he said to Him:

> I love Thee so, I know not how
> My transports to control;
> Thy love is like a burning fire
> Within my very soul.

A. W. Tozer, in *The Pursuit of God*

Not by Sight

We look not to the things that are seen
but to the things that are unseen.
(2 Corinthians 4:18, esv)

It's difficult for us to appreciate the reality of God sovereignly doing as He pleases in our lives because we don't *see* God doing anything. Instead we see ourselves or other people acting and events occurring, and we evaluate those actions and events according to our own preferences and plans. We see ourselves influencing or perhaps even controlling or being controlled by the actions of other people, but we don't see God at work. But over all the actions and events of our lives, God is in control, doing as He pleases — not apart from those events, or in spite of them, but *through* them. Joseph's brothers sold him into slavery — a malicious act in and of itself — but in due time Joseph recognized that through his brothers' actions God was acting. He could say to them, "So it was not you who sent me here, but God" (Genesis 45:8, esv). Joseph recognized the hand of God in his life sovereignly directing all the events to bring about God's plan for him.

You and I may never have the privilege in this life of seeing an obvious outcome of God's plan for us, as Joseph did. But God's plan for us is no less firm and its outcome is no less certain than was God's plan for Joseph. God did not give us the story of Joseph's life just to inform us but to encourage us. "For whatever was written in former days was written for our instruction, that through endurance and *through the encouragement of the Scriptures* we might have hope" (Romans 15:4, esv, emphasis added). What God did for Joseph, He will do for us. But to derive the comfort and encouragement from this truth that God has provided, we must learn to trust God. We must learn to live, as Paul said, "by faith, not by sight" (2 Corinthians 5:7, esv).

Jerry Bridges, in *Trusting God*

Waiting for More Than We Know

And now, O Lord, for what do I wait? My hope is in you.
(Psalm 39:7-8, esv)

There may be times when we feel as if we know not what we are waiting for. There may be other times we think we do know, yet it would be so good for us to realize we do not know what to ask as we ought. God is able to do for us exceeding abundantly above what we ask or think, and we are in danger of limiting Him when we confine our desires and prayers to our own thoughts of them. It is a great thing at times to say, with Psalm 39:7, "And now, Lord, what wait I for?" I scarce know or can tell; this only I can say: "My hope is in thee" (kjv).

When Moses promised meat to Israel in the wilderness, they doubted, saying, "Can God furnish a table in the wilderness? Behold, he smote the rock, that the water gushed out . . . can he give bread also? can he provide flesh for his people?" (Psalm 78:19-20, kjv). If they had been asked whether God could provide streams in the desert, they would have answered, Yes. God had done it: He could do it again. But when the thought came of God doing something new, they limited Him; their expectation could not rise beyond their past experience, or their own thoughts of what was possible.

Even so we may be limiting God by our conceptions of what He has promised or is able to do.

Let us beware of limiting the Holy One of Israel in our prayer. Let us believe that the very promises of God we plead have a divine meaning, infinitely beyond our thoughts of them. Let us believe that His fulfillment of them can be, in a power and an abundance of grace, beyond our largest grasp of thought. And let us wait on God for all that His grace and power are ready to do for us.

Andrew Murray, in *Waiting on God*

He Calls Us "Friend"

I have called you friends, for all that I have heard from my Father I have made known to you.

(John 15:15, ESV)

On the evening before His crucifixion, Jesus assured His little band of followers that although He was leaving them, He would continue to manifest Himself to all who loved Him. Then a disciple asked Him just the right question (see John 14:22): *How* would this manifesting take place? Jesus' reply was that He and His Father would come to them and make Their home with them (see John 14:23).

This abiding of the Son and the Father in the faithful heart certainly involves conscious communication or conversation, in a manner and a measure our Lord Himself considers to be appropriate. It is simply beyond belief that two Persons so intimately related as indicated in Jesus' answer in John 14:23 would not explicitly speak to one another. The Spirit who inhabits us is not mute, restricting Himself to an occasional nudge, a hot flash, a brilliant image, or a case of goosebumps.

Such simple reasonings add further weight to the examples set by well-known Christians that confirm the thought that ideally we should be engaged in personal communion with God. We might well ask, "How could there be a personal relationship, a personal walk with God—or with anyone else—*without* individualized communication?"

Sometimes today it seems that our personal relationship with God is treated as no more than a mere arrangement or understanding that Jesus and His Father have about us. Our personal relationship then means only that each believer has his or her own unique account in heaven, which allows them to draw on the merits of Christ to pay their sin bills. Or possibly it means that God's general providence for His creation is adequate to provide for each person.

But who does not think there should be much more to a personal relationship than that? A mere benefactor, however powerful, kind, and thoughtful, is not the same thing as a *friend.*

Dallas Willard, in *Hearing God*

WAIT FOR HIS WONDERS

My hope is in you. Deliver me from all my transgressions.
(PSALM 39:7-8, ESV)

In every true prayer there are two hearts in exercise. The one is your heart, with its little, dark, human thoughts of what you need and what God can do. The other is God's great heart, with its infinite, its divine purposes of blessing.

To which of these two ought the larger place be given in your approach to Him? Undoubtedly, to the heart of God: everything depends upon knowing and being occupied with that. But how little this is done.

This is what waiting on God is meant to teach you. Just think of God's wonderful love and redemption, in the meaning these words must have to Him. Confess how little you understand what God is willing to do for you. Wait on God to do for you more than you can ask or think.

Apply this to the prayer in Psalm 39:8: "Deliver me from all my transgressions" (ESV). You have prayed to be delivered from temper, or pride, or self-will. It is as if it is in vain. Have you had your own thoughts about the way or the extent of God's doing it, without waiting on the God of glory, according to the riches of His glory, to do for you what hath not entered the heart of man to conceive?

Learn to worship God as the God who doeth wonders, who wishes to prove in you that He can do something supernatural and divine. Bow before Him, wait upon Him, until your soul realizes that you are in the hands of a divine and almighty Worker. Consent but to know what and how He will work; expect it to be something altogether Godlike, something to be waited for in deep humility, and received only by His divine power. He will in His time do His work.

He is teaching you to leave all in His hands, and to wait on Him alone.

ANDREW MURRAY, IN *WAITING ON GOD*

The Privilege Open to All

I will give them a heart to know that I am the Lord. . . .
They shall return to me with their whole heart.
(Jeremiah 24:7, esv)

God is so vastly wonderful, so utterly and completely delightful that He can, without anything other than Himself, meet and overflow the deepest demands of our total nature, mysterious and deep as that nature is.

Hearts that are "fit to break" with love for the Godhead are those who have been in the Presence and have looked with opened eye upon the majesty of Deity. Men with these breaking hearts had a quality about them not known to or understood by common men. They habitually spoke with spiritual authority. They had been in the Presence of God, and they reported what they saw there. The great of the kingdom have been those who loved God more than others did. We all know who they have been and gladly pay tribute to the depths and sincerity of their devotion.

The type of Christianity now in vogue knows this Presence only in theory. It fails to stress the Christian's privilege of present realization. According to its teachings we are in the Presence of God positionally, and nothing is said about the need to experience that Presence actually. The fiery urge that drove men like Robert Murray McCheyne is wholly missing. And the present generation of Christians measures itself by this imperfect rule. Ignoble contentment takes the place of burning zeal. We are satisfied to rest in our *judicial* possessions and for the most part we bother ourselves very little about the absence of personal experience.

In the deep spirit of a man the fire must glow or his love is not the true love of God. The Church waits for the tender voice of the saint who has penetrated the veil and has gazed with inward eye upon the Wonder that is God. And yet, thus to penetrate, to push in sensitive living experience into the holy Presence, is a privilege open to every child of God.

A. W. Tozer, in *The Pursuit of God*

God Is Working

My Father is working until now, and I am working.

(John 5:17, esv)

God did not create the world and then abandon it to run itself. He is not sitting in a heavenly throne room passively observing activity on earth. God is orchestrating history. He is present and in the middle of human activity. God is actively at work redeeming a lost world, and He chooses to involve His servants in carrying out His redemptive plans.

One of the greatest tragedies among God's people is that even though they long to experience Him, they do not know how to recognize Him at work in their midst. These are extremely exciting days to be walking with the Lord! You don't want to miss out on what He is doing. The Holy Spirit will instruct you and help you know when and where God is working. Once you know where He is working, you can adjust your life to join Him in His divine purposes.

I've heard stories from people all around the world who suddenly discovered God had been present and active in their workplace or church or family or neighborhood all along, but they had not recognized it. When God revealed where He was at work, suddenly they were able to start a noon hour Bible study at their job site, see revival come to their church, help a spouse draw closer to the Lord, or lead a neighbor to faith in Christ. Before, these Christians had assumed God was not doing anything significant around them. After God revealed to them what He was doing, they realized they had been missing out on God's great work.

Watch to see where God is at work around you. When He shows you, join Him in His work. Keep your attention on God's call to an assignment rather than on your spiritual gifts, personal desires, skills, abilities, or resources. Once you understand God's call to an assignment, obey Him, and He will work through you to accomplish His divine, eternal purposes.

Henry Blackaby and Richard Blackaby, in *Experiencing God*

True Patience

I waited patiently for the Lord; he inclined to me and heard my cry.

(Psalm 40:1, esv)

The word *patience* is derived from the Latin word for suffering. It suggests the thought of being under the constraint of some power from which we wish to be free. At first we submit against our will; experience teaches us that when it is vain to resist, patient endurance is our wisest course. In waiting on God it is of infinite consequence that we submit not only because we are compelled to, but because we lovingly and joyfully consent to be in the hands of our blessed Father. Patience then becomes our highest blessedness and our highest grace. It honors God and gives Him time to have His way with us. It is the highest expression of our faith in His goodness and faithfulness. It brings the soul perfect rest in the assurance that God is carrying on His work. It is the token of our full consent that God should deal with us in such a way and time as He thinks best. True patience is the losing of our self-will in His perfect will.

Such patience is the growth and fruit of lessons in the school of waiting. To many it will appear strange how difficult it is truly to wait upon God. The great stillness of soul before God that sinks into its own helplessness and waits for Him to reveal Himself; the deep humility that is afraid to let one's own will or one's own strength work anything except as God works to will and to do; the meekness that is content to be and to know nothing except as God gives His light; the entire resignation of the will that only wants to be a vessel in which His holy will can move and mold: all these elements of perfect patience are not found at once. But they will come in measure as the soul waits upon God.

Andrew Murray, in *Waiting on God*

A NEW PASSION FOR HIS PRESENCE

The kingdom of heaven is like treasure hidden in a field, which a man found and covered up. Then in his joy he goes and sells all that he has and buys that field.

(MATTHEW 13:44, ESV)

We may speak of the "joy of faith" at three levels.

First, there is the new spiritual taste created by the Spirit of God for the glory of God. This new taste is the seed and root of joy. Thus, it is the "joy of faith" in embryo, as it were.

Second, there is the shoot, the stem, of faith itself reaching out actively for all that God is for us in Christ. The pith of this stem is joy in God. It is not possible for vital, genuine faith in the Fountain of Joy not to partake of that joy. Joyless embracing of the God of hope, for who He really is, is impossible.

Third, there is the fruit of daily gladness that Paul speaks of in Romans 15:13: "May the God of hope fill you with all *joy* and peace *in believing*" (ESV, emphasis added). Here joy and peace flow out *from* faith into the whole of life.

In conversion we find the hidden Treasure of the kingdom of God. We venture all on it. And year after year in the struggles of life, we prove the value of the treasure again and again, and we discover depths of riches we had never known. And so the joy of faith grows. When Christ calls us to a new act of obedience that will cost us some temporal pleasure, we call to mind the surpassing value of following Him, and by faith in His proven worth, we forsake the worldly pleasure. The result? More joy! More faith! Deeper than before. And so we go on from joy to joy and faith to faith.

Behind the repentance that turns away from sin, and behind the faith that embraces Christ, is the birth of a new taste, a new longing, a new passion for the pleasure of God's presence. This is the root of conversion. This is the creation of a Christian Hedonist.

JOHN PIPER, IN *DESIRING GOD*

A Veil Remaining

You have said, "Seek my face."
My heart says to you, "Your face, Lord, do I seek."
(Psalm 27:8, esv)

With the veil removed by the rending of Jesus' flesh, with nothing on God's side to prevent us from entering, why do we tarry without? Why do we consent to abide all our days just outside the Holy of Holies and never enter at all to look upon God? We sense His call, but still we fail to draw near, and the years pass and we grow old and tired in the outer courts of the tabernacle. What hinders us?

The answer usually given — that we are "cold" — will not explain all the facts. There is something more serious than coldness of heart. What is it? What but the presence of a *veil in our hearts*? A veil not taken away as the first veil was, but which remains there still shutting out the light and hiding the face of God from us. It is the veil of our fleshly fallen nature living on, unjudged within us, uncrucified and unrepudiated. It is the close-woven veil of the self-life which we have never truly acknowledged, of which we have been secretly ashamed, and which for these reasons we have never brought to the judgment of the cross.

It is not too mysterious, this opaque veil, nor is it hard to identify. We have but to look in our own hearts and we shall see it there, sewn and patched and repaired it may be, but there nevertheless, an enemy to our lives and an effective block to our spiritual progress.

This veil is not a beautiful thing and it is not a thing about which we commonly care to talk, but I am addressing the thirsting souls who are determined to follow God, and I know they will not turn back because the way leads temporarily through the blackened hills. They will face the facts however unpleasant and endure the cross for the joy set before them.

A. W. Tozer, in *The Pursuit of God*

For a New Song

May you be strengthened with all power, according to his glorious might, for all endurance and patience with joy.
(Colossians 1:11, ESV)

Yes, we need to be strengthened with all God's might — according to the measure of His glorious power — if we are to wait on God in all patience. It is God revealing Himself in us as our life and strength that will enable us with perfect patience to leave all in His hands. If any are inclined to despond because they have not such patience, let them be of good courage; it is in the course of our feeble and imperfect waiting that God Himself by His hidden power strengthens us and works out in us the patience of the saints, the patience of Christ Himself.

Listen to the voice of one who was deeply tried: "I waited patiently for the Lord; and he inclined unto me, and heard my cry" (Psalm 40:1, KJV). Hear what he passed through: "He brought me up also out of an horrible pit, out of the miry clay, and set my feet upon a rock, and established my goings. *And he hath put a new song in my mouth, even praise unto our God*" (40:2-3, KJV, emphasis added). Patient waiting upon God brings a rich reward; the deliverance is sure; God Himself will put a new song into your mouth.

O soul, be not impatient! — whether it be in the exercise of prayer and worship that you find it difficult to wait, or in respect to certain requests, or in the fulfilling of your heart's desire for the revelation of God Himself in a deeper spiritual life — fear not, but rest in the Lord, and wait patiently for Him.

And if you sometimes feel as if patience is not your gift, remember it is *God's* gift, and take it: "The Lord direct your hearts into . . . the patient waiting for Christ" (2 Thessalonians 3:5, KJV). Into the patience with which you are to wait on God, He Himself will guide you.

Andrew Murray, in *Waiting on God*

No Contingencies

For I know the plans I have for you, declares the Lord, plans for welfare and not for evil, to give you a future and a hope.

(Jeremiah 29:11, esv)

Jeremiah 29:11 is a passage that has been meaningful to me for several years. Although its words were directed to the nation of Judah in its captivity, they express a principle about God, a principle affirmed elsewhere throughout the Bible: God has a plan for you. Because He has a plan for you, and because no one can thwart that plan, you too can have hope and courage. You, too, can trust God.

From our limited vantage point, our lives are marked by an endless series of contingencies. We frequently find ourselves, instead of acting as we planned, reacting to an unexpected turn of events. We make plans but are often forced to change those plans.

Even those whose lives are free from major pain still experience the frequently frustrating or anxiety-producing events of daily life, which momentarily grab our attention and rob us of our peace of mind. A long-planned vacation has to be cancelled because of illness, the washing machine breaks down the day company arrives, your class notes are lost or stolen the day before a major exam, you tear your favorite dress on the way to church, and on and on. Instances of this magnitude are numerous. Life is full of them.

But there are no contingencies with God. Our unexpected, forced change of plans is a part of His plan. God is never surprised; never caught off guard; never frustrated by unexpected developments. God does as He pleases, and that which pleases Him is always for His glory and our good.

Our lives are also cluttered with a lot of "if onlys." "If only I had done this," or "if only that had not happened." But again, God has no "if onlys." God never makes a mistake; God has no regrets. "This God—his way is perfect" (Psalm 18:30, esv). We can trust God. He is trustworthy.

Jerry Bridges, in *Trusting God*

Waiting for His Counsel

But they soon forgot his works; they did not wait for his counsel.
(Psalm 106:13, esv)

God wonderfully redeemed His people Israel, and was prepared as wonderfully to supply their every need. But when the time of need came, "they waited not for his counsel" (Psalm 106:13, kjv). The Almighty God was their Leader and Provider, but they asked not what His plans might be. They simply thought the thoughts of their own heart, and tempted and provoked God by their unbelief.

This has been the sin of God's people in all ages! In the land of Canaan, in the days of Joshua, the only three failures of which we read were owing to this one sin. *They waited not for His counsel* in going up against Ai, then in making a covenant with the Gibeonites, then in settling down without going up to possess the whole land.

Even the advanced believer is in danger from this most subtle of temptations. Let us be warned. And let us very specially regard it as a danger not only to the individual, but to God's people in their collective capacity.

Our whole relation to God is ruled in this, that His will is to be done in us and by us as it is in heaven. He has promised to make known His will to us by His Spirit, the Guide into all truth. And our position is to be that of waiting for His counsel as the only guide of our thoughts and actions. In our church worship, in our prayer-meetings, in all our gatherings in any part of the work for God, our first object ought ever to be to ascertain the mind of God.

God always works according to the counsel of His will; the more that counsel of His will is sought and found and honored, the more surely and mightily will God do His work for us and through us.

Andrew Murray, in *Waiting on God*

Removing the Veil

Put to death therefore what is earthly in you.
(Colossians 3:5, ESV)

The veil in our hearts is woven of the fine threads of the self-life, the hyphenated sins of the human spirit. They are not something we do, they are something we *are*, and therein lies both their subtlety and their power. To be specific, the self-sins are these: self-righteousness, self-pity, self-confidence, self-sufficiency, self-admiration, self-love, and a host of others. They dwell too deep within us and are too much a part of our natures to come to our attention till the light of God is focused upon them.

One should suppose that proper instruction in the doctrines of man's depravity and the necessity for justification through the righteousness of Christ alone would deliver us from the power of the self-sins; but it does not work out that way. Self can live unrebuked at the very altar. It can watch the bleeding Victim die and not be in the least affected by what it sees. It can fight for the faith of the Reformers and preach eloquently the creed of salvation by grace, and gain strength by its efforts. To tell all the truth, it seems actually to feed upon orthodoxy and is more at home in a Bible conference than in a tavern. Our very state of longing after God may afford it an excellent condition under which to thrive and grow.

Self is the opaque veil that hides the Face of God from us. It can be removed only in spiritual experience, never by mere instruction. As well try to instruct leprosy out of our system. There must be a work of God in destruction before we are free. We must invite the cross to do its deadly work within us. We must bring our self-sins to the cross for judgment. We must prepare ourselves for an ordeal of suffering in some measure like that through which our Savior passed when He suffered under Pontius Pilate.

A. W. Tozer, in *The Pursuit of God*

DEATH AND LIFE

If by the Spirit you put to death the deeds of the body, you will live.
(ROMANS 8:13, ESV)

When we talk of rending of the veil, we are speaking in a figure, and the thought of it is poetical, almost pleasant; but in actuality there is nothing pleasant about it. In human experience that veil is made of living spiritual tissue; it is composed of the sentient, quivering stuff of which our whole beings consist, and to touch it is to touch us where we feel pain. To tear it away is to injure us, to hurt us and make us bleed. To say otherwise is to make the cross no cross and death no death at all. It is never fun to die. To rip through the dear and tender stuff of which life is made can never be anything but deeply painful. Yet that is what the cross did to Jesus and it is what the cross would do to every man to set him free.

Let us beware of tinkering with our inner life in hope ourselves to rend the veil. God must do everything for us. Our part is to yield and trust. We must confess, forsake, repudiate the self-life, then reckon it crucified. But we must be careful to distinguish lazy "acceptance" from the real work of God. We must insist upon the work being done. We dare not rest content with a neat doctrine of self-crucifixion. That is to imitate Saul and spare the best of the sheep and the oxen.

Insist that the work be done in very truth, and it will be done. The cross is rough, it is deadly, but it is effective. It does not keep its victim hanging there forever. There comes a moment when its work is finished and the suffering victim dies. After that is resurrection glory and power, and the pain is forgotten for joy that the veil is taken away and we have entered in actual spiritual experience the Presence of the living God.

A. W. TOZER, IN *THE PURSUIT OF GOD*

God Pursues Relationship with You

Whoever has my commandments and keeps them, he it is who loves me. And he who loves me will be loved by my Father, and I will love him and manifest myself to him.

(John 14:21, esv)

God created you for intimate fellowship with Him. A life spent walking closely with the Lord is both exciting and rewarding. God does not want you to miss out on what He has intended for you from eternity. Sin causes us to follow our own selfish desires, but in doing so we reject God's best for our lives. So God takes the initiative to draw us closer to Himself.

This love relationship, however, is not one-sided. As you accept His love and forgiveness, He wants you to know and worship Him. Most of all, He wants you to love Him. Your love for God and your obedience to His commands go hand in hand. Jesus declared, "If you love Me, you will keep My commandments" (John 14:15, hcsb). When you obey Jesus, you demonstrate that you trust Him. Obedience is the outward expression of your love for God. If you have an obedience problem, you have a love problem. Focus your attention on God's love. Could you stand before God and describe your relationship to Him by saying, "I love You with all my heart and all my soul and all my mind and all my strength"? Jesus said He would take those who respond to His love into an ever-deepening experience of love and fellowship with Him.

The daily presence of God should be the most practical aspect of a believer's life. His plan for the advance of His kingdom on earth includes working in real and tangible ways through relationships with His people. God can make a dramatic difference in your relationships, your home, your church, and your workplace. His involvement in your life should be visible and evident to you and to those around you, like it was in the lives of countless others revealed in the Scriptures.

Henry Blackaby and Richard Blackaby, in *Experiencing God*

The Battle Within

Truly, truly, I say to you, everyone who commits sin is a slave to sin.
(John 8:34, ESV)

"Sinner" is not some theological term contrived to explain away the presence of evil in this world; nor is it a cliché conceived by colonial hymn writers or backwoods preachers to frighten recalcitrant congregations.

R. C. Sproul often says, "We are not sinners because we sin; we sin because we are sinners." We are not theoretical sinners or honorary sinners or vicarious sinners. We are sinners indeed and in deed.

Man goes to great lengths to avoid his own responsibility. Many blame Satan for every imaginable evil—but Jesus states clearly that sin is in *us* (see Matthew 15:18-20). Others recoil with horror at the sins of the society around them, smugly satisfied that sinful abominations are not of their doing—not realizing that God holds *us* responsible for acts of omission as well as acts of commission. Still others believe, as did Socrates two thousand years ago, that sin is not man's moral responsibility, but is caused by ignorance. Hegel, whose philosophy so enormously influenced nineteenth and twentieth century thought, argued that man is "evolving" through increasing knowledge to superior moral levels.

But history continues to validate the biblical account that man is by his own nature sinful—indeed, imprisoned by his sin.

The war to end all wars is a battle for eternal stakes between spiritual forces—and it is being waged *in* you and *in* me.

When we truly smell the stench of sin within us, it drives us helplessly and irresistibly to despair. *But God* has provided a way for us to be freed from the evil within: it is through the door of repentance. When we truly comprehend our own nature, repentance is no dry doctrine, no frightening message. It is a gift God grants which leads to life (see Acts 11:18). It is the key to the door of liberation, to the only real freedom we can ever know.

Charles Colson, in *Loving God*

Best Boast, Greatest Treasure

In God we have boasted continually,
and we will give thanks to your name forever.
(Psalm 44:8, esv)

The knowledge of God is our greatest privilege. Hear Jeremiah: "Thus says the Lord: 'Let not the wise man boast in his wisdom, let not the mighty man boast in his might, let not the rich man boast in his riches, but let him who boasts boast in this, that he understands and knows me, that I am the Lord who practices steadfast love, justice, and righteousness in the earth. For in these things I delight, declares the Lord'" (9:23-24, esv).

This declaration is from the same man whose speech had begun with, "Oh that my head were waters, and my eyes a fountain of tears" (Jeremiah 9:1, esv). No ivory-tower theologian or author was Jeremiah! Here was a man suffering for the sake of his people, seeing things with the clarity of one who was an outsider in every society, except in the society of God. He penetrated through all the superficialities of life to the heart of the matter. Who cares for the wisdom of this world, or the strength of men, or the riches and fame some attain, if all these things are to be had without knowing God? With devastating honesty, Jeremiah reduced all these things men desire to their proper (and very secondary) place in his "Jeremiad." Life is only worth boasting about if at its center is the knowledge of God, controlling all our aspirations. That *is* something to boast about.

What do you and I boast about? What subject of conversation most arouses us and fills our hearts? Do we consider knowing God to be the greatest treasure in the world?

How sensitive are you to this issue? Knowing God is your single greatest privilege as a Christian, and the one that sensitizes you to every other issue of importance. But is this the issue that lies at the center of *your* thinking?

Sinclair Ferguson, in *A Heart for God*

The God Who Governs

You alone, whose name is the Lord, are the Most High over all the earth.

(Psalm 83:18, esv)

The God we're invited to trust is the One who governs the universe — including all actions of all creatures, both men and animals. Jesus tells us He is the One apart from whose will the sparrow cannot fall to the ground (see Matthew 10:29). Paul calls Him "the blessed and only Sovereign" (1 Timothy 6:15, esv). In the book of Daniel, we read that "the Most High rules the kingdom of men and gives it to whom he will," and that He "does according to his will among the host of heaven and among the inhabitants of the earth; and none can stay his hand or say to him, 'What have you done?'" (4:32,35, esv). As David says to Him, "You are exalted as head above all . . . and you rule over all" (1 Chronicles 29:11-12, esv). Jeremiah asks, "Who has spoken and it came to pass, unless the Lord has commanded it?" (Lamentations 3:37, esv).

No one can act outside God's sovereign will or against it. As Augustine wrote centuries ago, "Nothing . . . happens unless the Omnipotent wills it to happen: he either permits it to happen, or he brings it about himself."[6] Philip Hughes said, "Under God . . . all things are without exception fully controlled — despite all appearances to the contrary."[7] Nothing is too large or small to escape God's governing hand. The spider building its web in the corner and Napoleon marching his army across Europe are both under God's control.

As God's rule is invincible, so it is incomprehensible. His ways are higher than our ways (see Isaiah 55:9). His judgments are unsearchable, and His paths are beyond tracing out (see Romans 11:33). We're therefore wrong to question His sovereignty simply because we do not understand what God is doing. God's plan and His ways of working out His plan are frequently beyond our ability to fathom and understand. We must learn to trust when we don't understand.

Jerry Bridges, in *Trusting God*

Waiting to Hear

We are all here in the presence of God
to hear all that you have been commanded by the Lord.
(Acts 10:33, esv)

Peter came to the house of Cornelius and preached the good news of Christ. And "while Peter yet spake these words, the Holy Ghost fell on all them which heard the word" (Acts 10:44, kjv). Why? They had testified, "Now . . . are we all here *present before God, to hear all things that are commanded thee of God*" (10:33, kjv, emphasis added).

In all our gatherings we need to believe in the Holy Spirit as the Guide and Teacher of God's saints when they wait to be led by Him into the things which God hath prepared, and which the heart cannot conceive.

The great danger in our assemblies is that in our consciousness of having our Bible, and our past experience of God's leading, and our sound creed, and our honest wish to do God's will, *we trust in these*, and do not realize that with every step we need and may have a heavenly guidance.

There may be elements of God's will, application of God's word, experience of the close presence and leading of God, and manifestations of His Spirit's power of which we know nothing as yet. God is willing to open these up to souls intently set upon allowing Him to have His way entirely.

When we come together praising God for all He has done and taught and given, we may at the same time be limiting Him by not expecting greater things. While we think that we know and trust the power of God for what we may expect, we may be hindering Him by not cultivating the habit of waiting for His counsel.

More stillness of soul to realize God's presence . . . more consciousness of our ignorance of what God's great plans may be . . . more faith in the certainty that God has greater things to show us, that He Himself will be revealed in new glory . . . these must be the marks of the assemblies of God's saints.

Andrew Murray, in *Waiting on God*

Improving, Humbling, Consoling

Let us know; let us press on to know the Lord.

(Hosea 6:3, esv)

These words spoken in 1855 by Charles H. Spurgeon were true then, and they are true now:

"It has been said by someone that 'the proper study of mankind is man.' I will not oppose the idea, but I believe it is equally true that the proper study of God's elect is God; the proper study of a Christian is the Godhead. . . .

"There is something exceedingly *improving to the mind* in a contemplation of the Divinity. It is a subject so vast that all our thoughts are lost in its immensity; so deep that our pride is drowned in its infinity. . . . No subject of contemplation will tend more to humble the mind than thoughts of God. . . .

"But while the subject *humbles* the mind, it also *expands* it. He who often thinks of God will have a larger mind than the man who simply plods around this narrow globe. . . . The most excellent study for expanding the soul is the science of Christ and Him crucified, and the knowledge of the Godhead in the glorious Trinity. Nothing will so enlarge the intellect, nothing so magnify the whole soul of man, as a devout, earnest, continued investigation of the great subject of the Deity.

"And while humbling and expanding, this subject is eminently *consolatory*. Oh, there is in contemplating Christ a balm for every wound; in musing on the Father, there is a quietus for every grief; and in the influence of the Holy Ghost, there is a balsam for every sore."[8]

It is as we enter more and more deeply into this experience of being humbled and exalted that our knowledge of God increases, and with it our peace, our strength, and our joy. God help us then to put our knowledge about God to this use, that we all may in truth "know the Lord."

J. I. Packer, in *Knowing God*

Worship as Honor

This people honors me with their lips, but their heart is far from me; in vain do they worship me.
(Matthew 15:8-9, esv)

Worship is essentially a way of honoring God. It means recognizing His honor and feeling the worth of it and ascribing it to Him in all the ways appropriate to His character.

Worship is a way of gladly reflecting back to God the radiance of His worth. The reason for saying *gladly* is that even mountains and trees reflect back to God the radiance of His worth: "Praise the Lord from the earth . . . mountains and all hills, fruit trees and all cedars!" (Psalm 148:7,9, esv). Yet this reflection of God's glory in nature is not conscious. The mountains and hills do not willingly worship. In all the earth, only humans have this unique capacity.

If we do not gladly reflect God's glory in worship, we will nevertheless reflect the glory of His justice in our own condemnation: "Surely the wrath of man shall praise you" (Psalm 76:10, esv). But this unwilling reflection of God's worth is *not* worship. Therefore, it is necessary to define worship not simply as a way of reflecting back to God the radiance of His worth, but, more precisely, as a way of doing it *gladly.*

The word *gladly* is liable to misunderstanding because (as we will see in a moment) worship at times involves contrition and brokenness, which we do not usually associate with gladness. But I keep the word because if we say only, for example, that worship is a "willing" reflection back to God of His worth, then we are on the brink of a worse misunderstanding; namely, that worship can be willed when the heart has no real desire, or as Jesus says, when the heart is "far from me." Moreover, I think we will see that in genuine biblical contrition there is at least a seed of gladness that comes from the awakening hope that God will "revive the heart of the contrite" (Isaiah 57:15, esv).

John Piper, in *Desiring God*

A Paradox

He goes before them, and the sheep follow him, for they know his voice.
(John 10:4, ESV)

It is not an exaggeration to speak of a *paradox* in the contemporary experience and understanding of hearing God. It is a paradox that seriously hinders our practical faith.

On one hand we have massive testimony to and widespread faith in God's personal, guiding communication with us—far more than mere providential and blindly controlling guidance. This is not only recorded in Scripture and emblazoned upon the history of the church; it also lies at the heart of our worship services and our individualized relationships with God, and it actually serves as the basis of authority for our teachers and leaders. Only very rarely will someone profess to teach and lead the people of God on the basis of his or her education, natural talents, and denominational connections alone. Authority in spiritual leadership derives from a life in the Spirit, from the minister's personal encounter and ongoing relationship with God.

On the other hand we also find a pervasive and often painful uncertainty about how hearing God's voice actually works today and what its place is in the church and in the Christian's life. Even those who firmly believe they have been addressed or directly spoken to by God may be at a loss to know what is happening or what to do about it.

This paradox must be resolved and removed by providing believers with a *clear understanding* and a *confident, practical orientation toward God's way of guiding us and communicating with us.* Our failure to hear God has its deepest roots in a failure to understand, accept, and grow into a conversational relationship with God, the sort of relationship suited to friends who are mature personalities in a shared enterprise, no matter how different they may be in other respects.

Within such a relationship, our Lord surely intends us to recognize His voice speaking in our hearts as occasion demands.

Dallas Willard, in *Hearing God*

LEARNING TO TRUST

Trust in him at all times, O people;
pour out your heart before him; God is a refuge for us.
(PSALM 62:8, ESV)

It's difficult to believe God is in control when we're in the midst of heartache or grief. I've struggled with this many times myself, including two recent occasions. Each time I've had to decide if I would trust Him, even when my heart ached. I realized anew that we must learn to trust God one circumstance at a time.

It's not a matter of my feelings but of my will. I never feel like trusting God when adversity strikes, but I can choose to do so anyway. That act of the will must be based on belief, and belief must be based on the truth that God is sovereign. He carries out His own good purposes without ever being thwarted, and nothing is outside of His sovereign will. We must cling to this in the face of adversity and tragedy, if we're to glorify God by trusting Him.

I'll say this as gently and compassionately as I know how: Our first priority in adversity is to honor and glorify God by trusting Him. Gaining relief from our feelings of heartache or disappointment or frustration is a natural desire, and God has promised to give us grace sufficient for our trials and peace for our anxieties (see 2 Corinthians 12:9; Philippians 4:6-7). But just as God's will is to take precedence over our will ("Yet not as I will, but as you will"—Matthew 26:39, NIV), so God's honor is to take precedence over our feelings. We honor God by choosing to trust Him when we don't understand what He is doing or why He has allowed some adverse circumstance to occur. As we seek God's glory, we may be sure He has purposed our good and that He won't be frustrated in fulfilling that purpose.

JERRY BRIDGES, IN *TRUSTING GOD*

Accepting the Light

For the Lord *God is a sun and shield;*
the Lord *bestows favor and honor.*
(Psalm 84:11, esv)

Our waiting on God can have no higher object than simply having His light shine on us, and in us, and through us, all the day.

God is Light. God is a Sun. Paul says: "God . . . hath shined in our hearts, to give the light," What light? "The light of the . . . glory of God in the face of Jesus Christ" (2 Corinthians 4:6, kjv). Just as the sun shines its beautiful, life-giving light on and into our earth, so God shines into our hearts the light of His glory, of His love, in Christ His Son.

Our heart is meant to have that light filling and gladdening it all the day, because God is our sun, and it is written, "Thy sun shall no more go down" (Isaiah 60:20, kjv). God's love shines on us without ceasing.

But can we indeed enjoy it all the day? We can. How? Let nature give us the answer. Those beautiful trees and flowers and green grass — what do they do to keep the sun shining on them? They do nothing; they simply bask in the sunshine when it comes. The sun is millions of miles away, but over all that distance it comes, its own light and joy; and the tiniest flower that lifts its little head upward is met by the same exuberance of light and blessing as flood the widest landscape.

What the trees and the flowers do unconsciously is to be with us a voluntary and a loving acceptance. Faith, simple faith in God's word and love, is to be the opening of the eyes, the opening of the heart, to receive and enjoy the unspeakable glory of His grace.

It is the very highest exercise of our Christian life just to abide in the light of God, and let it, and let Him, fill us with the life and the brightness it brings.

Andrew Murray, in *Waiting on God*

Inference or Reality?

Oh, taste and see that the Lord is good!
Blessed is the man who takes refuge in him!
(Psalm 34:8, esv)

Canon Holmes of India decades ago called attention to the inferential character of the average man's faith in God. To most people God is an inference, not a reality. He is a deduction from evidence which they consider adequate; but He remains personally unknown to the individual. "He *must* be," they say, "therefore we believe He is." Others do not go even so far as this; they know of Him only by hearsay. They have never bothered to think the matter out for themselves, but have heard about Him from others, and have put belief in Him into the back of their minds along with the various odds and ends that make up their total creed. To many others God is but an ideal, another name for goodness, or beauty, or truth; or He is law, or life, or the creative impulse back of the phenomena of existence.

These notions about God are many and varied, but they who hold them have one thing in common: they do not know God in personal experience. The possibility of intimate acquaintance with Him has not entered their minds. While admitting His existence they do not think of Him as knowable in the sense that we know things or people.

Christians, to be sure, go further than this, at least in theory. Their creed requires them to believe in the personality of God, and they have been taught to pray, "Our Father, which art in heaven." Now personality and fatherhood carry with them the idea of the possibility of personal acquaintance. This is admitted, I say, in theory, but for millions of Christians, nevertheless, God is no more real than He is to the non-Christian. They go through life trying to love an ideal and be loyal to a mere principle.

Over against all this cloudy vagueness stands the clear scriptural doctrine that God can be known in personal experience.

A. W. Tozer, in *The Pursuit of God*

More Than Watchmen for the Morning

My soul waits for the Lord more than watchmen for the morning.
(Psalm 130:6, ESV)

With what intense longing morning light is often waited for. By mariners in a shipwrecked vessel; by a benighted traveler in a dangerous country; by an army finding itself surrounded by an enemy. Morning light will show what hope of escape there may be. Morning may bring life and liberty. And so the saints of God in darkness have longed for the light of His countenance.

Dear soul! Learn to wait on the Lord more than watchers for the morning. All within you may be very dark; is that not the very best reason for waiting for the light of God? The first beginnings of light may be just enough to discover the darkness, and painfully to humble you on account of sin. Can you not trust the light to expel the darkness?

Bow, even now, in stillness before God, and wait on Him to shine into you.

God is light: the Father, the eternal, inaccessible, and incomprehensible light; the Son, the light concentrated, and embodied, and manifested; the Spirit, the light entering and dwelling and shining in our hearts. *God is light*, and is here shining on my heart.

Say, in humble faith, *God is light,* infinitely brighter and more beautiful than that of the sun. I have been so occupied with my thoughts and efforts. I have never opened the shutters to let His light in. Unbelief has kept it out. I bow in faith: God, light, is shining into my heart. What would I think of a sun that could not shine? What shall I think of a God that does not shine? No, God shines! *God is light!* I will rest in the light of God. My eyes are feeble, my windows unclean, but the light will shine in me, and I shall learn to walk all the day in the joy of it.

Andrew Murray, in *Waiting on God*

His Way Is Always Best

My people did not listen to my voice. . . . So I gave them over to their stubborn hearts, to follow their own counsels.
(Psalm 81:11-12, esv)

To live a God-centered life, you must focus on God's purposes, not your own plans. Try to see things from God's perspective rather than from your distorted human view. When God starts to do something in the world, He takes the initiative to tell someone what He is doing. Out of His grace, God involves His people in accomplishing His purposes.

In the Bible, God rebukes those who propose their own best thinking over His commands. Those in the Bible who received praise from God were not brilliant planners. They were humble "heroes of faith" (see Hebrews 11). God commended them for their compliance, not for their performance.

Why don't we realize that doing things God's way is always best? We cause a great deal of pain in our relationships and division in our churches because *we* decide what *we* think is best for our family or business or church. *We* develop *our* plans. *We* implement *our* strategies, at times imposing them on others and then experiencing the meager — or even destructive — results of our limited knowledge, reasoning, and power. Oh, that we would discover the difference when we acknowledge Christ as Head of His body, the church. He will accomplish more in six months through a people yielded to Him than we could in sixty years in our own strength and wisdom.

God wants us to align our lives with Him so He will accomplish His divine purposes in and through us. God is not our servant to bless our plans and desires. He is our Lord, and we must adjust our lives to what He is doing and to the ways He chooses to accomplish His work. If we will not submit to God and His ways, He will allow us to follow our own devices. But be sure of this: we will miss God's activity, and we will not experience what God wants to do through us to bless others.

Henry Blackaby and Richard Blackaby, in *Experiencing God*

Waiting on Behalf of His Church

I will wait for the Lord, who is hiding his face from the house of Jacob, and I will hope in him.

(Isaiah 8:17, esv)

In Isaiah 8 we have a servant of God waiting upon Him, not on behalf of himself, but of his people, from whom God was hiding His face. It suggests to us how our waiting upon God — though it commences with our personal needs, with the desire for the revelation of Himself, or for the answer to personal petitions — need not, may not, stop there. We may be walking in the full light of God's countenance, and God yet be hiding His face from His people around us; far from being content to think that this is nothing but the just punishment of their sin, or the consequence of their indifference, we are called with tender hearts to think of their sad estate, and to wait on God on their behalf. The privilege of waiting upon God is one that brings great responsibility. Even as Christ, when He entered God's presence, at once used His place of privilege and honor as intercessor, so we no less, if we know what it is really to enter in and wait upon God, must use our access for our less favored brethren.

If others fail in doing it, give yourself doubly to it. The deeper the darkness, the greater the need of appealing to the one only Deliverer. Instead of the tone of judgment or condemnation toward them, of despondency or despair, realize your calling to wait upon God.

Let us wait on God, in the humble confession of the sins of His people. Let us wait on God in tender, loving intercession for all saints, our beloved brethren, however wrong their lives or their teaching may appear. Let us wait on God in faith and expectation, until He shows us that He will hear. Let us wait on God, and give Him no rest till He makes Zion a joy in the earth.

Andrew Murray, in *Waiting on God*

Lifelong Seeking

I press on to make it my own,
because Christ Jesus has made me his own.
(Philippians 3:12, ESV)

The seeking of God *begins* at conversion. Though we may proclaim to the world that we "found it," the finding of God is, ironically, the beginning of seeking after God. To seek God is a lifelong pursuit. The seeking after God is what Jonathan Edwards called "the main business of the Christian life."

To seek God's kingdom is to fulfill the last command of Jesus as well as the crucial petition of the Lord's Prayer: "Your kingdom come. Your will be done on earth as it is in heaven" (Matthew 6:10, NKJV).

The last question His disciples asked Jesus was, "Lord, will you at this time restore the kingdom to Israel?" (Acts 1:6, ESV). Just moments before Jesus departed this planet in His glorious ascension, His students pressed Him with one last question. The question was about the kingdom. Jesus answered the question first with a mild rebuke and then with a command: "You shall be witnesses to Me" (Acts 1:8, NKJV).

We are called to seek the kingdom by bearing witness to the kingdom. We are to seek to show the world what the kingdom of God looks like. For the kingdom to come on earth as it is in heaven means that loyal children of the King do the King's will here and now. We bear witnesses to God's kingdom by serving God's King. This is the will of God. This is what pleases Him. There is a reason why Jesus links the coming of the kingdom with the doing of the will of God. "Your kingdom come" and "Your will be done" belong together. They are two sides of the same coin. The kingdom comes on earth where God's will is done on earth.

The conclusion we reach is this: The great overarching goal of the Christian life is *obedience to the King.* And He is pleased when we obey.

R. C. Sproul, in *Pleasing God*

United Waiting

Behold, this is our God; we have waited for him,
that he might save us. This is the Lord; we have waited for him;
let us be glad and rejoice in his salvation.
(Isaiah 25:9, esv)

In Isaiah 25:9, we have two precious thoughts. (1) This is the language of God's people who have been *unitedly* waiting on Him. (2) The fruit of their waiting is that God has so revealed Himself that they could joyfully say, "Lo, this is our God . . . this is the Lord" (Isaiah 25:9, kjv).

Note this repeated phrase, "We have waited for him." In time of trouble the hearts of the people had been drawn together, and ceasing from all human hope or help, they had with one heart set themselves to wait for their God.

Is this not just what we need in our churches? Is not the need of the church and the world great enough to demand it? Are there not evils in the church of Christ to which no human wisdom is equal, evils that are robbing the church of its power? Have we not culture and money and pleasure threatening its spiritual life? Are not the powers of the church utterly inadequate to cope with the powers of infidelity and iniquity and wretchedness?

And is there not a provision made in the promise of God, and in the power of the Holy Spirit, that can meet this need? And would not united waiting upon God for the supply of His Spirit most certainly seem the needed blessing? We cannot doubt it.

The object of a more definite waiting upon God in our gatherings would be very much the same as in personal worship. It would mean a deeper conviction that God must and will do all. It would require a more humble and abiding entrance into our deep helplessness, and the need of entire and unceasing dependence upon Him. We need a more living consciousness that the essential thing is to give God His place of honor and of power.

Andrew Murray, in *Waiting on God*

OUR FACULTIES FOR KNOWING GOD

Long for the pure spiritual milk . . . if indeed you have tasted that the Lord is good.

(1 PETER 2:2-3, ESV)

A loving Personality dominates the Bible, walking among the trees of the garden and breathing fragrance over every scene. Always a living Person is present, speaking, pleading, loving, working, and manifesting Himself whenever and wherever His people have the receptivity necessary to receive the manifestation.

The Bible assumes as a self-evident fact that men can know God with at least the same degree of immediacy as they know any other person or thing that comes within the field of their experience. The same terms are used to express the knowledge of God as are used to express knowledge of physical things. "O *taste* and see that the LORD is good" (Psalm 34:8, KJV, emphasis added). "All thy garments *smell* of myrrh, and aloes, and cassia, out of the ivory palaces" (Psalm 45:8, KJV, emphasis added). "My sheep *hear* my voice" (John 10:27, KJV, emphasis added). "Blessed are the pure in heart: for they shall *see* God" (Matthew 5:8, KJV, emphasis added). These are but four of countless such passages from the Word of God. And more important than any proof text is the fact that the whole import of the Scripture is toward this belief.

What can all this mean except that we have in our hearts organs by means of which we can know God as certainly as we know material things through our familiar five senses? We possess spiritual faculties by means of which we can know God and the spiritual world if we will obey the Spirit's urge and begin to use them.

That a saving work must first be done in the heart is taken for granted here. The spiritual faculties of the unregenerate man lie asleep in his nature, unused and for every purpose dead; that is the stroke which has fallen upon us by sin. They may be quickened to active life again by the operation of the Holy Spirit in regeneration; that is one of the immeasurable benefits which come to us through Christ's atoning work on the cross.

A. W. TOZER, IN *THE PURSUIT OF GOD*

Our Feelings in Worship

Whom have I in heaven but you?
And there is nothing on earth that I desire besides you.
(Psalm 73:25, esv)

What are the feelings or affections that make the outward acts of worship authentic? For an answer, we turn to the inspired psalms and hymns of the Old Testament. An array of different and intertwined affections may grip the heart at any time.

Perhaps the first response of the heart at seeing the majestic holiness of God is stunned silence: "Be still, and know that I am God" (Psalm 46:10, esv). "The Lord is in his holy temple; let all the earth keep silence before him" (Habakkuk 2:20, esv).

In the silence arises a sense of awe and reverence and wonder at the sheer magnitude of God: "Let all the earth fear the Lord; let all the inhabitants of the world stand in awe of him!" (Psalm 33:8, esv).

And because we are all sinners, there is in our reverence a holy dread of God's righteous power: "The Lord of hosts, him you shall honor as holy. Let him be your fear, and let him be your dread" (Isaiah 8:13, esv). "I will bow down toward your holy temple in the fear of you" (Psalm 5:7, esv).

But this dread is not a paralyzing fright full of resentment against God's absolute authority. It finds release in brokenness and contrition and grief for our ungodliness: "The sacrifices of God are a broken spirit; a broken and contrite heart, O God, you will not despise" (Psalm 51:17, esv).

Mingled with the feeling of genuine brokenness and contrition, there arises a longing for God: "As a deer pants for flowing streams, so pants my soul for you, O God. My soul thirsts for God, for the living God" (Psalm 42:1-2, esv). "My flesh and my heart may fail, but God is the strength of my heart and my portion forever" (Psalm 73:26, esv). "O God, you are my God; earnestly I seek you; my soul thirsts for you; my flesh faints for you, as in a dry and weary land where there is no water" (Psalm 63:1, esv).

John Piper, in *Desiring God*

More of Our Feelings in Worship

In your presence there is fullness of joy;
at your right hand are pleasures forevermore.
(Psalm 16:11, esv)

God is not unresponsive to the contrite longing of the soul. He comes and lifts the load of sin and fills our heart with gladness and gratitude. "You have turned for me my mourning into dancing; you have loosed my sackcloth and clothed me with gladness, that my glory may sing your praise and not be silent. O Lord my God, I will give thanks to you forever!" (Psalm 30:11-12, esv).

But our joy does not just rise from the backward glance in gratitude. It also rises from the forward glance in hope: "Why are you cast down, O my soul, and why are you in turmoil within me? Hope in God; for I shall again praise him, my salvation and my God" (Psalm 42:5-6, esv).

In the end the heart longs not for any of God's good gifts, but for God Himself. To see Him and know Him and be in His presence is the soul's final feast. Beyond this there is no quest. Words fail. We call it pleasure, joy, delight. But these are weak pointers to the unspeakable experience: "One thing have I asked of the Lord, that will I seek after: that I may dwell in the house of the Lord all the days of my life, to gaze upon the beauty of the Lord and to inquire in his temple" (Psalm 27:4, esv).

These are some of the affections of the heart that keep worship from being "in vain" (Matthew 15:9, esv). Worship is not a mere act of willpower by which we perform outward acts. Without the engagement of the heart, we do not really worship. The engagement of the heart in worship is the coming alive of the feelings and emotions and affections of the heart. Where feelings for God are dead, worship is dead.

True worship must include inward feelings that reflect the worth of God's glory.

John Piper, in *Desiring God*

In the Lord's Hand

The king's heart is a stream of water in the hand of the Lord;
he turns it wherever he will.
(Proverbs 21:1, esv)

How are we to respond when we find ourselves desperately needing a favorable decision or action on another person's part? Can we trust God that He will work in the heart of that individual to bring about His plan for us? Or consider the instance when someone is out to ruin our reputation or jeopardize our career. Can we trust God to intervene in that person's heart so he doesn't carry out his evil intent?

According to the Bible, the answer is yes. God does sovereignly intervene in people's hearts so that their decisions and actions accomplish His purpose for our lives. Yet God does this in such a way that these people act by their own free and voluntary choices.

Perhaps the clearest biblical statement that God does sovereignly influence the decisions of people is found in Proverbs 21:1. Charles Bridges comments that here the "general truth" of God's sovereignty over the hearts of all people "is taught by the strongest illustration — his uncontrollable sway upon the most absolute of all wills — *the king's heart*."[9]

In our day of limited monarchies, it may be difficult for us to appreciate fully the force of what Charles Bridges is saying. But in Solomon's time the king was an absolute monarch. There was no separate legislative body to make laws he wouldn't like or a supreme court to restrain him. The king's word was law. His authority over his realm was unconditional and unrestrained.

Yet God controls that king's heart. The stubborn will of the most powerful monarch on earth is directed by God as easily as the farmer directs the flow of water in his irrigation canals. The argument, then, is from the greater to the lesser — if God controls the king's heart, surely He controls everyone else's. All must move before His sovereign influence.

Jerry Bridges, in *Trusting God*

JUDGMENT COMES

For it is time for judgment to begin at the household of God;
and if it begins with us, what will be the outcome
for those who do not obey the gospel of God?
(1 PETER 4:17, ESV)

Among those who seek to learn the blessed art of waiting on God, let no one wonder if at first the attempt to wait on Him only reveals more of unconquered sins, evil thoughts, or great darkness. Through His own beloved Son, the gift and bearer of His mercy and justice on Calvary, submit and sink down deep under the judgment of your every sin! Judgment prepares the way and breaks out in wonderful mercy. It is written, "Zion shall be redeemed with judgment" (Isaiah 1:27, KJV). Wait on God, in the faith that His tender mercy is working out His redemption in the midst of judgment. Wait for Him; He will be gracious to you.

Meanwhile, we are expecting God, in the way of His judgments, to visit his earth; we are waiting for Him. What a thought of unspeakable solemnity! We know of these coming judgments. We know of those around us who live on in carelessness, and who, if no change comes, must perish under God's hand. Will we not do our utmost to warn them, to plead with and for them, if God may have mercy on them? Will we not ask Him to so reveal Himself in the judgments that are coming on our very friends, that we may be inspired with a new fear of Him and for them, and constrained to speak and pray as never yet before?

Verily, waiting on God is not meant to be a spiritual self-indulgence. Its object is to let God and His holiness, Christ and the love that died on Calvary, the Spirit and fire that burns in heaven and came to earth, get possession of us to warn and arouse men with the message that we are waiting for God in the way of His judgments.

Oh, Christian, prove that you really believe in the God of judgment!

ANDREW MURRAY, IN *WAITING ON GOD*

FEAR OF THE FUTURE

Fear not, nor be afraid; have I not told you from of old and declared it?

(ISAIAH 44:8, ESV)

We may have the wrong motives for seeking to hear from God. We all in some measure share in the general human anxiety about the future. By nature we live in the future, constantly hurled into it whether we like it or not. Knowing what we will meet there is a condition of our being prepared to deal with it — or so it would seem from the human point of view. Francis Bacon's saying that knowledge is power is never more vividly realized than in our concern about our own future.

Within the Christian community, teaching on the will of God and how to know it continues to be one of the most popular subjects. But is not a self-defeating motive at work here — one that keeps people from coming to peace about their place in the will of God?

I fear that many people seek to hear God solely as a device for securing their own safety, comfort, and righteousness. For those who busy themselves to know the will of God, however, it is still true that "whoever would save his life will lose it, but whoever loses his life for my sake will find it" (Matthew 16:25, ESV). My extreme preoccupation with knowing God's will for me may indicate only that I am overconcerned with myself, and not that I have a Christlike interest in the well-being of others or in the glory of God.

Frederick B. Meyer writes, "So long as there is some thought of personal advantage, some idea of acquiring the praise and commendation of men, some aim of self-aggrandizement, it will be simply impossible to find out God's purpose concerning us."[10] Nothing will go right in our effort to hear God if this false motivation is its foundation. God will not cooperate. We must discover a different motivation for knowing God's will and listening to His voice.

DALLAS WILLARD, IN *HEARING GOD*

THE NEXT LEVEL

For it is God who works in you,
both to will and to work for his good pleasure.
(PHILIPPIANS 2:13, ESV)

Have you ever said something like, "Lord, if You will just tell me what You want me to do, I will serve You to the best of my ability"? If God *were* to put you in that kind of assignment, could He trust you to handle it? Are you ready to go to the next level of faith in God?

On the night before Jesus' crucifixion, Peter said to the Lord, "I'm ready to go with You both to prison and to death!" In response, Jesus warned him, "The rooster will not crow today until you deny three times that you know Me!" (Luke 22:33-34, HCSB). God also knows the exact limits of *your* faith. He knows what you can handle.

Our own hearts can deceive us (see Jeremiah 17:9). We can often have a higher estimate of our faithfulness and trust in God than we should. God is never fooled. He always matches His assignments with our character and faith in Him. So trust Him. Don't insist that God put you in a position you think you should have. Don't strive to gain a position you think you deserve or can handle. That could lead to your ruin. You might inadvertently manipulate yourself right into a position or responsibility that is beyond what your character can manage. Rather, trust Him and obey wholeheartedly where He has put you, and watch to see where He leads you next.

Remember: God is far more interested in accomplishing His kingdom purposes than you are. He will move you into every assignment He knows you are ready to take on. Let God orient you to Himself. Be patient and wait. Let God use times of waiting to mold and shape your character. Let Him purify your life and make you into a clean vessel for His service.

As you obey Him, God will prepare you for the assignment that is just right for you.

HENRY BLACKABY AND RICHARD BLACKABY, IN *EXPERIENCING GOD*

When You Depend on Others

It is God who executes judgment,
putting down one and lifting up another.
(Psalm 75:6-7, esv)

The Bible's consistent teaching is that God is able and does move upon the hearts and minds of people to accomplish His purposes. Yet it also seems equally clear from Scripture that God does this without violating or coercing their wills, but rather that He works in His mysterious way through their wills to accomplish His purposes.

God is never at a loss because He cannot find someone to cooperate with Him in carrying out His plan. He so moves in the hearts of people — either Christians or non-Christians, it makes no difference — that they willingly, of their own free will carry out His plans. Do you need the good favor of a certain professor in order to get a good recommendation for a job? If that job is God's plan for you, God is able to and will move in the heart of that professor to give you a good recommendation.

Are you dependent upon your boss (or your commanding officer, or some other person) for advancement in your career? God will move in the heart of that person one way or the other, depending on His plan for you (see Psalm 75:6-7).

Your promotion, or lack of it, is in the hand of God. Your superiors are simply His agents to carry out His will. They are not conscious of doing His will and never intended to do it (unless, of course, they are Christians prayerfully seeking to follow the will of God), but that does not alter the result in your life.

You can trust God in all the areas of your life where you are dependent upon the favor or frown of another person. God will move in that person's heart to carry out His will for you.

Jerry Bridges, in *Trusting God*

God or Chance?

The heart of man plans his way, but the Lord establishes his steps.
(Proverbs 16:9, esv)

In divine providence, God sustains and governs His universe, bringing all events to their appointed end. This doctrine, however, is scarcely accepted among people today.

The non-Christian, for the most part, has ruled out both the creating act of God and His providence. Randomness, luck, chance, fate — that is modern man's answer to the age-old question, "Why?" Of course, there's no other alternative if one dismisses the whole idea of God, as many do.

Many others, while not dismissing the idea of God, have fabricated a God of their own speculation. Seventeenth-century deism constructed a God who created a universe and then walked away to leave it running according to its natural laws and man's devices. Many people today are practical deists. Even Christians often think as deists, accepting the concept that God is sovereign but believing He chooses not to exercise His sovereignty in the daily affairs of our lives.

In His well-known statement about sparrows, Jesus said, "Are not two sparrows sold for a penny? And not one of them will fall to the ground apart from your Father. . . . Fear not, therefore; you are of more value than many sparrows" (Matthew 10:29,31, esv). According to Jesus, God does exercise His sovereignty in very minute events — even the life and death of an almost worthless sparrow. And Jesus' whole point is: If God so exercises His sovereignty in regard to sparrows, most certainly He will exercise it in regard to His children. While it is certainly true that God's love for us does not protect us from pain and sorrow, it's also true that all occasions of pain and sorrow are under the absolute control of God. If God controls the circumstances of the sparrow, how much more does He control the circumstances that affect us? God does not walk away and leave us to the mercy of uncontrolled random or chance events.

Jerry Bridges, in *Trusting God*

Who Waits on Us

The Lord waits to be gracious to you. . . .
Blessed are all those who wait for him.
(Isaiah 30:18, esv)

We must think not only of our waiting upon God, but also of what is more wonderful still, of *God's waiting upon us.* This will give new impulse and inspiration to our waiting upon Him. If He waits for us, then we may be sure that we are more than welcome — that He rejoices to find those He has been seeking for.

Let us seek even now, at this moment, in the spirit of lowly waiting on God, to find out something of what it means that the Lord waits to be gracious to us (see Isaiah 30:18). Then we will accept and echo back the message, "Blessed are all they that wait for him" (kjv).

Look up and see the great God upon His throne. He is love, with an unceasing and inexpressible desire to communicate His own goodness and blessedness to all His creatures. He longs and delights to bless. He has inconceivably glorious purposes concerning every one of His children, by the power of His Holy Spirit, to reveal in them His love and power. He waits with all the longings of a father's heart. He waits that He may be gracious unto you. And, each time you come to wait upon Him, or seek to maintain in daily life the holy habit of waiting, you may look up and see Him ready to meet you. He will be waiting so that He may be gracious unto you. Yes, connect every exercise, every breath of the life of waiting, with faith's vision of your God waiting for you.

Yes, it is blessed when a waiting soul and a waiting God meet each other. Let waiting be our work, as it is His. And if His waiting is nothing but goodness and graciousness, let ours be nothing but a rejoicing in that goodness, and a confident expectancy of that grace.

Andrew Murray, in *Waiting on God*

Forgetting the Dung

Whatever gain I had, I counted as loss for the sake of Christ.

(Philippians 3:7, esv)

Not many of us, I think, would ever naturally say that we have known God. The words imply a definiteness and matter-of-factness of experience to which most of us, if we are honest, have to admit that we are still strangers. We claim, perhaps, to have a testimony, and can rattle off our conversion story with the best of them; we say that we *know* God—this, after all, is what evangelicals are expected to say; but would it occur to us to say, without hesitation, and with reference to particular events in our personal history, that we *have known* God? I doubt it, for I suspect that with most of us our experience of God has never become so vivid as that.

Nor, I think, would many of us ever naturally say that in the light of the knowledge of God which we have come to enjoy, past disappointments and present heartbreaks (as the world counts heartbreaks) *don't matter.* For the plain fact is that to most of us they do matter.

But those who really know God never brood on might-have-beens; they never think of the things they have missed, only of what they have gained. "What things were gain to me, those I counted loss for Christ," wrote Paul. "I count all things but loss for the excellency of the knowledge of Christ Jesus my Lord: for whom I have suffered the loss of all things, and do count them but dung, that I may win Christ . . . that I may know him" (Philippians 3:7-10, kjv). When Paul says he counts the things he lost as "dung," he means not merely that he does not live with them constantly in his mind; what normal person spends his time nostalgically dreaming of manure? Yet this, in effect, is what many of us do. It shows how little we have in the way of true knowledge of God.

J. I. Packer, in *Knowing God*

Awaken to Reality

You . . . I have chosen, that you may know and believe me and understand that I am he.

(Isaiah 43:10, ESV)

Why do the very ransomed children of God know so little of that habitual conscious communion with God that the Scriptures seem to offer?

The answer is our chronic unbelief. Faith enables our spiritual sense to function. Where faith is defective the result will be inward insensibility and numbness toward spiritual things. This is the condition of vast numbers of Christians today. No proof is necessary to support that statement. We have but to converse with the first Christian we meet or enter the first church we find open to acquire all the proof we need.

A spiritual kingdom lies all about us, enclosing us, embracing us, altogether within reach of our inner selves, waiting for us to recognize it. God Himself is here waiting our response to His Presence. This eternal world will come alive to us the moment we begin to *reckon* upon its *reality*.

By *reality*, I mean that which has existence apart from any idea any mind may have of it, and which would exist if there were no mind anywhere to entertain a thought of it. That which is real has being in itself. It does not depend upon the observer for its validity.

By our definition, God is real in the absolute and final sense that nothing else is. All other reality is contingent upon His. The great Reality is God who is the Author of that lower and dependent reality which makes up the sum of created things, including ourselves. God has objective existence independent of and apart from any notions which we may have concerning Him.

The worshipping heart does not create its Object. It finds Him here when it wakes from its moral slumber in the morning of its regeneration.

A. W. Tozer, in *The Pursuit of God*

Our Destiny in His Hands

If God is for us, who can be against us?
(Romans 8:31, esv)

How shall we respond to the fact that God is able to and does in fact move in the minds and hearts of people to accomplish His will?

Our first response should be one of trust. Our careers and destinies are in His hands not the hands of bosses, commanding officers, professors, coaches, and all other people who, humanly speaking, are in a position to affect our futures. No one can harm you or jeopardize your future apart from the sovereign will of God.

Moreover, God is able to and will grant you favor in the eyes of people who are in a position to do you good. You can entrust your future to God.

We should then look to God in prayer in all those situations where some aspect of our futures lies in the hands of another individual. As Alexander Carson said, "If we need the protection of men, let us first ask it from God. If we prevail with him, the power of the most mighty and of the most wicked must minister to our relief."[11]

When Queen Esther was to go before King Xerxes without being summoned—an act that would normally result in her being put to death—she asked Mordecai to gather all of the Jews together to fast (and presumably to pray) that the king would grant her favor. Esther did not presume to know God's will—she said, "If I perish, I perish" (Esther 4:16, esv)—but she certainly knew that God controlled the king's heart.

Obviously we do not always know how God will answer our prayers, or whether He will move in the heart of another individual. But it is enough to know that our destiny is in His hands, not those of other people.

Jerry Bridges, in *Trusting God*

Why He Waits

The Lord, the Lord, a God merciful and gracious, slow to anger, and abounding in steadfast love and faithfulness.

(Exodus 34:6, esv)

You ask, "How is it, if God waits to be gracious to us (see Isaiah 30:18), that even after I come and wait upon Him, He does not give the help I seek, but waits still longer and longer?"

There is a double answer.

First, God is a wise husbandman, who "waiteth for the precious fruit of the earth, and hath long patience for it" (James 5:7, kjv). He cannot gather the fruit until it is ripe. He knows when we are spiritually ready to receive the blessing to our profit and His glory. Waiting in the sunshine of His love is what will ripen the soul for His blessing. Waiting under the cloud of trial, that breaks in showers of blessing, is just as necessary. Be assured that if God waits longer than you could wish, it is only to make the blessing doubly precious. God waited four thousand years, until the fullness of time, before He sent His Son. Our times are in His hands. He will avenge His elect speedily. He will make haste for our help and not delay one hour too long.

The other answer: The giver is more than the gift; God is more than the blessing. And our being kept waiting on Him is the only way for our learning to find our life and joy in Himself.

Oh, if God's children only knew what a glorious God they have, and what a privilege it is to be linked in fellowship with Him, then they would rejoice in Him! Even when He keeps them waiting, they will learn to understand better than ever: His waiting will be the highest proof of His graciousness.

What a dignity and blessedness to be waiting on the everlasting God, ever on the watch for every indication of His will or favor, ever conscious of His nearness, His goodness, and His grace!

Andrew Murray, in *Waiting on God*

THE SPIRITUAL IS REAL

The things that are seen are transient,
but the things that are unseen are eternal.
(2 CORINTHIANS 4:18, ESV)

Imagination is not faith. The two not only are different from each other, but stand in sharp opposition. Imagination projects unreal images out of the mind and seeks to attach reality to them. Faith creates nothing; it simply reckons upon that which is already *there.* God and the spiritual world are real. We can reckon upon them with as much assurance as we reckon upon the familiar world around us. Spiritual things are there (or rather we should say *here*) inviting our attention and challenging our trust.

Our trouble is that we have established bad thought habits. We habitually think of the visible world as real and doubt the reality of any other. We do not deny the existence of the spiritual world but we doubt that it is real in the accepted meaning of the word. The world of sense intrudes upon our attention day and night for the whole of our lifetime. It is clamorous, insistent, self-demonstrating. It does not appeal to our faith; it is here, assaulting our five senses, demanding to be accepted as real and final.

Sin has so clouded the lenses of our hearts that we cannot see that other reality, the City of God, shining around us. The world of sense triumphs. The visible becomes the enemy of the invisible; the temporal, of the eternal. That is the curse inherited by every member of Adam's tragic race.

Our uncorrected thinking, influenced by the blindness of our natural hearts and the intrusive ubiquity of visible things, tends to draw a contrast between the spiritual and the real; but actually no such contrast exists. The antithesis lies elsewhere: between the real and the imaginary, between the spiritual and the material, between the temporal and the eternal; but between the spiritual and the real, never. The spiritual is real.

A. W. TOZER, IN *THE PURSUIT OF GOD*

WHEN WE'RE TREATED UNJUSTLY

He will rejoice over you with gladness; he will quiet you by his love; he will exult over you with loud singing.

(ZEPHANIAH 3:17, ESV)

Confidence in God's sovereignty in the lives of people should keep us from becoming resentful and bitter when we're treated unjustly or maliciously by others. Bitterness usually stems not so much from the other person's actions as from the effects of those actions on our lives.

Consider the following scenario. You've just been unjustly fired from your job for reasons unrelated to your performance. After months of fruitless job hunting, you find yourself standing in the unemployment line. Standing there, you brood over the injustice perpetrated on you by your former boss. You're resentful and bitter.

But suppose on the day you were fired, as you walked out the door, you met a man looking for someone with your skill and experience who offers you a better job at twice the salary. There is one additional qualification: You must have had the experience of being unjustly fired. You gladly accept the job and thoroughly enjoy your new position. Do you become bitter? No. Instead you think how fortunate you are that you were fired. It's the effects of being fired, not the act itself, that determines whether you're tempted to become bitter.

God sometimes allows people to treat us unjustly. Sometimes He even allows their actions to seriously affect our careers or our futures viewed on a human plane. But God never allows people to make decisions about us that undermine His plan for us. God is *for* us, we are His children, He delights in us (see Zephaniah 3:17). And the Scripture says, "If God is for us, who can be against us?" (Romans 8:31, ESV). We can put this down as a bedrock truth: God will never allow any action against you that is not in accord with His will for you. And His will is always directed to our good.

JERRY BRIDGES, IN *TRUSTING GOD*

SOARING HIGH

They who wait for the LORD shall renew their strength;
they shall mount up with wings like eagles.
(ISAIAH 40:31, ESV)

Our waiting on God will depend greatly on our faith's understanding of who He is.

In Isaiah 40:31, we have the close of a passage in which God reveals Himself as the everlasting and almighty One. As that revelation enters into our soul, the waiting will become the spontaneous expression of what we know Him to be—a God altogether most worthy to be waited upon.

Listen to the words: "Why sayest thou, O Jacob . . . My way is hid from the LORD . . . ? Hast thou not known? hast thou not heard, that the everlasting God, the LORD, the Creator of the ends of the earth, fainteth not, neither is weary?" (Isaiah 40:27-28, KJV). So far from it: "He giveth power to the faint; and to them that have no might he increaseth strength. Even the youths shall faint . . . and the young men shall utterly fall" (verses 29-30, KJV). And consider that "the glory of young men is their strength" (Proverbs 20:29, KJV). All that is deemed strong with man shall come to nothing. "But they that wait upon the LORD," on the Everlasting One, who does not faint, and is not weary, they "shall renew their strength; they shall mount up with wings as eagles; they shall run"—and listen now, for they will be strong with the strength of God, and even as He, "they shall run, and not be weary; and they shall walk, and"—even as He—"not faint" (Isaiah 40:31, KJV).

Yes, "they shall mount up with wings as eagles." You know what this means. The eagle is the king of birds; it soars the highest into the heavens. Believers are to live a heavenly life, in the very presence and love and joy of God. They are to live where God lives; they need God's strength to rise there. And it will be given to them that wait on Him.

ANDREW MURRAY, IN *WAITING ON GOD*

Otherworldliness

Whoever would draw near to God must believe that he exists and that he rewards those who seek him.

(Hebrews 11:6, esv)

At the root of the Christian life lies belief in the invisible. The object of the Christian's faith is unseen reality.

For apprehending this reality, the soul has eyes with which to see and ears with which to hear. Feeble they may be from long disuse, but by the life-giving touch of Christ they are now alive and capable of sharpest sight and most sensitive hearing.

If we would rise into that region of light and power plainly beckoning us through the Scriptures of truth, we must break the evil habit of ignoring the spiritual. We must shift our interest from the seen to the unseen. For the great unseen Reality is God. "He that cometh to God must believe that he is, and that he is a rewarder of them that diligently seek him" (Hebrews 11:6, kjv). This is basic in the life of faith. From there we can rise to unlimited heights. "Ye believe in God," said our Lord Jesus Christ, "believe also in me" (John 14:1, kjv). Without the first there can be no second.

If we truly want to follow God we must seek to be otherworldly. This I say knowing well that that word has been used with scorn by the sons of this world and applied to the Christian as a badge of reproach. So be it. Every man must choose his world. If we who follow Christ, with all the facts before us and knowing what we are about, deliberately choose the kingdom of God as our sphere of interest I see no reason why anyone should object. If we lose by it, the loss is our own; if we gain, we rob no one by so doing. The "other world," which is the object of this world's disdain and the subject of the drunkard's mocking song, is our carefully chosen goal and the object of our holiest longing.

A. W. Tozer, in *The Pursuit of God*

IDENTIFYING GOD'S ACTIVITY

I have spoken, and I will bring it to pass; I have purposed, and I will do it.

(ISAIAH 46:11, ESV)

God is at work when you see someone coming to Christ, asking about spiritual matters, beginning to understand spiritual truth, experiencing conviction of sin, or being convinced of the righteousness of Christ or of God's judgment.

God wants to use you to influence others for the kingdom. When you want to know what God is doing around you, *start by praying.* Only the Father knows what He has purposed for the people around you, and He knows the best way to accomplish His will for them. After you pray, watch to see what God does next. Take note of what people are saying when they approach you. *Make the connection* between your prayer and what happens next.

Then, *ask questions.* Ask the kind of probing questions that will reveal what is happening in people's lives, without being intrusive or aggressive. *Listen attentively.* And *be prepared to respond.* If someone confides a personal need, pray for that person and ask God how you might minister practically in response. Be ready to share clearly how Christ's presence has made a difference in your life and how Christ is ready to enter their life and change them as well. Be ready to make whatever adjustments are required to join God in what He is doing.

Keep in mind, the final completion of God's work may be a long time off. He does this on His timetable, not ours.

He's the One who is already at work in our world. When He opens your spiritual eyes to see where He is at work, that revelation is your invitation to join Him. You will know where He is working when you see Him doing things only God can do. When God reveals His work to you, that is the time He wants you to begin adjusting to Him and His activity. What God purposes, He guarantees to complete.

HENRY BLACKABY AND RICHARD BLACKABY, IN *EXPERIENCING GOD*

Words of Caution

The secret things belong to the Lord our God, but the things that are revealed belong to us and to our children forever.

(Deuteronomy 29:29, ESV)

Here are some words of caution we need to consider lest we wrongly use the doctrine of God's sovereignty over people.

First, we should never use the doctrine as an excuse for our own shortcomings. If you failed to get the promotion you had hoped for, or worse yet, you are fired from your job or fail an important exam, you need to first examine your life to see if perhaps the reason lay in your own performance.

Second, we should not allow the doctrine of God's sovereignty to cause us to respond passively to the actions of other people that affect us. We should take all reasonable steps within the will of God to protect and advance our situation. The doctrine of God's sovereignty, considered by itself, should never be used to promote passivity.

Third, we must never use the doctrine of God's sovereignty to excuse our own sinful actions or decisions that hurt another person. God is indeed sovereign in that other person's life, and He may choose to use our sinful actions to accomplish His will. But He will still hold us accountable for our harmful decisions and sinful actions.

We do not know what God's sovereign will is. We do not know how He will work in the heart of another individual, whether favorably or unfavorably from our viewpoint. That is in the realm of God's "secret things" that are not revealed to us. We do know He will work to accomplish His purpose, which is ultimately for our good. Our duty, then, is to obey the "things that are revealed"—the will of God as revealed in Scripture for every area of life (Deuteronomy 29:29, ESV). Scripture teaches us to be prudent, conscientious, and responsible, and to do our jobs or our studies as best we can.

Jerry Bridges, in *Trusting God*

Carried on Eagle's Wings

You yourselves have seen . . . how I bore you on eagles' wings and brought you to myself.
(Exodus 19:4, esv)

Eagles obtain their wings in only one way—by their birth as eagles.

You are born of God. You have the eagle's wings. You may not have known it; you may not have used them; but God can and will teach you how to use them.

You know how eagles are taught the use of their wings. See yonder cliff rising a thousand feet out of the sea. High up a ledge on the rock, see an eagle's nest with its treasure of two young eaglets. See the mother come and stir up her nest, and with her beak push the timid birds over the precipice. See how they flutter and fall and sink toward the depth. See how she "fluttereth over her young, spreadeth abroad her wings, taketh them, beareth them on her wings" (Deuteronomy 32:11, kjv). And so, as they ride upon her wings, she brings them to a place of safety. And she does this again and again. "So the Lord alone did lead him" (verse 12, kjv). Yes, the instinct of that eagle mother was God's gift, a single ray of that love in which the Almighty trains His people to mount as on eagles' wings.

He stirs up your nest. He disappoints your hopes. He brings down your confidence. He makes you fear and tremble, as all your strength fails, and you feel utterly weary and helpless. All the while He is spreading His strong wings for you to rest your weakness on, and offering His everlasting Creator-strength to work in you. All He asks is that you sink down in your weariness and wait on Him. Allow Him in His Jehovah-strength to carry you as you ride upon the wings of His omnipotence.

Lift up your eyes, and behold your God! Listen to Him who says that He "fainteth not, neither is weary" (Isaiah 40:28, kjv), who asks only that you should wait on Him.

Andrew Murray, in *Waiting on God*

Enlarging Our Horizons

He does according to his will . . . among the inhabitants of the earth.
(Daniel 4:35, esv)

Most Christians tend to think of the sovereignty of God only in terms of its immediate effect upon us, or our families or friends. We're not too interested in the sovereignty of God over the nations and over history unless we're consciously and personally affected by that history.

But we must remember that God promised to Abraham and to his seed that all nations will be blessed through Christ (see Genesis 12:3; 22:18; Galatians 3:8). Someday that promise will be fulfilled for, as recorded in Revelation 7:9, John saw "a great multitude that no one could count, from every nation, tribe, people and language, standing before the throne and in front of the Lamb" (niv). God has a plan to redeem people from all nations and to bless all nations through Christ.

As we look around the world today, we see over one-half of the world's population living in countries whose governments are hostile to the gospel, where missionaries are not allowed, and where national Christians are hindered from proclaiming Christ. How do we trust God for the fulfillment of His promises when the current events and conditions of the day seem so directly contrary to their fulfillment?

We must also look at the sovereignty of God and at His promises. He has promised to redeem people from every nation, and He has commanded us to make disciples of all nations. We must trust God by praying. We must learn to trust God for the spread of the gospel, even in those areas where it is severely restricted.

God is sovereign over the nations. He is sovereign even where every attempt is made to stamp out true Christianity. In all of these areas, we can and must trust God.

Jerry Bridges, in *Trusting God*

The Certainty of Blessing

Then you will know that I am the Lord;
those who wait for me shall not be put to shame.
(Isaiah 49:23, esv)

God seeks to draw us by the most positive assurance that waiting on Him can never be in vain: "They shall not be ashamed that wait for me" (Isaiah 49:23, kjv). How strange that, though we should so often have experienced it, we are yet so slow to learn that this blessed waiting must and can be the very breath of our life — a continuous resting in God's presence and His love, an unceasing yielding of ourselves for Him to perfect His work in us.

Listen and meditate, until our heart says with new conviction, "Blessed are all they that wait for him" (Isaiah 30:18, kjv).

The very prayer of Psalm 25:3 — "Let none that wait on thee be ashamed" (kjv) — shows how we fear that it might not be true. Let us listen to God's answer, until every fear is banished, and we send back to heaven the words God speaks. *Yes, Lord, we believe what You say: "All they who wait for Me will not be ashamed."*

In times when God's people were in great straits, and to human eyes there were no possibilities of deliverance, God interposed with His word of promise, and pledged His almighty power for the deliverance of His people. As the God who has Himself undertaken the work of their redemption, He invited them to wait on Him, and assured them that disappointment is impossible.

We, too, are living in days in which there is much in the state of the church that is indescribably sad. Amid all we praise God for, alas, there is much to mourn over! Were it not for God's promises, we might well despair. But in His promises the living God has given and bound Himself to us. He calls us to wait on Him; He assures us we will not be put to shame.

Andrew Murray, in *Waiting on God*

A NEW GOD-CONSCIOUSNESS

You have come to Mount Zion and to the city of the living God, the heavenly Jerusalem.
(HEBREWS 12:22, ESV)

We must avoid the common fault of pushing the "other world" into the future. It is not future, but present. It parallels our familiar physical world, and the doors between the two worlds are open.

"Ye are come," says the writer to the Hebrews (and the tense is plainly present), "unto mount Sion, and unto the city of the living God, the heavenly Jerusalem, and to an innumerable company of angels, to the general assembly and church of the firstborn, which are written in heaven, and to God the Judge of all, and to the spirits of just men made perfect, and to Jesus the mediator of the new covenant, and to the blood of sprinkling, that speaketh better things than that of Abel" (Hebrews 12:22-24, KJV). All these things are contrasted with "the mount that might be touched" (verse 18) and "the sound of a trumpet, and the voice of words" (verse 19) that might be heard.

May we not safely conclude that, as the realities of Mount Sinai were apprehended by the senses, so the realities of Mount Zion are to be grasped by the soul? And this not by any trick of the imagination, but in downright actuality.

As we begin to focus upon God, the things of the spirit will take shape before our inner eyes. Obedience to the word of Christ will bring an inward revelation of the Godhead (see John 14:21-23). It will give acute perception enabling us to see God even as is promised to the pure in heart. A new God-consciousness will seize upon us, and we shall begin to taste and hear and inwardly feel the God who is our life and our all. More and more, as our faculties grow sharper and more sure, God will become to us the great All, and His Presence the glory and wonder of our lives.

A. W. TOZER, IN *THE PURSUIT OF GOD*

Brutalizing God

Master, I knew you to be a hard man . . . so I was afraid.

(Matthew 25:24-25, esv)

Far too commonly we think of God as did the man in the parable of the talents who regarded his lord as "a harsh man." In the same way we demean God immeasurably by casting Him in the role of the cosmic boss, whose chief joy in relation to humans is ordering them around, taking pleasure in seeing them jump at His command, and painstakingly noting any failures.

When we come to learn how we can hear God and what divine guidance *really* is, we must come in such a way that we do justice to the revelation of God in Christ. Hearing God and seeking guidance are an almost universal human preoccupation. It's hard, however, to cleanse our minds of those motives, images, and concepts that would brutalize the very God we hope to approach.

In the primitive rituals and the "Bible roulette" (picking verses at random for guidance) frequently practiced by present-day believers, we see both the desperate urgency and the superstitious character of human efforts to get a word from God, especially a word on what is going to happen and what we should do about it. If necessary, some people are prepared to *force* such a word from Him. Like King Saul, many of us have our own versions of a witch of Endor (see 1 Samuel 28).

Hearing God cannot be a reliable and intelligible fact of life *except* when we see His speaking as one aspect of His presence with us, of His life in us. Only our *communion* with God provides the appropriate context for *communications* between us and Him. And within those communications, guidance will be given in a manner suitable to our particular lives and circumstances. It will fit into our life together with God in His earthly and heavenly family. This is our first preliminary insight to help us in learning to discern God's voice.

Dallas Willard, in *Hearing God*

Unquestionable Love

The Lord is . . . kind in all his works.

(Psalm 145:17, esv)

The apostle John said, "God is love" (1 John 4:8, esv). This succinct statement, along with its parallel one, "God is light" (1 John 1:5, esv; that is, God is holy), sums up the essential character of God, as revealed to us in the Scriptures. Just as it is impossible in the very nature of God for Him to be anything but perfectly holy, so it is impossible for Him to be anything but perfectly good.

Because God is love, an essential part of His nature is to do good and show mercy to His creatures. Psalm 145 speaks of His "abundant goodness," of His "abounding in steadfast love" and being "good to all," of how "his mercy is over all that he has made" (verses 7-9, esv). Even in His role of Judge of rebellious men, He declares, "I take no pleasure in the death of the wicked" (Ezekiel 33:11, niv).

When calamity after calamity seems to surge in upon us, we'll be tempted to doubt God's love. Not only do we struggle with our own doubts, but Satan seizes these occasions to whisper accusations against God: "If He loved you, He wouldn't have allowed this to happen." My own experience suggests that Satan attacks us far more in the area of God's love than either His sovereignty or His wisdom.

If we're to honor God by trusting Him, we must not allow such thoughts to lodge in our minds. As Philip Hughes said, "To question the goodness of God is, in essence, to imply that man is more concerned about goodness than is God. . . . To suggest that man is kinder than God is to subvert the very nature of God. . . . It is to deny God; and this is precisely the thrust of the temptation to question the goodness of God."[12]

Jerry Bridges, in *Trusting God*

WHAT IS OURS EVEN NOW

Our soul waits for the LORD; he is our help and our shield.
(PSALM 33:20, ESV)

Our mind may have beautiful visions of what God has promised to do, and our lips may speak of them in stirring words, but these are not really the measure of our faith or power. No, the real measure of the spiritual blessing we expect from Him — and the blessing we bring to our fellow men — is what we really know of God in our personal experience, of His conquering the enemies within, reigning and ruling, revealing Himself in His holiness and power in our innermost being.

As we know how blessed the waiting on God has become to our own souls, we will confidently hope in the blessing to come upon ourselves and on the church around us. The keyword of all our expectations will be what He has said. In the promises, He reveals Himself in His hidden glory! And from what He has done *in* us, we will trust Him to do mighty things *around* us.

While the promised blessings for ourselves or for others may tarry, what is ours even now is the unutterable blessedness of knowing and having *Him who has promised* — the divine Blesser, the living Fountain of the coming blessings. Let this truth acquire full possession of your souls — that waiting on God is itself the highest privilege of man, the highest blessedness of His redeemed child.

In waiting on God, His greatness and your littleness suit and meet each other most wonderfully. Just bow in emptiness and poverty and utter weakness, in humility and meekness, and surrender to His will before His great glory . . . and be still. As you wait on Him, God draws near. He will reveal Himself as the God who will mightily fulfill His every promise.

May God increase the company of those who say: "Our soul waiteth for the LORD: he is our help and our shield" (Psalm 33:20, KJV).

ANDREW MURRAY, IN *WAITING ON GOD*

THE BEGINNING

One God and Father of all, who is over all and through all and in all.

(EPHESIANS 4:6, ESV)

God dwells in His creation and is everywhere, indivisibly present in all His works. This is boldly taught by prophet and apostle and is accepted by Christian theology generally.

While God dwells in His world, He is separated from it by a gulf forever impassable. However closely He may be identified with the work of His hands, they are and must eternally be *other than* He, and He is and must be antecedent to and independent of them. He is transcendent above all His works even while He is immanent within them.

What now does the divine immanence mean in direct Christian experience? It means simply that *God is here*. Wherever we are, God is here. There is no place, there can be no place, where He is not. Ten million intelligences standing at as many points in space and separated by incomprehensible distances can each one say with equal truth, God is here. No point is nearer to God than any other point. It is exactly as near to God from any place as it is from any other place. No one is in mere distance any further from or any nearer to God than any other person is.

These are truths believed by every instructed Christian. It remains for us to think on them and pray over them until they begin to glow within us.

"In the beginning God." Not *matter*, for matter is not self-causing. It requires an antecedent cause, and God is that Cause. Not *law*, for law is but a name for the course which all creation follows. That course had to be planned, and the Planner is God. Not *mind*, for mind also is a created thing and must have a Creator back of it.

In the beginning God, the uncaused Cause of matter, mind, and law. There we must begin.

A. W. TOZER, IN *THE PURSUIT OF GOD*

Recognizing God's Voice

Let me hear what God the Lord will speak,
for he will speak peace to his people.
(Psalm 85:8, ESV)

Sin has affected us so deeply (see Romans 3:10-11) that you and I cannot understand the truth of God unless the Holy Spirit reveals it to us. He is our teacher. As you read your Bible, be open to the Spirit as He teaches you the Word of God. As you pray, watch how the Holy Spirit uses Scripture to confirm in your heart what God is saying. Observe what He is doing around you in the circumstances of life. The God who is speaking to you as you pray and the God who is speaking to you in the Scriptures is the same God who is at work around you daily.

The evidence of the Scriptures can encourage you at this point. The Bible illustrates that when God chose to speak to an individual, that person had no doubt it was God, and it was clear what God was saying. When God speaks to you, you can know He is the One speaking, and you, too, can understand clearly what He is saying. Jesus explained, "The one who enters by the door is the shepherd of the sheep . . . and the sheep hear his voice. He calls his own sheep by name and leads them out. . . . I am the good shepherd. I know My own sheep, and they know Me" (John 10:2-4,14, HCSB).

Knowing God's voice is not a matter of honing a method or discovering a formula. Recognizing God's voice comes from an intimate love relationship with Him. Those who do not have the relationship do not hear what God is saying (see John 8:47). Since God will uniquely communicate with you in the intimacy of your walk with Him, your relationship with Him is of utmost importance.

There is no substitute for an intimate relationship with God.

Henry Blackaby and Richard Blackaby, in *Experiencing God*

Made Personally

Blessed be the Lord . . . who alone does wondrous things.

(Psalm 72:18, esv)

David said, "I praise you because I am fearfully and wonderfully made" (Psalm 139:14, niv). We might say, "That's well enough for David; he was handsome, athletic, skilled in war, and a gifted musician. But look at me. I'm very ordinary physically and mentally." In fact, some people feel they don't even measure up to ordinary.

I understand people who feel that way. In addition to having hearing and vision disabilities, I've never been excited about my physical appearance. But God didn't give His own Son handsome features in His human body: "He had no beauty or majesty to attract us to him, nothing in his appearance that we should desire him" (Isaiah 53:2, niv). Jesus, at best, was apparently nondescript in His physical appearance. This never bothered Him nor interfered with His carrying out His Father's will.

David praised God not because he was handsome but because *God made him*. Dwell on that thought: The eternal God, infinite in His wisdom and perfect in His love, personally made you and me. He gave you your body, your mental abilities, and your basic personality because that's the way He wanted you to be — and He loves you and wants to glorify Himself through you.

This is our foundation for self-acceptance. God sovereignly and directly created us to be who we are, disabilities or physical flaws and all. We need to learn to think like George MacDonald, who said, "I would rather be what God chose to make me than the most glorious creature that I could think of; for to have been thought about, born in God's thought, and then made by God, is the dearest, grandest, and most precious thing in all thinking."[13]

Jerry Bridges, in *Trusting God*

He Will Do Unlooked-for Things

What no eye has seen, nor ear heard, nor the heart of man imagined, what God has prepared for those who love him.

(1 Corinthians 2:9, esv)

As we wait upon God, things that the human heart cannot conceive — what "eye hath not seen, nor ear heard, neither have entered into the heart of man" (1 Corinthians 2:9, kjv) — will be revealed to us. These things, Paul says (in 2:10), are the things the Holy Spirit is to reveal.

Paul is quoting Isaiah 64:4. The previous verses in Isaiah refer to the low state of God's people. Prayer has been poured out: "Look down from heaven" (63:15, kjv); "Why hast thou . . . hardened our heart from thy fear? Return for thy servants' sake" (63:17, kjv). And still more urgent, "Oh that thou wouldst rend the heavens, that thou wouldst come down . . . as when the melting fire burneth . . . to make thy name known to thine adversaries!" (64:1-2, kjv).

Then follows the plea from the past: "When thou didst terrible things which we looked not for, thou camest down, the mountains flowed down at thy presence" (64:3, kjv). And now faith has been awakened by the thought of things "we looked not for" — for He is still the same God. For those "that waiteth for him," God has prepared what "men have not heard, nor perceived by the ear, neither hath the eye seen" (64:4, kjv).

God alone knows what He can do for His waiting people. As Paul expounds and applies it: "The things of God knoweth no man, but the Spirit of God" (1 Corinthians 2:11, kjv). "But God hath revealed them unto us by his Spirit" (verse 10, kjv).

The need of God's people, and the call for His intervention, are as urgent in our day as in Isaiah's time. What is to be done? We must wait upon God. We must desire and believe, we must ask and expect, that He will do unlooked-for things. The wonder-doing God, who can surpass all our expectations, must be the God of our confidence.

Andrew Murray, in *Waiting on God*

As a Melting Fire

Now to him who is able to do far more abundantly than all that we ask or think.

(Ephesians 3:20, ESV)

Yes, let God's people enlarge their hearts to wait on a God able to do exceeding abundantly above what we can ask or think. Let us band ourselves together as His elect who cry day and night to Him for things men have not seen. He is able to arise and to make His people a name and a praise in the earth. "Therefore will the Lord wait, that he may be gracious unto you . . . blessed are all they that wait for him" (Isaiah 30:18, KJV).

There is now — as there was in Isaiah's day, as there has been at all times — a few who seek after God with their whole hearts. But if we look at Christendom as a whole, at the state of the church of Christ, there is infinite cause for beseeching God to rend the heavens and come down. Nothing but a special interposition of almighty power will avail. Unless God comes down "as when the melting fire burneth . . . to make [his] name known to [his] adversaries" (Isaiah 64:2, KJV), our labors are comparatively fruitless.

Look at the ministry: how much it is in the wisdom of man and of literary culture; how little in demonstration of the Spirit and of power. Think of the unity of the body: how little there is of the manifestation of the power of a heavenly love binding God's children into one. Think of holiness — the holiness of Christlike humility and crucifixion to the world. How little the world sees that they have men among them who live in Christ in heaven, in whom Christ and heaven live.

We must cry, with a cry that never rests, "Oh that thou wouldst rend the heavens . . . [and] come down, that the mountains might flow down at thy presence" (Isaiah 64:1, KJV). We must set our faith on a God of whom men do not know what He has prepared for them who wait for Him.

Andrew Murray, in *Waiting on God*

An End in Itself

Let us go to his dwelling place; let us worship at his footstool!
(Psalm 132:7, esv)

We do not eat the feast of worship as a means to anything else. Happiness in God is the end of all our seeking. Nothing beyond it can be sought as a higher goal. John Calvin put it like this: "If God contains the fullness of all good things in himself like an inexhaustible fountain, nothing beyond him is to be sought by those who strike after the highest good and all the elements of happiness."[14]

True worship cannot be performed as a means to some other experience. Feelings are not like that. Genuine feelings of the heart cannot be manufactured as stepping stones to something else.

All genuine emotion is an end in itself. This does not mean we cannot or should not seek to have certain feelings. We should and we can. But in the moment of authentic emotion, we are transported (perhaps only for seconds) above the reasoning work of the mind, and we experience feeling without reference to logical or practical implications.

This is what keeps worship from being "in vain." Worship is authentic when affections for God arise in the heart as an end in themselves.

If God's reality is displayed to us in His Word or His world and we do not then feel in our heart any grief or longing or hope or fear or awe or joy or gratitude or confidence, then we may dutifully sing and pray and recite and gesture as much as we like, but it will not be real worship. We cannot honor God if our "heart is far from [him]" (Matthew 15:8, esv).

Worship is a way of gladly reflecting back to God the radiance of His worth. This cannot be done by mere acts of duty. It can be done only when spontaneous affections arise in the heart. And these affections for God are an end in themselves. They are the essence of eternal worship.

John Piper, in *Desiring God*

Righteousness, Not Spirituality

Blessed are those who hunger and thirst for righteousness,
for they shall be satisfied.
(Matthew 5:6, ESV)

Spirituality can be a cheap substitute for righteousness.

Over the years I've had many young Christians ask me how to be more spiritual or more pious. Rare has been the earnest student who said, "Teach me how to be righteous." *Why,* I wondered, *does anybody want to be spiritual? What is the purpose of spirituality? What use is there in piety?*

Spirituality and piety are not ends in themselves. In fact they are worthless *unless* they are means to a higher goal. The goal must go beyond spirituality to righteousness.

Spiritual disciplines are vitally necessary to achieve righteousness. Bible study, prayer, church attendance, evangelism are necessary for Christian growth, but they cannot be the final goal. I cannot achieve righteousness without spirituality. But it is possible to be "spiritual," at least on the surface, without attaining righteousness.

Jesus was a man of prayer. His prayer life was intense and powerful. He was a man of vast knowledge of the Scriptures. He obviously mastered the Word of God. He was spiritual. But His spirituality ultimately showed itself by authentic righteousness. It was not merely a surface thing. His inner life displayed itself in outward obedience, obedience even unto death.

What is righteousness? *Righteousness is doing what is right in the sight of God.* This is a simple definition that is far more complex under the surface. To be righteous is to do everything that God calls us to do. The demands of true righteousness are so great and so many that none of us ever in this world achieves it perfectly. It involves following the whole counsel of God.

Righteousness means right living, treating people right, living with personal integrity. A righteous person is moral without being moralistic. And he has the overarching desire to please a loving God.

R. C. Sproul, in *Pleasing God*

THE UNIVERSAL PRESENCE

Where shall I go from your Spirit?
Or where shall I flee from your presence?
(PSALM 139:7, ESV)

Adam sinned and, in his panic, frantically tried to do the impossible: He tried to hide from the Presence of God. David also must have had wild thoughts of trying to escape from the Presence, for he wrote, "Whither shall I go from thy spirit? or whither shall I flee from thy presence?" (Psalm 139:7, KJV).

Then he proceeded through one of his most beautiful psalms to celebrate the glory of the divine immanence. "If I ascend up into heaven, thou art there: if I make my bed in hell, behold, thou art there. If I take the wings of the morning, and dwell in the uttermost parts of the sea; even there shall thy hand lead me, and thy right hand shall hold me" (verses 8-10, KJV). And he knew that God's *being* and God's *seeing* are the same — that the seeing Presence had been with him even before he was born, watching the mystery of unfolding life.

Paul assured the Athenians that God is not far from any one of us: for "in him we live, and move, and have our being" (Acts 17:28, KJV).

If God is present at every point in space, if we cannot go where He is not, cannot even conceive of a place where He is not, why then has not that Presence become the one universally celebrated fact of the world? The patriarch Jacob gave the answer to that question. He saw a vision of God and cried out in wonder, "Surely the LORD is in this place; and I knew it not" (Genesis 28:16, KJV). Jacob had never been for one small division of a moment outside the circle of that all-pervading Presence. But he knew it not. That was his trouble, and it is ours. Men do not know that God is here.

What a difference it would make if they knew.

A. W. TOZER, IN *THE PURSUIT OF GOD*

KNOWING HIS GOODNESS

The LORD is good to those who wait for him,
to the soul who seeks him.
(LAMENTATIONS 3:25, ESV)

There is none good but God (see Matthew 19:17). His goodness is in the heavens. "Oh how great is thy goodness, which thou hast laid up for them that fear thee" (Psalm 31:19, KJV). "O taste and see that the LORD is good" (Psalm 34:8, KJV). And in Lamentations 3:25 is the true way of entering into and rejoicing in this goodness of God—waiting upon Him.

The Lord is good—even His children often do not know this, for they do not wait in quietness for Him to reveal it. But to those who persevere in waiting, whose souls do wait, it will come true.

One might think that it is just those who have to wait who might doubt His goodness. But this is only when they do not wait, but grow impatient. The truly waiting ones will all say, "The LORD is good unto them that wait for him" (Lamentations 3:25, KJV). If you want to fully know the goodness of God, give yourself more than ever to a life of waiting on Him.

At our first entrance into the school of waiting upon God, the heart is mainly set on the blessings which we wait for. God graciously uses our needs and desires to help educate us for something higher than we were thinking of. We were seeking gifts; He, the Giver, longs to give Himself and to satisfy the soul with His goodness. It is just for this reason that He often withholds the gifts, and that the time of waiting is made so long. He is constantly seeking to win the heart of His child for Himself. He wishes that we would say, "How good is God!" not only when He bestows the gift, but that long before it comes—and even if it never comes—we should all the time be experiencing: "The LORD is good unto them that wait for him."

ANDREW MURRAY, IN *WAITING ON GOD*

An Extraordinary Assurance

Let them make me a sanctuary, that I may dwell in their midst.
(Exodus 25:8, esv)

The same remarkable promise that God made to Moses — that He would *pitch His tent* and dwell in the midst of His people (see Exodus 29:44-45) — is a central theme throughout Scripture. In the familiar passage of John's gospel, "The Word became flesh, and *dwelt* among us" (John 1:14, nasb, emphasis added), the Greek word for *dwelt* literally means to "pitch a tent." So now, through Christ, God comes to "pitch His tent" among His people. And to carry the theme to its conclusion, John, in describing his apocalyptic vision of the new heaven and new earth, writes, "The tabernacle of God is among men, and He will dwell among them, and they shall be His people" (Revelation 21:3, nasb). Again the word *dwell* is literally translated to "pitch a tent."

Thus, from Exodus to Revelation we find the identical imagery, a holy God "pitching His tent" among His people: first in the tabernacle, then in Christ and Christ in us, and ultimately in His kingdom.

Salvation, therefore, is not simply a matter of being separated from our past and freed from our bondage to sin; salvation means that we are joined to a holy God. By pitching His tent in our midst, God identifies with His people through His very presence. The reality of a "God who is here" — personal and in our midst — is an extraordinary assurance, one which distinguished the Judeo-Christian faith from all other religions.

But God demands something in return for His presence. He demands that we identify with Him — that we be holy because He is holy.

Holiness is not an option. God will not tolerate our indifference to His central command. It is the central covenant and command of Scripture, the "cardinal point on which the whole of Christianity turns," William Wilberforce wrote.[15]

Charles Colson, in *Loving God*

FACE-TO-FACE WITH GOD

Moses hid his face, for he was afraid to look at God.

(EXODUS 3:6, ESV)

We cannot know ourselves unless we see ourselves as we are in the presence of God. Nor can we come to know God without viewing ourselves in a new light. The presence of God, therefore, does two things: It makes us conscious of who He is, and it makes us aware of who we are in His glorious presence.

As Moses stood in the presence of the God who is a consuming fire, but found that he was not consumed, he must have felt as though every last element of superficiality was being stripped from his being. In that context there could be no pretense; nor, in the desert, was there anywhere to hide. He was alone, with God, awed by his presence as the One who called Himself "I AM WHO I AM" (Exodus 3:14, ESV).

What does it really mean to stand in the presence of God? In the Old Testament, to be "in the presence of God" often translates a Hebrew expression meaning "before the face of God." It conveys the idea of coming face-to-face with Him. More than that, because no man can see God's face and live (as Moses learned — see Exodus 33:20), being in the presence of God may carry the sense of standing before One who is able to scrutinize us, who can see all our actions and reactions, even though we can never know or understand Him. For God dwells in unapproachable light. What could be more awesome than to stand in the presence of God — and live? There was nothing in the world more awesome that Moses could have done than to stand before the mystery of God's being and the majesty of His glory, yet not die.

One of our greatest needs in coming to know God in our day is to recover a sense of what it really means to stand in the presence of God.

SINCLAIR FERGUSON, IN *A HEART FOR GOD*

THE MANIFEST PRESENCE

The LORD descended in the cloud and stood with him there, and proclaimed the name of the LORD.

(EXODUS 34:5, ESV)

The Presence and the manifestation of the Presence are not the same. There can be the one without the other. God is here when we are wholly unaware of it; He is *manifest* only when and as we are aware of His Presence. On our part there must be surrender to the Spirit of God, for His work is to show us the Father and the Son. If we cooperate with Him in loving obedience, God will manifest Himself to us, and that manifestation will be the difference between a nominal Christian life and a life radiant with the light of His face.

Always, everywhere God is present, and always He seeks to discover Himself. To each one He would reveal not only that He is, but *what* He is as well.

He did not have to be persuaded to discover Himself to Moses. "The LORD descended in the cloud and stood with him there, and proclaimed the name of the LORD" (Exodus 34:5, ESV). He not only made a verbal proclamation of His nature but He revealed His very Self to Moses so that the skin of Moses' face shone with the supernatural light. It will be a great moment for some of us when we begin to believe that God's promise of self-revelation is literally true: that He promised much, but promised no more than He intends to fulfill.

Our pursuit of God is successful just because He is forever seeking to manifest Himself to us.

When we sing, "Draw me nearer, nearer, blessed Lord," we are not thinking of the nearness of place, but of the nearness of relationship. It is for increasing degrees of awareness that we pray, for a more perfect consciousness of the divine Presence. We need never shout across the spaces to an absent God. He is nearer than our own soul, closer than our most secret thoughts.

A. W. TOZER, IN *THE PURSUIT OF GOD*

FACING PHYSICAL AFFLICTION

Though he cause grief, he will have compassion
according to the abundance of his steadfast love;
for he does not willingly afflict or grieve the children of men.
(LAMENTATIONS 3:32-33, ESV)

God does not willingly bring affliction or grief to us. He does not delight in causing us to experience pain or heartache. He always has a purpose for the grief He brings or allows to come into our lives. Most often we do not know what that purpose is, but it is enough to know that His infinite wisdom and perfect love have determined that the particular sorrow is best for us. God never wastes pain. He always uses it to accomplish His purpose. And His purpose is for His glory and our good. Therefore, we can trust Him when our hearts are aching or our bodies are racked with pain.

Trusting God in the midst of our pain and heartache means that we accept it from Him. There is a vast difference between acceptance and either resignation or submission. We can resign ourselves to a difficult situation, simply because we see no other alternative. Many people do that all the time. Or we can submit to the sovereignty of God in our circumstances with a certain amount of reluctance. But to truly accept our pain and heartache has the connotation of willingness. An attitude of acceptance says that we trust God, that He loves us and knows what is best for us.

Acceptance does not mean that we do not pray for physical healing, or for the conception and birth of a little one to our marriage. We should indeed pray for those things, but we should pray in a trusting way. We should realize that, though God can do all things, for infinitely wise and loving reasons, He may not do that which we pray that He will do. How do we know how long to pray? As long as we can pray trustingly, with an attitude of acceptance of His will, we should pray as long as the desire remains.

JERRY BRIDGES, IN *TRUSTING GOD*

TWO THIEVES

Jesus, remember me when you come into your kingdom.
(LUKE 23:42, ESV)

Golgotha — what a grim set on which to play out the crucial act in the drama of redemption. Golgotha — from the Aramaic meaning "skull" and the Hebrew implying "a skull-like mound" — was well-named in light of the bloody business conducted there.

The central drama of Golgotha was played out upon the three crosses there.

"Are you not the Christ? Save yourself and us!" cried one thief hanging there, angry to the end (Luke 23:39, ESV). He might even have believed that the limp figure beside him was the Son of God. But so what? If He couldn't save Himself, He certainly couldn't save anyone else.

The other thief, convicted by the Holy Spirit, realized that he deserved to die. He understood that no matter what he had done or not done, no matter what the circumstances, "no punishment comes to us in this life on earth which is undeserved."[16]

And therein lies the crucial distinction between the two thieves. It has nothing to do with their crimes, their moral values, the relative goodness or badness of their lives. In fact, Scripture suggests the irrelevance of these criteria by the stark lack of detail describing their lives. The distinction was that one recognized his own sin. His reply to the other, "We are receiving the due reward of our deeds; but this man has done nothing wrong" (Luke 23:41, ESV) is one of the purest expressions of repentance of all Scripture. And his words to Jesus — "Remember me" (23:42, ESV) — are the classic statement of faith. With such simplicity and power this man repented and believed and died trusting in Christ.

Those two men who actually died alongside my Savior are representative of all mankind. We either recognize our sinful selves, our sentence of death, and our deserving of that sentence, which leads us to repent and believe — or we curse God and die.

CHARLES COLSON, IN *LOVING GOD*

The Breath of the Soul

I wait for the Lord, my soul waits, and in his word I hope.
(Psalm 130:5, esv)

Knowing God's goodness, what a blessed life the life of waiting becomes — the continual worship of faith, adoring, and trusting His goodness. As the soul learns its secret, every act or exercise of waiting becomes just a quiet entering into the goodness of God, to let it do its blessed work and satisfy our every need. And, every experience of God's goodness gives new attractiveness to the work of waiting. Instead of only taking refuge in time of need, there comes a great longing to wait continually and all day. And, however duties and engagements occupy the time and the mind, the soul gets more familiar with the secret art of always waiting. Waiting becomes the habit and disposition, the very second nature and breath of the soul.

Dear Christian, begin to see that waiting is not one among a number of Christian virtues, to be thought of from time to time. It expresses that disposition that lies at the very root of the Christian life. It gives a higher value and a new power to our prayers and worship, to our faith and surrender, because it links us in unalterable dependence to God Himself. And it gives us the unbroken enjoyment of the goodness of God.

Many of us are too occupied with our work. As with Martha, the very service we want to render the Master separates us from Him. It is neither pleasing to Him nor profitable to ourselves. The more work, the more need of waiting upon God. The doing of God's will would then be, instead of exhausting, our meat and drink, our nourishment and refreshment and strength. "The Lord is good unto them that wait for him" (Lamentations 3:25, kjv). How good is known only by those who prove it in waiting on Him. How good none can fully tell but those who have proved Him to the utmost.

Andrew Murray, in *Waiting on God*

THE ONE VITAL QUALITY

You have said, "Seek my face." My heart says to you, "Your face, LORD, do I seek."
(PSALM 27:8, ESV)

Why do some persons "find" God in a way that others do not? Why does God manifest His Presence to some and let multitudes of others struggle along in the half-light of imperfect Christian experience? Of course the will of God is the same for all. He has no favorites within His household. All He has ever done for any of His children He will do for all of His children. The difference lies not with God but with us.

Pick at random a score of great saints whose lives and testimonies are widely known. Let them be Bible characters or well known Christians of post-biblical times. You will be struck instantly with the fact that the saints were not alike. Sometimes the unlikenesses were so great as to be positively glaring. How different for example was Moses from Isaiah, Elijah from David; how unlike were John and Paul, Saint Francis and Luther, Finney and Thomas à Kempis. The differences are as wide as human life itself: differences of race, nationality, education, temperament, habit, and personal qualities. Yet they all walked, each in his day, upon a high road of spiritual living far above the common way.

Their differences must have been incidental and in the eyes of God of no significance. In some vital quality they must have been alike. What was it?

I venture to suggest that the one vital quality which they had in common was *spiritual receptivity.* Something in them was open to heaven, something which urged them Godward. Without attempting anything like a profound analysis I shall say simply that they had spiritual awareness and that they went on to cultivate it until it became the biggest thing in their lives. They differed from the average person in that when they felt the inward longing they *did something about it.* They acquired the lifelong habit of spiritual response. They were not disobedient to the heavenly vision.

A. W. TOZER, IN *THE PURSUIT OF GOD*

RESPOND NOW

Take care then how you hear, for to the one who has, more will be given, and from the one who has not, even what he thinks that he has will be taken away.

(LUKE 8:18, ESV)

When God spoke to Moses in Exodus 3, Moses' next move was crucial. After Jesus spoke to the disciples in the Gospels, what they did next was pivotal. What you do after the Holy Spirit speaks will have enormous consequences for you and those around you. Too often when the Spirit of God speaks to us, we launch into a protracted discussion with Him, questioning the correctness of His directions. Moses tried it at the burning bush (see Exodus 3:11–4:13), and it limited him for the rest of his life. Because of Moses' objections, God assigned Aaron to be a spokesman for Moses. He had to speak to the people through his brother Aaron (see 4:14-16). Eventually, Aaron caused Moses considerable grief when he made a golden calf for the rebellious Hebrews (see 32:1-6). Aaron, together with Miriam, led a challenge to Moses' leadership. Moses paid a high price for arguing with God (see Numbers 12:1-8).

I encourage you to review on a regular basis what you sense God has been saying to you. If God speaks and you hear but do not respond, a time could come when you will not hear His voice. Disobedience can lead to a "famine . . . of hearing the words of the LORD" (Amos 8:11, HCSB).

When Samuel was a young boy, God began to speak to him. The Scriptures say, "Samuel grew, and the LORD was with him and let nothing he said prove false" (1 Samuel 3:19, HCSB). Be like Samuel. Don't let a single word from the Lord fail to bear fruit in your life. Then God will do in you and through you everything He promises.

If you hear the Word of God and do not apply it to produce fruit in your life, your disobedience will cost you. Make up your mind now that when the Spirit of God speaks, you are going to do what He says.

HENRY BLACKABY AND RICHARD BLACKABY, IN *EXPERIENCING GOD*

A Reason to Pray

They lifted their voices together to God and said, "Sovereign Lord, who made the heaven and the earth and the sea and everything in them."

(Acts 4:24, esv)

Prayer assumes the sovereignty of God. If God is not sovereign, we have no assurance that He is able to answer our prayers. Our prayers would become nothing more than wishes. But while God's sovereignty, along with His wisdom and love, is the foundation of our trust in Him, prayer is the expression of that trust.

The Puritan preacher Thomas Lye, in a sermon entitled "How Are We to Live by Faith on Divine Providence?" said, "As prayer without faith is but a beating of the air, so trust without prayer [is] but a presumptuous bravado. He that promises to give, and bids us trust his promises, commands us to pray, and expects obedience to his commands. He will give, but not without our asking."[17]

The apostle Paul, while imprisoned in Rome, wrote to his friend Philemon, "Prepare a guest room for me, because I hope to be restored to you in answer to your prayers" (Philemon 22, niv). Paul did not presume to know God's secret will. He *hoped* to be restored. He did not say, "I will be restored." But he did know that God in His sovereignty was well able to effect his release, so he asked Philemon to pray. Prayer was the expression of his confidence in the sovereignty of God.

John Flavel was a Puritan preacher and a prolific writer (six volumes of collected works). He wrote a classic treatise titled *The Mystery of Providence*, first published in 1678. It is instructive to note that Flavel begins this treatise on the sovereign providence of God with a discourse on Psalm 57:2: "I cry out to God Most High, to God, who fulfills his purpose for me" (niv). That is, Flavel says to us, because God is sovereign, we should pray. God's sovereignty does not negate our responsibility to pray, but rather makes it possible to pray with confidence.

Jerry Bridges, in *Trusting God*

Quietly, in Faith

It is good that one should wait quietly for the salvation of the Lord.
(Lamentations 3:26, esv)

"Take heed, and be quiet; fear not, neither be fainthearted" (Isaiah 7:4, kjv). "In quietness and in confidence shall be your strength" (Isaiah 30:15, kjv). Such words reveal to us the close connection between quietness and faith. They show us what a deep need there is of quietness, as an element of true waiting upon God.

God is a being of such infinite greatness and glory, and our nature has become so estranged from Him, that it requires our whole heart and desires set upon Him, even in some little measure, to know and receive Him. Everything that is not God, that excites our fears or stirs our efforts or awakens our hopes or makes us glad, hinders us in our perfect waiting on Him. The message is one of deep meaning: "It is good that a man should . . . quietly wait."

Scripture abundantly testifies how the very thought of God in His majesty and holiness should silence us: "The Lord is in his holy temple: let all the earth keep silence before him" (Habakkuk 2:20, kjv); "Hold thy peace at the presence of the Lord God" (Zephaniah 1:7, kjv); "Be silent, O all flesh, before the Lord: for he is raised up out of his holy habitation" (Zechariah 2:13, kjv).

As long as the waiting on God is chiefly regarded as an end toward more effectual prayer, and the obtaining of our petitions, this spirit of perfect quietness will not be obtained. But when it is seen that waiting on God is itself an unspeakable blessedness—one of the highest forms of fellowship with the Holy One—the adoration of Him in His glory will of necessity humble the soul into a holy stillness, making way for God to speak and reveal Himself. Then it comes to the fulfillment of the precious promise: "The haughtiness of men shall be bowed down, and the Lord alone shall be exalted in that day" (Isaiah 2:11, kjv).

Andrew Murray, in *Waiting on God*

Cultivating Our Spiritual Receptivity

Be still, and know that I am God.

(Psalm 46:10, esv)

Spiritual receptivity is not a single thing; it is a compound rather, a blending of several elements within the soul. It is an affinity for, a bent toward, a sympathetic response to, a desire to have. It can be present in degrees, depending upon the individual. It may be increased by exercise or destroyed by neglect. It is not a sovereign and irresistible force which comes upon us as a seizure from above. It is a gift of God, indeed, but one which must be recognized and cultivated as any other gift if it is to realize the purpose for which it was given.

Failure to see this is the cause of a very serious breakdown in modern evangelicalism. The idea of cultivation and exercise, so dear to the saints of old, has now no place in our total religious picture. It is too slow, too common. We now demand glamour and fast-flowing dramatic action. A generation of Christians reared among push buttons and automatic machines is impatient of slower and less direct methods of reaching their goals. We have been trying to apply machine-age methods to our relations with God. We read our chapter, have our short devotions, and rush away, hoping to make up for our deep inward bankruptcy by attending another gospel meeting or listening to another thrilling story told by a religious adventurer lately returned from afar.

The tragic results of this spirit are all about us. Shallow lives, hollow religious philosophies, the preponderance of the element of fun in gospel meetings, the glorification of men, trust in religious externalities, quasi-religious fellowships, salesmanship methods, the mistaking of dynamic personality for the power of the Spirit: these and such as these are the symptoms of an evil disease, a deep and serious malady of the soul.

A. W. Tozer, in *The Pursuit of God*

ACTING WISELY IN LIGHT OF GOD'S SOVEREIGNTY

Trust in the LORD, and do good.

(PSALM 37:3, ESV)

God's sovereignty doesn't set aside our responsibility to act prudently — to use all legitimate means at our disposal to avoid harm to ourselves or others and to bring about what we believe to be the right course of events.

We see this illustrated in Acts 27, the story of Paul's shipwreck. After many storm-battered days, when everyone had given up all hope of being saved, Paul stood before everyone and said: "Take heart, for there will be no loss of life among you, but only of the ship. For this very night there stood before me an angel of the God to whom I belong and whom I worship, and he said, 'Do not be afraid, Paul. . . . God has granted you all those who sail with you.' So take heart, men. . . . But we must run aground on some island" (Acts 27:22-26, ESV).

Yet some time later, when he saw the sailors trying to escape from the ship with the lifeboat, he said to the Roman centurion, "Unless these men stay with the ship, you cannot be saved" (Acts 27:31, ESV). Paul apparently realized that the presence of the skilled sailors was necessary for everyone's further safety. He took prudent action to bring about that which God by divine revelation had already promised would certainly come to pass. Paul did not consider God's sovereign purpose a reason to neglect his duty, though in that instance God's purpose had been revealed by an angel from heaven.

In our circumstances today, we don't know what God's sovereign purpose is in a specific situation. We should be even more aware not to use God's sovereignty as an excuse to shirk the duties that He has commanded in the Scriptures. God usually works through means, and He intends that we use the means He has placed at our disposal.

JERRY BRIDGES, IN *TRUSTING GOD*

Deeper Than Mind or Heart

Be careful, be quiet, do not fear, and do not let your heart be faint.
(Isaiah 7:4, esv)

Take time to be still and quiet before God—not only to secure stillness away from the world, but away from self and its energy. Let the Word and prayer be very precious. But remember, even these may hinder the quiet waiting. The activity of the mind in studying the Word or giving expression to its thoughts in prayer, and the activities of the heart with its desires and hopes and fears, may so engage us that we do not come to the still waiting on the All-Glorious One; our whole being is prostrate in silence before Him.

Though at first it may appear difficult to know how thus quietly to wait, with the activities of mind and heart for a time subdued, every effort after it will be rewarded. We will discover that it grows upon us, and the little season of silent worship will bring a peace and a rest that give a blessing not only in prayer, but all day.

"It is good that a man should . . . quietly wait for the salvation of the Lord" (Lamentations 3:26, kjv). Yes, it is good. The quietness is the confession of our meekness. It will not be done with all our willing and running (see Romans 9:16), with all our thinking and praying. We must receive it from God. It is the confession of our trust that our God will, in His time, come to our help—the quiet resting in Him alone. It is the confession of our desire to sink into our nothingness and to let Him work and reveal Himself. Do let us wait quietly. In daily life, let there be, in the soul that is waiting for the great God to do His wondrous work, a quiet reverence, an abiding watching against too deep engrossment with the world. Then, the whole character will come to bear the beautiful stamp—quietly waiting for the salvation of God.

Andrew Murray, in *Waiting on God*

Great Energy for God

They shall be like mighty men in battle, trampling the foe. . . .
They shall fight because the Lord is with them.
(Zechariah 10:5, esv)

Those who know God have great energy for God.

In one of the prophetic chapters of Daniel we read: "the people who know their God shall stand firm and take action" (11:32, esv). In the context, this statement is introduced by "but," and set in contrast to the activity of the "contemptible person" (verse 21, esv) who sets up "the abomination that makes desolate" (verses 31-32, esv). This shows us that the action taken by those who know God is their *reaction* to the anti-God trends they see operating around them. While their God is being defied or disregarded, they cannot rest; they feel they must do something; the dishonor done to God's name goads them into action.

This is exactly what we see happening in the narrative chapters of Daniel. Daniel and his three friends were men who knew God, and who in consequence felt compelled from time to time actively to stand out against the conventions and dictates of irreligion and false religion. Daniel in particular appears as one who would not let a situation of that sort slide, but felt bound openly to challenge it. Those who know their God are sensitive to situations in which God's truth and honor are being directly or tacitly jeopardized, and rather than let the matter go by default will force the issue on men's attention and seek thereby to compel a change of heart about it — even at personal risk.

Men who know their God are before anything else men who pray, and the first point where their zeal and energy for God's glory come to expression is in their prayers. The invariable fruit of true knowledge of God is energy to pray for God's cause — energy, indeed, which can find an outlet and a relief of inner tension only when channeled into such prayer — and the more knowledge, the more energy!

J. I. Packer, in *Knowing God*

IDEAL WORSHIP

My soul will be satisfied as with fat and rich food,
and my mouth will praise you with joyful lips.
(PSALM 63:5, ESV)

I see three stages of movement toward the ideal experience of worship.

1. There is a final stage in which we feel an unencumbered joy in the manifold perfection of God — the joy of gratitude, wonder, hope, admiration. In this stage we are satisfied with the excellency of God, and we overflow with the joy of His fellowship.
2. In a prior stage that we often taste, we do not feel fullness, but rather longing and desire. Having tasted the feast before, we recall the goodness of the Lord — but it seems far off. We preach to our souls not to be downcast, because we are sure we shall again praise the Lord (see Psalm 42:5). Yet, for now, our hearts are not very fervent. Even though this falls short of the ideal of vigorous, heartfelt adoration and hope, yet it is a great honor to God. We honor the water from a mountain spring not only by the satisfied "ahhh" after drinking our fill, but also by the unquenched longing to be satisfied while still climbing to it.
3. The lowest stage of worship — where all genuine worship starts, and where it often returns for a dark season — is the barrenness of soul that scarcely feels any longing, and yet is still granted the grace of repentant sorrow for having so little love: "When my soul was embittered, when I was pricked in heart, I was brutish and ignorant; I was like a beast toward you" (Psalm 73:21-22, ESV). Even in the miserable guilt we feel over our beastlike insensitivity, the glory of God shines. If God were not gloriously desirable, why would we feel sorrowful for not feasting fully on His beauty?

God surely is more glorified when we delight in His magnificence. Yet He is also glorified by the spark of anticipated gladness that gives rise to the sorrow we feel when our hearts are lukewarm.

JOHN PIPER, IN *DESIRING GOD*

A Return to Biblical Ways

They shall build up the ancient ruins; they shall raise up the former devastations; they shall repair the ruined cities, the devastations of many generations.

(Isaiah 61:4, esv)

For the great sickness that is upon modern evangelicalism, no one person is responsible, and no Christian is wholly free from blame. We have all contributed, directly or indirectly, to this sad state of affairs. We have been too blind to see, too timid to speak out, too self-satisfied to desire anything better than the poor average diet with which others appear satisfied. We have accepted one another's notions, copied one another's lives, and made one another's experiences the model for our own. And for a generation the trend has been downward.

It will require a determined heart and more than a little courage to wrench ourselves loose from the grip of our times and return to biblical ways. But it can be done. Every now and then in the past Christians have had to do it. History has recorded several large-scale returns. Whether or not another such return may be expected before the coming of Christ is a question upon which Christians are not fully agreed, but that is not of too great importance to us now.

What God in His sovereignty may yet do on a world-scale I do not claim to know; but what He will do for the plain man or woman who seeks His face I believe I do know and can tell others. Let any man turn to God in earnest, let him begin to exercise himself unto godliness, let him seek to develop his powers of spiritual receptivity by trust and obedience and humility, and the results will exceed anything he may have hoped in his leaner and weaker days.

Any man who by repentance and a sincere return to God will break himself out of the mold in which he has been held, and will go to the Bible itself for his spiritual standards, will be delighted with what he finds there.

A. W. Tozer, in *The Pursuit of God*

Depending on God in Everything

Unless the Lord builds the house, those who build it labor in vain.
Unless the Lord watches over the city, the watchman stays awake in vain.
(Psalm 127:1, esv)

All of our plans, all of our efforts, and all of our prudence are of no avail unless God prospers those means.

In Psalm 127:1, there is the concept of both offensive and defensive efforts — of both building for progress and watching against destruction. In a sense, the verse sums up all of our responsibilities in life. Whether it be in the physical, the mental, or the spiritual, we should always be building and watching. And Psalm 127:1 says none of those efforts will prosper unless God intervenes in them.

We must depend upon God to do for us what we cannot do for ourselves. We must, to the same degree, depend on Him to *enable* us to do what we must do for ourselves. The farmer must use all of his skills, experience, and resources to produce a harvest. Yet he is utterly dependent upon forces outside of himself. Those forces of nature — moisture, insects, sun — are, as we have already seen, under the direct sovereign control of God. The farmer is dependent upon God to control nature so that his crop will grow. But he is just as dependent upon God to enable him to plow, plant, fertilize, and cultivate properly. From where did he get his skills, his ability to learn from his experience, the financial resources to buy the equipment and fertilizer he uses? Where does even his physical strength to do his tasks come from? Are not all these things from the hand of God who "gives all men life and breath and everything else" (Acts 17:25, niv)? In every respect, we are utterly dependent upon God.

There are times when we can do nothing, and there are times when we must work. In both instances we are equally dependent upon God.

Jerry Bridges, in *Trusting God*

In Holy Expectancy

As for me, I will look to the Lord; I will wait for the God of my salvation; my God will hear me.

(Micah 7:7, esv)

Waiting for the answer to prayer is not the whole of waiting, but only a part—and a very important one. When we have special petitions, in connection with which we are waiting on God, our waiting must be very definitely in the confident assurance, "My God will hear me."

A holy, joyful expectancy is of the very essence of true waiting. This is true not only in reference to the many varied requests every believer has to make, but most especially to the one great petition which ought to be the chief thing every heart seeks for itself—that the life of God in the soul may have full sway, that Christ may be fully formed within, and that we may be filled to all the fullness of God.

This is what God has promised. This is what God's people too little seek, very often because they do not believe it possible. This is what we ought to seek and dare to expect, because God is able and waiting to work it in us.

Just notice how the threefold use of the name of God in our text points us to Himself as the one from whom alone is our expectation. "I will look unto the Lord; I will wait for the God of my salvation: my God will hear me" (Micah 7:7, kjv). Everything that is salvation, everything that is good and holy, must be the direct, mighty work of God Himself within us.

In every moment of a life in the will of God, there must be the immediate operation of God. And, the one thing I have to do is this: to look to the Lord, to wait for the God of my salvation, to hold fast the confident assurance, "my God will hear me."

Andrew Murray, in *Waiting on God*

The Speaking Voice

In the beginning was the Word, and the Word was with God, and the Word was God.

(John 1:1, esv)

An intelligent plain man, untaught in the truths of Christianity, coming upon the text of John 1:1, would likely conclude that John meant to teach that it is the nature of God to speak, to communicate His thoughts to others. And he would be right. A word is a medium by which thoughts are expressed, and the application of the term to the Eternal Son leads us to believe that self-expression is inherent in the Godhead, that God is forever seeking to speak Himself out to His creation. The whole Bible supports the idea. God is speaking. Not God *spoke*, but *God is speaking.* He is by His nature continuously articulate. He fills the world with His speaking Voice.

One of the great realities with which we have to deal is the Voice of God in His world. And this word of God which brought all worlds into being cannot be understood to mean the Bible, for it is not a written or printed word at all, but the expression of the will of God spoken into the structure of all things. This word of God is the breath of God filling the world with living potentiality. It is the most powerful force in nature, indeed the only force in nature, for all energy is here only because the power-filled Word is being spoken.

The Bible is the written word of God, and because it is written it is confined and limited by the necessities of ink and paper and leather. The Voice of God, however, is alive and free as the sovereign God is free. God's word in the Bible can have power only because it corresponds to God's word in the universe. It is the present Voice which makes the written Word all-powerful. Otherwise it would lie locked in slumber within the covers of a book.

A. W. Tozer, in *The Pursuit of God*

Dependence on God and Our Responsibility

Through sloth the roof sinks in, and through indolence the house leaks.
(Ecclesiastes 10:18, esv)

Sometimes, God reduces us to a *conscious*, utter dependence upon Him. A loved one is desperately ill, beyond the expertise and skill of medical service. Unemployment has persisted to the point that the cupboard is bare and no job prospects are in sight. At such times we readily recognize our dependence and cry out to God for His intervention. But we are just as dependent on God when the physician diagnoses a routine illness and prescribes a successful medication. We are just as dependent when the paycheck comes regularly and all our material needs are met.

At the same time we are responsible. The Bible never allows us to use our utter dependence on God as an excuse for indolence. "A sluggard does not plow in season; so at harvest time he looks but finds nothing" (Proverbs 20:4, niv). We're absolutely dependent upon God, but, at the same time, we are responsible to diligently use whatever means are appropriate for the occasion.

Our duty is found in the revealed will of God in the Scriptures. Our trust must be in the sovereign will of God, as He works in the ordinary circumstances of our daily lives for our good and His glory.

There is no conflict between trusting God and accepting our responsibility. The Puritan preacher Thomas Lye said that trust uses "such means as God prescribes for the bringing about his appointed end. . . . God's means are to be used, as well as God's blessing to be expected."[18]

Alexander Carson made a similar observation: "Let us learn . . . that as God has promised to protect us and provide for us, it is through the means of his appointment, vigilance, prudence, and industry, that we are to look for these blessings."[19]

Jerry Bridges, in *Trusting God*

No Greater Stillness

Be silent, all flesh, before the Lord, for he has roused himself from his holy dwelling.

(Zechariah 2:13, esv)

There is no stillness like that of the grave. In the grave of Jesus, in the fellowship of His death, in death to self with its own will and wisdom, its own strength and energy—there is rest.

As we cease from self and our soul becomes still to God, God will arise and show Himself. "Be still, and know"; then you will know "that I am God" (Psalm 46:10, kjv). There is no stillness like the stillness Jesus gives when He speaks. "Peace, be still" (Mark 4:39, kjv). In Christ, in His death, in His life, in His perfected redemption, the soul may be still, and God will come in, take possession, and do His perfect work.

But God Himself must work it. And for this end our working must cease. We must see how entirely it is to be the faith of the operation of God, who raised Jesus from the dead. Just as much as the resurrection, the perfecting of God's life in our souls is to be directly His work.

Waiting has to become, more than ever, a tarrying before God in stillness of soul, counting upon Him who raises the dead and calls the things that are not as though they were (see Romans 4:17).

My soul, be thou still only unto God! God says, "Be still, and know that I am God" (Psalm 46:10, kjv). Let us be still and wait and worship till we know how near He is, and then say, "On thee do I wait all the day" (Psalm 25:5, kjv).

And then, let it be very clear that we are waiting. Let that become so much our consciousness that the utterance comes spontaneously: "I wait on Thee." This will indeed imply sacrifice and separation, a soul entirely given up to God as its all, its only joy.

Andrew Murray, in *Waiting on God*

He Speaks, and It Is Done

By faith we understand that the universe was created by the word of God.
(Hebrews 11:3, esv)

We take a primitive view of things when we conceive of God at the creation coming into physical contact with things, shaping and fitting and building like a carpenter. The Bible teaches otherwise: "For he spake, and it was done; he commanded, and it stood fast" (Psalm 33:9, kjv). God is referring here not to His written Word, but to His speaking Voice. His world-filling Voice is meant, that Voice which antedates the Bible by uncounted centuries, that Voice which has not been silent since the dawn of creation, but is sounding still throughout the full far reaches of the universe.

The Word of God is quick and powerful. In the beginning He spoke to nothing, and it became *something.* Chaos heard it and became order, darkness heard it and became light. "And God said — and it was so." These twin phrases, as cause and effect, occur throughout the Genesis story of the creation. The *said* accounts for the *so.* The *so* is the *said* put into the continuous present.

That God is here and that He is speaking — these truths are back of all other Bible truths; without them there could be no revelation at all. God did not write a book and send it by messenger to be read at a distance by unaided minds. He spoke a Book and lives in His spoken words, constantly speaking His words and causing the power of them to persist across the years. God breathed on clay and it became a man; He breathes on men and they become clay. "Return, ye children of men" was the word spoken at the Fall by which God decreed the death of every man, and no added word has He needed to speak (Psalm 90:3, kjv). The sad procession of mankind across the face of the earth from birth to the grave is proof that His original Word was enough.

A. W. Tozer, in *The Pursuit of God*

THE RIGHT TO INTERRUPT

Well done, good and faithful servant. You have been faithful over a little; I will set you over much. Enter into the joy of your master.

(MATTHEW 25:21, ESV)

Do you want to experience God working mightily in and through you? Then adjust your life to God in the kind of relationship where you follow Him wherever He leads you—even if the assignment seems small or insignificant. Wouldn't you love to hear: "Well done, good and faithful slave! You were faithful over a few things; I will put you in charge of many things. Share your master's joy!" (Matthew 25:21, HCSB)?

Do not misunderstand the point here. Don't assume an assignment must be from God just because it is small or unexpected. Whether the assignment is large or small in your eyes, you will still have to determine whether it is from God. God is the One who can tell you that. The important thing is not to rule out an assignment on the basis of your preconceived ideas. God may well give you an assignment that takes you outside your experience or comfort level. Remember—you will know what His will is through your relationship with God. *Don't bypass the relationship.*

I have known people who wouldn't interrupt a fishing trip or a football game for anything. They say they want to serve God, but they keep eliminating from their lives anything that might interfere with their own plans. They are so self-centered, they don't recognize when God comes to them. There are Christians who spend great time and energy to make their lives as comfortable as possible. They immediately reject any initiative God brings into their lives that could create discomfort.

God has a right to interrupt your life. He is Lord. When you surrender to Him, you acknowledge His right to help Himself to your life at His prerogative. If you are God-centered, you will adjust your plans to what God wants to do.

HENRY BLACKABY AND RICHARD BLACKABY, IN *EXPERIENCING GOD*

When We Fail

For this purpose I have raised you up, to show you my power, so that my name may be proclaimed in all the earth.

(Exodus 9:16, esv)

Does failure on our part to act prudently frustrate the sovereign plan of God?

The Scriptures never indicate that God is frustrated to any degree by our failure to act as we should. In His infinite wisdom, God's sovereign plan includes our failures and even our sins.

When Mordecai asked Queen Esther to intercede with King Xerxes on behalf of the Jews, she demurred, explaining that she could enter the king's presence unbidden only on the threat of death (see Esther 4:10-11). However, Mordecai sent word back to her, "if you keep silent at this time, relief and deliverance will rise for the Jews from another place, but you and your father's house will perish. And who knows whether you have not come to the kingdom for such a time as this?" (Esther 4:14, esv). The key phrase here is "relief and deliverance will rise for the Jews from another place."

The options available to God to bring about deliverance for the Jews were as infinite as His wisdom and power. He literally did not need Esther's cooperation. But in this instance, He chose to use her. Mordecai's closing words in that verse assume that God uses people and means to accomplish His sovereign purpose.

As subsequent events proved, God had indeed raised up Esther to accomplish His purpose. But He could just as easily have raised up someone else or used an altogether different means. God usually works through ordinary events (as opposed to miracles) and the voluntary actions of people. But He always provides the means necessary and guides them by His unseen hand. He is sovereign, and He cannot be frustrated by our failure to act or by our actions, which in themselves are sinful. We must always remember, however, that God still holds us accountable for the very sins that He uses to accomplish His purpose.

Jerry Bridges, in *Trusting God*

For Redemption

Simeon . . . was righteous and devout, waiting for the consolation of Israel, and the Holy Spirit was upon him.

(Luke 2:25, esv)

Here we have the mark of a waiting believer. Righteous in all his conduct; devoted to God, ever walking as in His presence; looking for the fulfillment of God's promises; "and the Holy Ghost was upon him" (Luke 2:25, kjv). In the devout waiting, he had been prepared for the blessing.

And Simeon was not the only one. Anna (see Luke 2:36-38) spoke to all who looked for redemption in Jerusalem. This was the one mark, amid surrounding formalism and worldliness, of a godly band of men and women in Jerusalem. They were waiting on God, looking for His promised redemption.

And now that the consolation of Israel has come, and the redemption has been accomplished, do we still need to wait? We do indeed. But we now wait on God in the full power of the redemption, and we wait for its full revelation.

The Epistles teach us to present ourselves to God as "dead indeed unto sin, but alive unto God through Jesus Christ" (Romans 6:11, kjv), "blessed . . . with all spiritual blessings in heavenly places in Christ" (Ephesians 1:3, kjv). Our waiting on God may now be in the wonderful consciousness maintained by the Holy Spirit within us, that we are accepted in the Beloved, that the love that rests on Him rests on us, that we are living in that love, in the very nearness and presence and sight of God.

The old saints took their stand on the Word of God, and waiting, hoping on that Word, we rest on the Word, too—but, oh, under what exceedingly greater privileges, as one with Christ Jesus!

In our waiting on God, let this be our confidence: in Christ we have access to the Father. How sure, therefore, we may be that our waiting cannot be in vain.

Andrew Murray, in *Waiting on God*

VOICE OF LIGHT, VOICE OF WISDOM

The true light, which enlightens everyone, was coming into the world.

(JOHN 1:9, ESV)

The Word of God affects the hearts of all men as light in the soul. In the hearts of all men the light shines, the Word sounds, and there is no escaping them. Something like this would of necessity be so if God is alive and in His world. And John says that it is so. Even those persons who have never heard of the Bible have still been preached to with sufficient clarity to remove every excuse from their hearts forever. "Which shew the work of the law written in their hearts, their conscience also bearing witness, and their thoughts the mean while accusing or else excusing one another" (Romans 2:15, KJV). "For the invisible things of him from the creation of the world are clearly seen, being understood by the things that are made, even his eternal power and Godhead; so that they are without excuse" (Romans 1:20, KJV).

This universal Voice of God was by the ancient Hebrews often called Wisdom, and was said to be everywhere sounding and searching throughout the earth, seeking some response from the sons of men. The eighth chapter of the Book of Proverbs begins, "Doth not wisdom cry? and understanding put forth her voice?" (KJV). The writer then pictures wisdom as a beautiful woman standing "in the top of the high places, by the way in the places of the paths" (verse 2, KJV). She sounds her voice from every quarter so that no one may miss hearing it. "Unto you, O men, I call; and my voice is to the sons of man" (verse 4, KJV). Then she pleads for the simple and the foolish to give ear to her words. It is spiritual response for which this Wisdom of God is pleading, a response which she has always sought and is but rarely able to secure. The tragedy is that our eternal welfare depends upon our hearing, and we have trained our ears not to hear.

A. W. TOZER, IN *THE PURSUIT OF GOD*

BEAUTY FROM ASHES

To grant to those who mourn in Zion . . . a beautiful headdress instead of ashes, the oil of gladness instead of mourning.

(ISAIAH 61:3, ESV)

As we watch tragic events unfolding, or experience adversity ourselves, we often fail to see any possible good to us or glory to God that can come from it. But is not the wisdom of God — and thus the glory of God — more eminently displayed in bringing good out of calamity than out of blessing?

There's no question that God's people live in a hostile world. We have an enemy, the devil, who "prowls around like a roaring lion, seeking someone to devour" (1 Peter 5:8, ESV). He wants to sift us like wheat as he did Peter (see Luke 22:31), or make us curse God as he tried to get Job to do. God does not spare us from the ravages of disease, heartache, and disappointment of this sin-cursed world. But God is able to take all of these elements — the bad as well as the good — and make full use of every one.

As someone years ago said, "A lesser wisdom than the Divine would feel impelled to forbid, to circumvent, or to resist the outworking of these hellish plans. It is a fact that often God's people try to do this themselves, or cry unceasingly to the Lord that He may do it. So it is that prayers often seem to lie unanswered. For we are being handled by a wisdom which is perfect, a wisdom which can achieve what it [intends] by taking hold of things and people which are meant for evil and making them work together for good."[20]

God's infinite wisdom is displayed in bringing good out of evil, beauty out of ashes. It is displayed in turning all the forces of evil that rage against His children into good for them. But the good that He brings about is often different from the good we envision.

JERRY BRIDGES, IN *TRUSTING GOD*

He in Us, We in Him

Abide in me, and I in you. . . . Whoever abides in me and I in him, he it is that bears much fruit.

(John 15:4-5, ESV)

Christ said not only "Abide in me," but also "I in you" (John 15:4, ESV). The Epistles speak not only of us in Christ, but of Christ in us, as the highest mystery of redeeming love. As we maintain our place in Christ day by day, God waits to reveal Christ in us in such a way that He is formed in us, that His mind and disposition and likeness acquire form and substance in us, so that in truth we can say, "Christ liveth in me" (Galatians 2:20, KJV).

My life in Christ up there in heaven, and Christ's life in me down here on earth—these two are the complement of each other. And the more my waiting on God is marked by the living faith, *I in Christ*, the more the heart thirsts for and claims the *Christ in me*. The waiting on God, which began with special needs and prayer, will increasingly be concentrated, as far as our personal life is concerned, on this one thing: *Lord, reveal Your redemption fully in me; let Christ live in me.*

For this, we wait on God, from whom alone is our expectation in regard to the revelation of Christ in us. We are absolutely helpless to bring it about. God did not work out the great redemption in Christ as a whole and leave its application in detail to us.

The revelation of Christ in every individual believer, and in each one the daily revelation, step by step and moment by moment, is as much the work of God's omnipotence as the birth or resurrection of Christ. Until this truth enters and fills us, and we feel that we are just as dependent upon God for each moment of our life in the enjoyment of redemption as they were in their waiting for it, our waiting upon God will not bring its full blessing.

Andrew Murray, in *Waiting on God*

Worship Is a Feast

My people . . . have forsaken me, the fountain of living waters, and hewed out cisterns for themselves, broken cisterns that can hold no water.
(Jeremiah 2:13, esv)

The revolt against hedonism has killed the spirit of worship in many churches and many hearts. The widespread notion that high moral acts must be free from self-interest is a great enemy of true worship. Worship is the highest moral act a human can perform, so the only basis and motivation for it that many people can conceive is the notion of morality as the disinterested performance of duty. But when worship is reduced to disinterested duty, it ceases to be worship. For worship is a feast.

Neither God nor my wife is honored when I celebrate the high days of our relationship out of a sense of duty. They are honored when I delight in them! Therefore, to honor God in worship, we must not seek Him disinterestedly for fear of gaining some joy in worship and so ruining the moral value of the act. Instead we must seek Him hedonistically, the way a thirsty deer seeks the stream—precisely for the joy of seeing and knowing Him!

Worship is nothing less than obedience to the command of God: "Delight yourself in the Lord" (Psalm 37:4, esv).

Misguided virtue smothers the spirit of worship. The person who has the vague notion that it is virtue to overcome self-interest, and that it is vice to seek pleasure, will scarcely be able to worship. For worship is the most hedonistic affair of life and must not be ruined with the least thought of disinterestedness. The great hindrance to worship is not that we are a pleasure-seeking people, but that we are willing to settle for such pitiful pleasures.

The heavens are "appalled" and "shocked" when people give up soon on their quest for pleasure and settle for "broken cisterns" (see Jeremiah 2:13).

John Piper, in *Desiring God*

The Ever-Sounding Voice

Then a voice came from heaven. . . . The crowd that stood there and heard it said that it had thundered.

(John 12:28-29, esv)

The universal Voice has ever sounded, and it has often troubled men even when they did not understand the source of their fears. Could it be that this Voice distilling like a living mist upon the hearts of men has been the undiscovered cause of the troubled conscience and the longing for immortality confessed by millions since the dawn of recorded history?

We need not fear to face up to this. The speaking Voice is a fact. How men have reacted to it is for any observer to note.

When God spoke out of heaven to our Lord, self-centered men who heard it explained it by natural causes: they said, "It thundered" (John 12:29, kjv). This habit of explaining the Voice by appeals to natural law is at the very root of modern science.

In the living, breathing cosmos there is a mysterious Something, too wonderful, too awful for any mind to understand. The believing man does not claim to understand. He falls to his knees and whispers, "God."

The man of earth kneels also, but not to worship. He kneels to examine, to search, to find the cause and the how of things.

Just now we happen to be living in a secular age. Our thought habits are those of the scientist, not those of the worshipper. We are more likely to explain than to adore. "It thundered," we exclaim, and go our earthly way.

But still the Voice sounds and searches. The order and life of the world depend upon that Voice, but men are mostly too busy or too stubborn to give attention.

A. W. Tozer, in *The Pursuit of God*

TO SHARE GOD'S MIND

I will delight in your statutes; I will not forget your word.
(PSALM 119:16, ESV)

Once the life of Christ has entered into us, there are many things we may do to increase the extent and depth of our identification and union with him. But the proper use of the written Word is most central to our cooperative efforts with God toward full conformity with Christ.

The person who wishes to grow in grace is advised to make a close and constant companion of *the book* — the Bible. I do not mean that it should be worshipped. Its uniquely sacred character is something that does not need to be exaggerated or even insisted on, because it is self-authenticating to any earnest and open-minded user. For just as openness to and hunger for God leads naturally to the Bible, if it is available, so the eager use of the Bible leads naturally and tangibly to the mind of God and the person of Christ.

The written Word of God is an expression of God's mind just as surely, though in a different manner, as are creation and Jesus, the living Word. As we read and study it intelligently, humbly, and openly, we come increasingly to share God's mind.

We will be spiritually safe in our use of the Bible if we follow a simple rule: *Read with a submissive attitude.* Read with a readiness to surrender all you are — all your plans, opinions, possessions, positions. Study as intelligently as possible, with all available means, but never study merely to find the truth and especially not just to prove something. Subordinate your desire to *find* the truth to your desire to *do* it, to act it out!

Those who wish to hear the word and know the truth are often not prompted by their desire to *do* it. The light that such people find frequently proves to be their own snare and condemnation.

DALLAS WILLARD, IN *HEARING GOD*

Sharing God's Holiness

He disciplines us for our good, that we may share his holiness.

(Hebrews 12:10, esv)

To share in God's holiness is an equivalent expression to being conformed to the likeness of Christ. God knows exactly what He intends we become and He knows exactly what circumstances, both good and bad, are necessary to produce that result in our lives.

Note the contrast drawn in Hebrews 12 between the finite, fallible wisdom of human parents and the infinite, infallible wisdom of God: "We have had earthly fathers who disciplined us . . . for a short time as it seemed best to them" (12:9-10, esv). As a parent, I can readily identify with the phrase "as it seemed best to them." We sometimes agonized over the proper discipline for our children, both in kind and amount. Even when we thought we knew what was best, there were many times when we erred.

But, the writer of Hebrews says without qualification, that God "disciplines us for our good." There is no agonizing by God, no hoping He has made the right decision, no wondering what's really best for us. God makes no mistakes. With infinite wisdom He knows infallibly what combination of good and bad circumstances will bring us more and more into sharing His holiness. He never puts too much of the "salt" of adversity into the recipe of our lives. His blending of adversity and blessing is always exactly right for us.

"For the moment," God's discipline of us "seems painful," but it is also assuredly profitable; it produces "the peaceful fruit of righteousness" (12:11, esv). The purpose of God's discipline is not to punish us but to transform us. He has already meted out punishment for our sins on Jesus at Calvary: "Upon him was the chastisement that brought us peace" (Isaiah 53:5, esv). But we must be transformed more and more into the likeness of Christ. That is the purpose of discipline.

Jerry Bridges, in *Trusting God*

Waiting for Christ's Coming

You turned to God from idols to serve the living and true God, and to wait for his Son from heaven.
(1 Thessalonians 1:9-10, ESV)

Waiting on God in heaven, and waiting for His Son from heaven — these two God has joined together, and no man may put them asunder. The waiting on God for His presence and power in daily life will be the only true preparation for waiting for Christ in humility and true holiness. The waiting for Christ coming from heaven to take us to heaven will give the waiting on God its true tone of hopefulness and joy. The Father, who, in His own time, will reveal His Son from heaven, is the God who, as we wait on Him, prepares us for the revelation of His Son. The present life and the coming glory are inseparably connected in God and in us.

It is always easier to be engaged with the Christianity of the past or the future than to be faithful in the Christianity of today. As we look to what God has done in the past, or will do in time to come, the personal claim of present duty and present submission to His working may be avoided. Waiting on God must always lead to waiting for Christ as the glorious consummation of His work. And, waiting for Christ must always remind us of the duty of waiting upon God as our only proof that the waiting for Christ is in spirit and in truth.

There is such a danger of our being more occupied with the things that are coming than with Him who is to come. Nothing but deeply humble waiting on God can save us from this mistake. Be sure that you wait on God now . . . while waiting for the revelation of His Son from heaven. The hope of that glorious appearing will strengthen you in waiting upon God for what He is to do in you now. The same omnipotent love that is to reveal that glory is working in you even now to prepare you for it.

Andrew Murray, in *Waiting on God*

Adversity's Value

It is good for me that I was afflicted, that I might learn your statutes.
(Psalm 119:71, ESV)

Psalm 119:71 speaks of experiential learning. We can learn God's will for our character intellectually through reading and studying the Scriptures — and we should do that. That is where change begins, as our minds are renewed. But real change — down in the depth of our souls — is produced as the tenets of Scripture are worked out in real life. This usually involves adversity. We may admire and even desire the character trait of patience, but we will never learn patience until we have been treated unjustly and learn experientially to "suffer long" (the meaning of *patience*) the one who treats us unjustly.

If you stop and think about it, you'll realize that most godly character traits can only be developed through adversity. The kind of love that gives freely of itself at great cost to itself can only be learned when we are confronted with situations that call forth a sacrificial love. The fruit of the Spirit that is called joy cannot be learned in the midst of circumstances that produce mere "natural" happiness.

God in His infinite wisdom knows exactly what adversity we need to grow more and more into the likeness of His Son. He not only knows what we need but when we need it and how best to bring it to pass in our lives. He is the perfect teacher or coach. His discipline is always exactly suited for our needs. He never overtrains us by allowing too much adversity in our lives.

"We know that for those who love God all things [including our adversities] work together for *good*" (Romans 8:28, ESV, emphasis added). From this verse and the next, we see that the "good" God works for in our lives is *conformity to the likeness of His Son*. It is not necessarily comfort or happiness, but conformity to Christ in ever-increasing measure in this life and in its fullness in eternity.

Jerry Bridges, in *Trusting God*

WAITING TOGETHER

Waiting for our blessed hope, the appearing of the glory of our great God and Savior Jesus Christ.

(TITUS 2:13, ESV)

Our "blessed hope" of waiting for Christ's glorious appearing is one of the great bonds of union given to God's church throughout the ages. When "he shall come to be glorified in his saints" (2 Thessalonians 1:10, KJV), the unity of the body of Christ will be seen in its divine glory. It will be the meeting place and the triumph of divine love: Jesus receiving His own and presenting them to the Father; our meeting Him and worshipping, in speechless love, that blessed face; our meeting each other in the ecstasy of God's own love.

Waiting for His coming means waiting for the glorious coming manifestation of the unity of the body, while we seek here to maintain that unity in humility and love. Those who love most are the most ready for His coming. Love to each other is the life and beauty of His bride, the church.

Beloved child of God, if you want to learn how to properly wait for His Son from heaven, live even now waiting on God in heaven. Remember how Jesus lived ever waiting on God. He could do nothing of Himself. It was God who perfected His Son through suffering and then exalted Him. It is God alone who can give you the deep spiritual life of one who is really waiting for His Son: wait on God for it. Waiting for Christ Himself is something God must work in you every day by His Holy Spirit. Therefore, as you wait on God, look to Him for grace to wait for His Son from heaven in the Spirit which is from heaven. And, as you wait for His Son, wait on God continually to reveal Christ in you.

The revelation of Christ in us, as it is given to them who wait upon God, is the true preparation for the full revelation of Christ in glory.

ANDREW MURRAY, IN *WAITING ON GOD*

Great Thoughts of God

The Most High God rules the kingdom of mankind
and sets over it whom he will.
(Daniel 5:21, esv)

The central truth which Daniel taught Nebuchadnezzar in Daniel chapters 2 and 4—and of which he reminded Belshazzar (see 5:18-23), and which Nebuchadnezzar acknowledged (see 4:34-37), and which Darius confessed (see 6:25-27), and which was the basis of Daniel's prayers in chapters 2 and 9, and of his confidence in defying authority in chapters 1 and 6, and of his friends' confidence in defying authority in chapter 3, and which formed the staple substance of all the disclosures which God made to Daniel in chapters 2, 4, 7, 8, 10, 11, and 12—is the truth that "the Most High rules the kingdom of men" (4:25, esv). He knows, and foreknows, all things, and His foreknowledge is foreordination; He, therefore, will have the last word, both in world history and in the destiny of every man; His kingdom and righteousness will triumph in the end, for neither men nor angels shall be able to thwart Him.

These were the thoughts of God which filled Daniel's mind, as witness his prayers (always the best evidence for a man's view of God): "Blessed be the name of God forever and ever, to whom belong wisdom and might. He changes times and seasons; he removes kings and sets up kings; he gives wisdom. . . . He knows what is in the darkness, and the light dwells with him" (2:20 22, esv). "O Lord, the great and awesome God, who keeps covenant and steadfast love with those who love him and keep his commandments. . . . To you, O Lord, belongs righteousness. . . . To the Lord our God belong mercy and forgiveness. . . . The Lord our God is righteous in all the works that he has done" (Daniel 9:4,7,9,14, esv).

Does this tremendous sense of His holy majesty, His moral perfection, and His gracious faithfulness keep us humble and dependent, awed and obedient, as it did Daniel? By this test, too, we may measure how much, or how little, we know God.

J. I. Packer, in *Knowing God*

GOD'S PURPOSES VERSUS OUR PLANS

Many are the plans in the mind of a man,
but it is the purpose of the LORD that will stand.
(PROVERBS 19:21, ESV)

We often dream our dreams of what we want to do for God. We formulate plans based on our priorities. Then we pray and ask God to bless our efforts and to help us accomplish our goals. (After all, we're doing it for Him!) We mobilize fellow believers to make our schemes successful. What is really important, however, is what God plans to do where we are and how He wants to accomplish His purposes through us.

Planning is a valuable exercise, but it can never become a substitute for hearing from God. Your plans have merit only when they are based on what God has told you He intends to do. Your relationship with God is far more important to Him than any scheming you can do. The biggest problem with planning is when we try to carry out in our own wisdom what only God has a right to determine. We cannot know the when or where or how of God's will until He tells us.

God expects us to get our directives from Him, and He wants to equip us to do the assignment he gives. If we try to spell out all the details of His will in a planning session, we'll have a tendency to forget the need for a daily, intimate relationship with God. We may accomplish our objectives but forgo the relationship. It is possible to achieve all our goals and yet be outside God's will. God created us for an eternal love relationship. Life is our opportunity to experience Him at work in us and in our world.

Planning is not wrong. Just be careful not to plan more than God intends for you. Remain in a close relationship with Him so you can always hear His voice when He speaks to you.

HENRY BLACKABY AND RICHARD BLACKABY, IN *EXPERIENCING GOD*

Asking God Why

Why do you hide your face and count me as your enemy?
(Job 13:24, esv)

Three of the psalms begin with *why*: "Why, O Lord, do you stand far away? Why do you hide yourself in times of trouble?" (10:1, esv); "My God, my God, why have you forsaken me? Why are you so far from saving me, from the words of my groaning?" (22:1, esv); "O God, why do you cast us off forever? Why does your anger smoke against the sheep of your pasture?" (74:1, esv).

But each of those psalms ends on a note of trust in God. The psalm writers did not allow their whys to drag on. They did not allow them to take root and grow into accusations against God. Their whys were really cries of anguish, a natural reaction to pain.

By contrast, there are sixteen whys in the book of Job, according to author Don Baker.[21] Sixteen times Job asked God why. He is persistent and petulant. He is accusatory toward God. And, as has been observed by many, God never answered Job's why. Instead He answered *who*.

Pastor Baker, in his book on Job, says, "I have long since quit seeking the answer to that question [why?] in my own life. . . . God owes me no explanation. He has the right to do what He wants, when He wants, and how He wants. Why? Because He's God. . . . Job didn't need to know why these things happened as they did—he just needed to know Who was responsible and Who was in control. He just needed to know God."[22]

Though we should never ask a demanding why, we may and should ask God to enable us to understand what He may be teaching us through a particular experience. But even here we must trust God that He is working in the experience for our good, even when we see no beneficial results. We must learn to trust God when He doesn't tell us why, when we don't understand what He is doing.

Jerry Bridges, in *Trusting God*

THE CERTAINTY OF HIS PROVIDENCE

You, O LORD, are on high forever.
(PSALM 92:8, ESV)

A Christian husband flew in a private plane to another city to give his testimony at an evangelistic meeting, taking his son with him. On the way home they ran into an electrical storm that caused the plane to crash. Both the father and son were killed. A Christian friend, in an effort to comfort the bereaved wife and mother, said, "One thing you can be sure of: God had no part in that accident." According to this friend, God was apparently looking the other way when the pilot got into trouble. A sparrow cannot fall to the ground without our Father's will, but apparently a plane with Christians aboard can.

I read a blasphemous statement by someone who said, "Chance is the pseudonym God uses when He'd rather not sign His own name." A lot of Christians are doing that for God today, unwilling to accept the fact that He is working because they don't understand *how* He is working.

It isn't easy to believe in the doctrine of God's providence, especially in these days when that doctrine seems to have fallen upon hard times. In *The Providence of God*, G. C. Berkouwer speaks of the "catastrophic terrors" of modern history, then asks, "Does not pure honesty force us to stop seeking escape in a hidden, harmonious supersensible world? Does not honesty tell us to limit ourselves realistically to what lies before our eyes, and, without illusions, face the order of the day?"[23]

All people — believers as well as unbelievers — experience anxiety, frustration, heartache, and disappointment. Some suffer intense physical pain and catastrophic tragedies. But that which should distinguish the suffering of believers from unbelievers is the confidence that our suffering has meaning and purpose in God's eternal plan, and He brings or allows to come into our lives only that which is for His glory and our good.

JERRY BRIDGES, IN *TRUSTING GOD*

Waiting for Further Fulfillment

He ordered them . . . to wait for the promise of the Father; ". . . you will be baptized with the Holy Spirit."

(Acts 1:4-5, esv)

In one sense, the fulfillment of the Father's promise (see Acts 1:4-5) can never come again as it came at Pentecost. In another sense—and in as deep a reality as with the first disciples—we need to wait daily for the Father to fulfill His promise in us.

The Holy Spirit is not a person distinct from the Father in the way two persons on earth are distinct. The Father and the Spirit are never without or separate from each other. The Father is always in the Spirit; the Spirit works nothing but as the Father works in Him. Each moment, the same Spirit that is in us is in God, too. And the person who is most full of the Spirit will be the first to wait on God most earnestly to further fulfill His promise and to still strengthen him mightily by His Spirit in the inner man.

The Spirit in us is not a power at our disposal. Nor is the Spirit an independent power, acting apart from the Father and the Son. The Spirit is the real, living presence and the power of the Father working in us. Therefore, it is the person who knows that the Spirit is in him who waits on the Father for the full revelation and experience of the Spirit's indwelling. It is he who waits for His increase and abounding more and more.

When God gives grace or strength or life, He gives it by giving Himself to work it—it is all inseparable from Himself. Much more so is the Holy Spirit. He is God, present and working in us. The true position in which we can count upon that working with an unceasing power is as we, praising Him for what we have, still unceasingly wait for the Father's promise to be still more mightily fulfilled.

Andrew Murray, in *Waiting on God*

The World as Battlefield

All that is in the world — the desires of the flesh and the desires of the eyes and pride in possessions — is not from the Father but is from the world.

(1 John 2:16, esv)

Martin Luther spoke of a threefold battle in the Christian life. The Christian is locked in combat with the world, the flesh, and the devil. These are formidable opponents. In living to please a righteous God, we do constant battle with these enemies. Part of the process of sanctification is fighting with and — if we are truly growing — frequently triumphing over these foes. Every sensitive believer knows only too well how difficult it can be to win such a victory.

The world spirit — the value systems of a fallen creation — may be distinguished from the flesh and the devil but not separated from them. The flesh is part of the fallen world and the devil is the prince of this world.

We live in this world. We are part of the world. We are to a certain degree products of this world. And the world is our battlefield. Wherever we live and move in this world, we are still engaged in combat. There is no demilitarized zone. The whole planet is fallen. The whole creation groans in travail waiting for redemption. We live in a world injured by tooth, claw, and fang. We look forward to a new world where the wolf will lie down with the lamb and the child will play safely by the nest of the rattlesnake. But right now we do not invite wolves to act as shepherds of our sheep.

The secular spirit of this world has its own modern trends and emphases, but in its essence it is not new. Every generation has its own form of secularism. We are earthbound creatures.

The same was true in Jesus' day. He repeatedly called His disciples to look beyond the present. He lifted our gaze to the eternal. "Lay up for yourselves treasures in heaven" (Matthew 6:20, esv); "For what will it profit a man if he gains the whole world and forfeits his soul?" (Matthew 16:26, esv).

R. C. Sproul, in *Pleasing God*

THE VOICE CALLING

The voice of the LORD is powerful; the voice of the LORD is full of majesty. . . . The voice of the LORD flashes forth flames of fire.

(PSALM 29:4,7, ESV)

Every one of us has had experiences which we have not been able to explain: a sudden sense of loneliness, or a feeling of wonder or awe in the face of the universal vastness. Or we have had a fleeting visitation of light like an illumination from some other sun, giving us in a quick flash an assurance that we are from another world, that our origins are divine.

Explain such things as we will, I think we have not been fair to the facts until we allow at least the possibility that such experiences may arise from the Presence of God in the world and His persistent effort to communicate with mankind. Let us not dismiss such an hypothesis too flippantly.

It is my own belief (and here I shall not feel bad if no one follows me) that every good and beautiful thing which man has produced in the world has been the result of his faulty and sin-blocked response to the creative Voice sounding over the earth. The moral philosophers who dreamed their high dreams of virtue, the religious thinkers who speculated about God and immortality, the poets and artists who created out of common stuff pure and lasting beauty: how can we explain them? It is not enough to say simply, "It was genius." What then is genius? Could it be that a genius is a man haunted by the speaking Voice, laboring and striving like one possessed to achieve ends which he only vaguely understands? That the great man may have missed God in his labors, that he may even have spoken or written against God does not destroy the idea I am advancing.

God's redemptive revelation in the Holy Scriptures is necessary to saving faith and peace with God. Faith in a risen Savior is necessary if the vague stirrings toward immortality are to bring us to restful and satisfying communion with God.

A. W. TOZER, IN *THE PURSUIT OF GOD*

SURRENDERING TO THE TRUTH ABOUT GOD

As the heavens are higher than the earth, so are my ways higher than your ways and my thoughts than your thoughts.

(ISAIAH 55:9, ESV)

In his commentary on Isaiah 55:8-9, Edward J. Young said, "The implication is that just as the heavens are so high above the earth that by human standards their height cannot be measured, so also are God's ways and thoughts so above those of man that they cannot be grasped by man in their fullness. In other words, the ways and thoughts of God are incomprehensible to man."[24] God's ways, being the ways of infinite wisdom, simply cannot be comprehended by our finite minds.

The apostle Paul states the same truth in his doxology at the end of Romans 11 when he exclaims in amazement, "Oh, the depth of the riches and wisdom and knowledge of God! How unsearchable are his judgments and how inscrutable his ways!" (verse 33, ESV).

God's wisdom is fathomless, His decisions are unsearchable, His methods are mysterious and untraceable. No one has ever even understood His mind, let alone advised Him on the proper course of action. How futile and even arrogant for us to seek to determine what God is doing in a particular event or circumstance. We simply cannot search out the reasons behind His decisions or trace out the ways by which He brings those decisions to pass.

If we are to experience peace in our souls in times of adversity, we must come to the place where we truly believe that God's ways are simply beyond us and stop asking Him why or even trying to determine it ourselves. This may seem like an intellectual "cop out," a refusal to deal with the really tough issues of life. In fact, it is just the opposite. It is a surrender to the truth about God and our circumstances as it is revealed to us by God Himself in His inspired Word.

JERRY BRIDGES, IN *TRUSTING GOD*

Fresh Fulfillment

When they had prayed . . . they were all filled with the Holy Spirit and continued to speak the word of God with boldness.

(Acts 4:31, ESV)

Not long after the disciples were filled with the Spirit at Pentecost, they prayed afresh for boldness to speak in His name (see Acts 4:23-30); a fresh coming down of the Holy Spirit was the Father's fresh fulfillment of His promise (see 4:31). So also we find Paul praying for those who have been sealed with the Spirit, that God would grant them the spirit of illumination (see Ephesians 1:13,17); and later on, that He would grant them, according to the riches of His glory, to be strengthened with might by the Spirit in the inner man (see 3:16).

What new meaning and promise does this give to our lives of waiting! It teaches us to continually keep the place where the disciples tarried at the footstool of the throne. It reminds us that, as helpless as they were to meet their enemies or to preach to Christ's enemies, until they were endued with power, we too can be strong in the life of faith or the work of love only as we are in direct communication with God and Christ. The omnipotent God will, through the glorified Christ, work in us a power that can bring unexpected things to pass, impossible things.

Oh, what the church will be able to do when her individual members unite in waiting with one accord for the promise of the Father, once so gloriously fulfilled, but still unexhausted! Let each of us be still in the presence of the inconceivable grandeur of this prospect: the Father waiting to fill the church with the Holy Spirit. *And willing to fill me,* let each one say. With this faith, let a hush and a holy fear come over the soul, as it waits in stillness to take it all in. And, let life increasingly become a deep joy in the hope of the ever fuller fulfillment of the Father's promise.

Andrew Murray, in *Waiting on God*

Glory All Around You

The heavens declare the glory of God,
and the sky above proclaims his handiwork.
(Psalm 19:1, ESV)

Don't let your worship decline to the performance of mere duty. Don't let the childlike awe and wonder be choked out by unbiblical views of virtue. Don't let the scenery and poetry and music of your relationship with God shrivel up and die. You have capacities for joy you can scarcely imagine. They were made for the enjoyment of God. He can awaken them no matter how long they have lain asleep. Pray for His quickening power. Open your eyes to His glory. It is all around you.

I was flying at night from Chicago to Minneapolis, almost alone on the plane. The pilot announced that there was a thunderstorm over Lake Michigan and into Wisconsin. He would skirt it to the west to avoid turbulence. As I sat there staring out into the total blackness, suddenly the whole sky was brilliant with light, and a cavern of white clouds fell away four miles beneath the plane and then vanished. A second later, a mammoth white tunnel of light exploded from north to south across the horizon, and again vanished into blackness. Soon the lightning was almost constant, and volcanoes of light burst up out of cloud ravines and from behind distant white mountains. I sat there shaking my head almost in unbelief. *O Lord, if these are but the sparks from the sharpening of Your sword, what will be the day of Your appearing!* And I remembered the words of Christ: "As the lightning flashes and lights up the sky from one side to the other, so will the Son of Man be in his day" (Luke 17:24, ESV).

Even now as I recollect that sight, the word *glory* is full of feeling for me. I thank God that again and again He has awakened my heart to desire Him, to see Him, and to sit down to the feast of Christian Hedonism and worship the King of Glory. The banquet hall is very large.

John Piper, in *Desiring God*

A FRIENDLY VOICE

And through him to reconcile to himself all things, whether on earth or in heaven, making peace by the blood of his cross.

(COLOSSIANS 1:20, ESV)

The Voice of God is a friendly Voice. No one need fear to listen to it unless he has already made up his mind to resist it. The blood of Jesus has covered not only the human race but all creation as well. We may safely preach a friendly Heaven. The heavens as well as the earth are filled with the good will of Him that dwelt in the bush. The perfect blood of atonement secures this forever.

Whoever will listen will hear the speaking Heaven. This is definitely not the hour when men take kindly to an exhortation to *listen*, for listening is not today a part of popular religion. We are at the opposite end of the pole from there. Religion has accepted the monstrous heresy that noise, size, activity, and bluster make a man dear to God.

But we may take heart. God still says, "Be still, and know that I am God" (Psalm 46:10, KJV), as if He means to tell us that our strength and safety lie not in noise but in silence. It is important that we get still to wait on God. And it is best that we get alone, preferably with our Bible outspread before us. Then, if we will, we may draw near to God and begin to hear Him speak to us in our hearts.

I think for the average person the progression will be something like this: First a sound as of a Presence walking in the garden. Then a voice, more intelligible, but still far from clear. Then the happy moment when the Spirit begins to illuminate the Scriptures, and that which had been only a sound, or at best a voice, now becomes an intelligible word, warm and intimate and clear as the word of a dear friend. Then will come life and light, and best of all, ability to see and rest in and embrace Jesus Christ as Savior and Lord and All.

A. W. TOZER, IN *THE PURSUIT OF GOD*

His Sovereignty Is for Our Benefit

Behold . . . his arm rules for him; behold, his reward is with him . . . He will tend his flock like a shepherd; he will gather the lambs in his arms.

(Isaiah 40:10-11, esv)

God's sovereignty over all His universe is exercised primarily for His glory. But because you and I are in Christ Jesus, His glory and our good are linked together. Because we're united with Christ, whatever is for His glory is also for our good. And whatever is for our good is for His glory.

Therefore, we can, with scriptural warrant, say that God exercises His sovereignty *on our behalf*. Paul says in Ephesians 1:22-23 that God "put all things under [Christ's] feet and gave him as head over all things to the church, which is his body, the fullness of him who fills all in all" (esv). That is, Christ reigns over the entire universe for the benefit of His body, the church. God's sovereignty —which is absolute over the most awesome earthly or spiritual powers and penetrates to the most mundane and minute details of life—is exercised by Christ on behalf of the church, which is His body.

The reason Christ thus exercises His power to govern the universe, as New Testament commentator William Hendriksen explains, is that "he is so intimately and indissolubly united" with the church, "and loves it with such profound, boundless, and steadfast love." Hendriksen further explains that it's this "closeness of the bond, the unfathomable character of the love between Christ and his church that is stressed by the head-body symbolism. . . . Since the church is Christ's body, with which he is organically united, he loves it so much that in its interest he exercises his infinite power in causing the entire universe with all that is in it to co-operate, whether willingly or unwillingly."[25]

Thus we can see that our union with Christ guarantees that God's sovereign power is exercised on our behalf.

Jerry Bridges, in *Trusting God*

Wait Continually

By the help of your God, return, hold fast to love and justice, and wait continually for your God.

(Hosea 12:6, esv)

To those who are content with a feeble Christian life, continual waiting on God appears to be a luxury beyond what is essential to be a good Christian. But all who are praying the prayer, "Lord, make me as holy as a pardoned sinner can be made! Keep me as near to You as it is possible for me to be! Fill me as full of Your love as You are willing to do!" — all such believers feel at once this is something that must be had. They feel there can be no unbroken fellowship with God, no full abiding in Christ, no maintaining of victory over sin and readiness for service, without waiting continually on the Lord.

Many think that with the duties of life, such continual waiting is out of the question. They cannot always be thinking of it. Even when they wish to, they forget.

They do not understand that this is a matter of the heart, and that what the heart is full of, occupies it — even when the thoughts are otherwise engaged. A father's heart may be continuously filled with intense love and longing for a sick wife or child at a distance, even though pressing business requires all his thoughts. When the heart has learned how entirely powerless it is, even for one moment, to keep itself or bring forth any good, when it has learned how surely and truly God will keep it — when in despair of self it has accepted God's promise to do for it the impossible — it learns to rest in God. In the midst of occupations and temptations, it can wait continually.

What God expects of me — what is well-pleasing in His sight — is what God wants me to be, and waits to make me. Let it be also what I want to be, and wait for Him to make me, every moment.

Andrew Murray, in *Waiting on God*

A Book Now Speaking

Is not my word like fire, declares the Lord,
and like a hammer that breaks the rock in pieces?
(Jeremiah 23:29, esv)

I believe that much of our religious unbelief is due to a wrong conception of and a wrong feeling for the Scriptures of Truth. A silent God suddenly began to speak in a book and when the book was finished lapsed back into silence again forever. Now we read the book as the record of what God said when He was for a brief time in a speaking mood. With notions like that in our heads how can we believe? The facts are that God is not silent, and has never been silent. It is the nature of God to speak. The second Person of the Holy Trinity is called the *Word*. The Bible is the inevitable outcome of God's continuous speech. It is the infallible declaration of His mind for us put into our familiar human words.

I think a new world will arise out of the religious mists when we approach our Bible with the idea that it is not only a book which was once spoken, but a book which is *now speaking*. The prophets habitually said, "Thus *saith* the Lord." They meant their hearers to understand that God's speaking is in the continuous present. We may use the past tense properly to indicate that at a certain time a certain word of God was spoken, but a word of God once spoken continues to be spoken, as a child once born continues to be alive, or a world once created continues to exist. And those are but imperfect illustrations, for children die and worlds burn out, but the Word of our God endureth forever.

If you would follow on to know the Lord, come at once to the open Bible expecting it to speak to you. Do not come with the notion that it is a *thing* which you may push around at your convenience. It is more than a thing, it is a voice, a word, the very Word of the living God.

A. W. Tozer, in *The Pursuit of God*

WHEN WE QUESTION GOD'S LOVE

He who did not spare his own Son but gave him up for us all, how will he not also with him graciously give us all things?
(ROMANS 8:32, ESV)

When we begin questioning the love of God, we need to remember who we are. We have absolutely no claim on His love. We don't deserve one bit of God's goodness to us. I once heard a speaker say, "Anything this side of hell is pure grace." Nothing cuts quicker the nerve of a petulant "Why did this happen to me?" attitude as a realization of who we are before God, considered in ourselves apart from Christ.

God loved us when we were totally unworthy, when there was nothing whatsoever within us that would call forth His love. Any time we're tempted to doubt God's love for us, we should go back to the Cross and reason in this fashion: *If God loved me enough to give His Son to die for me when I was His enemy, surely He loves me enough to care for me now that I am His child. Having loved me to the ultimate extent at the Cross, He cannot possibly fail to love me in my times of adversity. Having given such a priceless gift as His Son, surely He will also give all else that is consistent with His glory and my good.*

If we're to trust God in adversity, we must not allow our emotions to hold sway over our minds. Rather, we must use those times to reason through the great truths of God's sovereignty, wisdom, and love as they're revealed in Scripture. Our emotions must become subservient to God's truth.

This doesn't mean we do not feel the pain of adversity and heartache. We feel it keenly. Nor does it mean we should seek to bury our emotional pain in a stoic-like attitude. We are meant to feel the pain of adversity, but we must resist allowing that pain to cause us to lapse into hard thoughts about God.

JERRY BRIDGES, IN *TRUSTING GOD*

Trust That He Is Working

God . . . works in you, both to will and to work for his good pleasure.

(Philippians 2:13, esv)

When you first begin waiting on God, it is with frequent intermission and failure. But do believe God is watching over you in love and secretly strengthening you in it. There are times when waiting appears like just losing time, but it is not so. Waiting, even in darkness, is unconscious advance, because it is God you have to do with, and He is working in you. God, who calls you to wait on Him, sees your feeble efforts and works it in you.

Your spiritual life is in no respect your own work. It is God's Spirit who has begun the work in you of waiting upon God. He will enable you to wait continually. Waiting continually will be met and rewarded by God Himself working continually. God must, God will work continually. But our experience of His working is hindered by our unbelief. He, who by His Spirit teaches you to wait continually, will bring you also to experience how, as the Everlasting One, His work is never ceasing. In the love and the life and the work of God, there can be no break, no interruption.

Do not limit God in this by your thoughts of what may be expected. Fix your eyes upon this one truth: in His very nature, God, as the only Giver of life, cannot do anything other than work in His child every moment.

Place God first and say, "God works continually; every moment I may wait on Him continually." Take time, until your being is filled with the vision of your God working continually, without one moment's intermission. Your waiting continually will then come of itself. Full of trust and joy, the holy habit of the soul will be: "On thee do I wait all the day" (Psalm 25:5, kjv). The Holy Spirit will keep you ever waiting.

Andrew Murray, in *Waiting on God*

FAITH PRACTICALLY, NOT THEORETICALLY

These are written so that you may believe that Jesus is the Christ, the Son of God, and that by believing you may have life in his name.
(JOHN 20:31, ESV)

If faith is so vitally important, if it is an indispensable *must* in our pursuit of God, it is perfectly natural that we should be deeply concerned over whether or not we possess this most precious gift. And our minds being what they are, it is inevitable that sooner or later we should get around to inquiring after the nature of faith. "What *is* faith?" would lie close to the question "Do I *have* faith?" and would demand an answer if it were anywhere to be found.

In the Scriptures there is practically no effort made to define faith. Outside of a brief fourteen-word definition in Hebrews 11:1, I know of no biblical definition, and even there faith is defined functionally, not philosophically; that is, it is a statement of what faith is *in operation*, not what it is in essence. It assumes the presence of faith and shows what it results in, rather than what it is.

We will be wise to go just that far and attempt to go no further. We are told from whence it comes and by what means: Faith "is the gift of God" (Ephesians 2:8, KJV); and "Faith cometh by hearing, and hearing by the word of God" (Romans 10:17, KJV). This much is clear, and, to paraphrase Thomas à Kempis, "I had rather exercise faith than know the definition thereof."

So let the words "faith is" or their equivalent be understood to refer to what faith is in operation as exercised by a believing man. Right here we drop the notion of definition and think about faith as it may be experienced in action.

The complexion of our thoughts will be practical, not theoretical.

A. W. TOZER, IN *THE PURSUIT OF GOD*

INTO HIS FATHERLY LOVE

God has sent the Spirit of his Son
into our hearts, crying, "Abba! Father!"
(GALATIANS 4:6, ESV)

By God's grace, having trusted Christ as our Savior, we who are believers have been brought into the very family of God. He has covenanted with us to be our God, and we to be His people (see Hebrews 8:10). Through Christ He has adopted us as His children and has sent His Holy Spirit to live within us and to testify with our spirit that we are His children. The Holy Spirit bears witness within us to this filial relationship we have with God when He causes us to cry in our hearts, "Abba, Father" (see Romans 8:15-16). It was said that in the Jewish household, slaves were not allowed to use the word "Abba" to address the head of the family. It was a word reserved for the children. Paul's use of that word is intended to convey to us how deeply the Spirit assures us that we are indeed children of the Most High God, now our heavenly Father.

God loves His children with a very special love, a fatherly love. He calls us His "chosen ones, holy and beloved" (Colossians 3:12, ESV). As incredible as it may seem, He promises to "take great delight in you" (Zephaniah 3:17, NIV). On this last verse, Matthew Henry observed, "The great God not only loves his saints, but he *loves* to love them." God takes great delight in loving us because we are His very own.

David speaks of God's fatherly love being "as high as the heavens are above the earth" (Psalm 103:11, ESV). Just as God's wisdom, like the height of the heavens, cannot be measured, so God's love for us cannot be measured. It is not only perfect in its effect, it is infinite in its extent. No calamity that may come upon us, however great it may be, can carry us beyond the pale of God's fatherly love for us.

JERRY BRIDGES, IN *TRUSTING GOD*

ONLY

For God alone, O my soul, wait in silence, for my hope is from him. He only is my rock and my salvation, my fortress.

(PSALM 62:5-6, ESV)

It is possible to be waiting continually on God, but not *only* upon Him. There may be other secret confidences intervening and preventing the blessing that was expected. Yes, "my soul, wait thou only upon God" (Psalm 62:5, KJV). There is but one God, but one source of life and happiness for the heart.

You desire to be good: "There is none good but . . . God" (Matthew 19:17, KJV), and there is no possible goodness but what is received directly from Him. You have sought to be holy: "There is none holy as the LORD" (1 Samuel 2:2, KJV), and there is no holiness but what He by His Spirit of holiness every moment breathes in you. You would gladly live and work for God and His kingdom, for men and their salvation. Hear Him say, "The everlasting God, the LORD, the Creator of the ends of the earth, fainteth not, neither is weary. . . . He giveth power to the faint; and to them that have no might he increaseth strength. . . . They that wait upon the LORD shall renew their strength" (Isaiah 40:28-29,31, KJV). He only is God; He only is your Rock: "my soul, wait thou only upon God."

You are an immortal spirit, created not for this world but for eternity and for God. Oh, my soul, realize your destiny! Know your privilege, and "wait thou only upon God." Let not the interest of spiritual thoughts and exercises deceive you; they very often take the place of waiting upon God. God is for you; you are for God. Wait only upon Him.

Beware of two great enemies: the world and self. Beware of allowing any earthly satisfaction or enjoyment, however innocent it appears, keep you back from saying, "I go . . . unto God my exceeding joy" (Psalm 43:4, KJV). Remember and study what Jesus said about denying self (see Matthew 16:24). Gerhard Tersteegen says: "The saints deny themselves in everything." Pleasing self in little things may be strengthening it to assert itself in greater things.

ANDREW MURRAY, IN *WAITING ON GOD*

THE GAZE OF THE SOUL

Looking to Jesus, the founder and perfecter of our faith.
(HEBREWS 12:2, ESV)

In a dramatic story in Numbers, faith is seen in action. Israel became discouraged and spoke against God, and the Lord sent fiery serpents among them. "And they bit the people; and much people of Israel died." Moses sought the Lord for them; He heard, and gave them a remedy against the bite of the serpents. He commanded Moses to make a serpent of brass and put it upon a pole in sight of all the people, "that every one that is bitten, when he looketh upon it, shall live." Moses obeyed, "and it came to pass, that if a serpent had bitten any man, when he beheld the serpent of brass, he lived" (Numbers 21:6-9, KJV).

In the New Testament this important bit of history is interpreted for us by no less an authority than our Lord Jesus Christ Himself. He is explaining to His hearers how they may be saved. He tells them that it is by believing. To make it clear, He refers to this incident in the Book of Numbers: "As Moses lifted up the serpent in the wilderness, even so must the Son of man be lifted up: that whosoever believeth in him should not perish, but have eternal life" (John 3:14-15, KJV). Notice here that "look" and "believe" are synonymous terms. "Looking" on the Old Testament serpent is identical with "believing" on the New Testament Christ. The *looking* and the *believing* are the same thing; while Israel looked with their external eyes, believing is done with the heart. *Faith is the gaze of a soul upon a saving God.*

The whole tenor of the inspired Word regarding faith is summed up for us in the Hebrew epistle when we are instructed to run life's race "looking unto Jesus the author and finisher of our faith" (Hebrews 12:2, KJV). Faith is not a once-done act, but a continuous gaze of the heart at the Triune God.

A. W. TOZER, IN *THE PURSUIT OF GOD*

Grasping God's Love in Christ

He chose us in him before the foundation of the world. . . .
In love he predestined us for adoption as sons through Jesus Christ.
(Ephesians 1:4-5, esv)

It's very important that we grasp the crucial concept that God's love to us is *in Christ*. God's infinite, measureless love is poured out upon us not because of who or what we are, but because we are in Christ Jesus.

In Romans 8:38-39, Paul declares that *nothing* "will be able to separate us from *the love of God in Christ Jesus our Lord*" (esv, emphasis added). God's love flows to us entirely through, or in, Jesus Christ. Paul frequently uses the term *in Christ* to refer to our spiritually organic union with Jesus Christ. Jesus speaks of this same union in His metaphor of the vine and its branches in John 15. Just as the branches are organically related to the vine in a life-giving union, so believers, in a spiritual sense, are organically united to Christ.

Just as God's love to His Son cannot change, so His love to us cannot change because we are in union with the One He loves. God's love to us can no more waver than His love to His Son can waver.

We're constantly tempted to look within ourselves to seek to find some reason God should love us. Such searching is, of course, usually discouraging. We instead find reasons God should not love us. But the Bible is clear that God doesn't look within us for a reason to love us. Rather, as He looks at us, He sees us united to His beloved Son, clothed in His righteousness. He loves us, not because we are lovely in ourselves, but because we are in Christ.

Here then is another weapon of truth we should store up in our hearts to use against our doubts and the temptation to question God's love for us. God's love to us cannot fail any more than His love to Christ can fail.

Jerry Bridges, in *Trusting God*

Heroism or Holiness?

He chose us in him before the foundation of the world,
that we should be holy and blameless before him.
(Ephesians 1:4, esv)

Heroism is an extraordinary feat of the flesh; holiness is an ordinary act of the Spirit. One may bring personal glory; the other *always* gives God the glory.

The sure standard for holiness is Scripture. There God makes clear what He means by holy living or, as theologians call it, the process of sanctification.

The Ten Commandments, from which all other commandments flow, are the beginning; they apply today as much as they did when God engraved them on tablets of stone for Moses. Next, the life of Jesus provides holiness in the flesh; in His persevering self-denial, His unqualified obedience of the Father's will, and the fullness of the Holy Spirit in His daily life, Jesus remains our example. Then Paul and the other apostles give explicit guidelines in the remainder of the New Testament.

The quest for holiness, then, should begin with a search of the Scriptures. We next begin applying what we find, seeking His will for our lives. As the nineteenth-century Scottish theologian John Brown put it: "*Holiness* does not consist in mystic speculations, enthusiastic fervors, or uncommanded austerities; it *consists in thinking as God thinks and willing as God wills.*"[26]

That thinking and willing is a process requiring discipline and perseverance, and is a joint effort: God's and ours. On the one hand, the Holy Spirit convicts of sin and sanctifies. But that doesn't mean that we can sit back, relax, and leave the driving to God. God expects — demands — that we do our part. As Mother Teresa says, "Our progress in holiness depends on God and ourselves — on God's grace and on our will to be holy."[27]

Charles Colson, in *Loving God*

Your Only Expectation

"Therefore wait for me," declares the Lord.
(Zephaniah 3:8, esv)

"My soul, wait thou *only* upon God" (Psalm 62:5, kjv, emphasis added). Let Him be all your salvation and all your desire. Say continually and with an undivided heart, "He only is my rock . . . I shall not be greatly moved" (Psalm 62:2, kjv). Whatever your spiritual or temporal needs are, whatever the desire or prayer of your heart, whatever your interest in connection with God's work in the church or the world—in solitude or in the rush of the world, in public worship or other gatherings of the saints, wait thou only upon God. Let your expectations be from Him alone.

If you are ever inclined to think this waiting *only* upon God is too hard or too high, remember the two foundation truths on which this blessed waiting rests: your absolute helplessness and the absolute sufficiency of your God. Enter deeply into the entire sinfulness of all that is of self, and do not think of letting self have anything to say one single moment! Enter deeply into your utter and unceasing inability to ever change what is evil in you, or to bring forth anything that is spiritually good. Enter deeply into your relationship of dependence on God, to receive from Him every moment what He gives. Enter deeper still into His covenant of redemption, with His promise to restore more gloriously than ever what you have lost. And, by His Son and Spirit, He will unceasingly give you His actual divine presence and power.

And thus, wait upon your God—*continually* and *only.* No words can tell, no heart can conceive, the riches of the glory of this mystery of the Father and of Christ. Our God, in the infinite tenderness and omnipotence of His love, waits to be our life and joy.

Oh, my soul, let all that is in me rise and sing, "Truly my soul waiteth upon God" (Psalm 62:1, kjv). "On thee do I wait all the day" (Psalm 25:5, kjv).

Andrew Murray, in *Waiting on God*

GREAT BOLDNESS FOR GOD

We had boldness in our God to declare to you the gospel of God in the midst of much conflict.
(1 THESSALONIANS 2:2, ESV)

Those who know God show great boldness for God.

Daniel and his friends were men who stuck their necks out. This was not foolhardiness. They knew what they were doing. They had counted the cost. They had measured the risk. They were well aware what the outcome of their actions would be unless God miraculously intervened, as in fact He did. But these things did not move them.

Once they were convinced that their stand was *right,* and that loyalty to their God required them to take it, then, in Oswald Chambers's phrase, they "smilingly washed their hands of the consequences."

"We must obey God rather than men," said the apostles (Acts 5:29, ESV). "I do not account my life of any value nor as precious to myself, if only I may finish my course and the ministry that I received from the Lord," said Paul (Acts 20:24, ESV). This was precisely the spirit of Daniel, Shadrach, Meshach, and Abednego. It is the spirit of all who know God.

They may find the determination of the right course to take agonizingly difficult, but once they are clear on it they embrace it boldly and without hesitation. It does not worry them that others of God's people see the matter differently and do not stand with them. (Were Shadrach, Meshach, and Abednego the only Jews who declined to worship Nebuchadnezzar's image? Nothing in their recorded words suggests that they either knew, or, in the final analysis, cared. They were clear as to what they personally had to do, and that was enough for them.)

By this test also we may measure our own knowledge of God.

J. I. PACKER, IN *KNOWING GOD*

THE OVERFLOW OF JOY IN GOD

In a severe test of affliction, their abundance of joy and their extreme poverty have overflowed in a wealth of generosity on their part.

(2 CORINTHIANS 8:2, ESV)

Love is the overflow of joy in God that gladly meets the needs of others.

In 2 Corinthians 8:1-8, Paul does not set up the Macedonians as a model of love just because they sacrificed in order to meet the needs of others. What he stresses is how they *loved* doing this (remember Micah 6:8!). It was the overflow of *joy!* They begged earnestly to give (see 2 Corinthians 8:4). They found their pleasure in channeling the grace of God through their poverty to the poverty in Jerusalem. It is simply astonishing!

This is why a person can give his body to be burned and not have love (see 1 Corinthians 13:3). Love is the overflow of joy — *in God!* It is not duty for duty's sake or right for right's sake. It is not a resolute abandoning of one's own good with a view solely to the good of the other person. It is first a deeply satisfying experience of the fullness of God's grace, and then a doubly satisfying experience of sharing that grace with another person.

When poverty-stricken Macedonians beg Paul for the privilege of giving money to other poor saints, we may assume that this is not just what they ought to do or have to do, but what they really long to do. It is their joy — an extension of their joy in God. To be sure, they are denying themselves whatever pleasures or comforts they could have from the money they give away, but the joy of extending God's grace to others is a far better reward than anything money could buy. The Macedonians have discovered the labor of Christian Hedonism: love! It is the overflow of joy in God that gladly meets the needs of others.

JOHN PIPER, IN *DESIRING GOD*

Seeing Everything

Behold, the Lamb of God, who takes away the sin of the world!
(John 1:29, ESV)

Believing is directing the heart's attention to Jesus. It is lifting the mind to "behold the Lamb of God," and never ceasing that beholding for the rest of our lives. At first this may be difficult, but it becomes easier as we look steadily at His wondrous Person, quietly and without strain. Distractions may hinder, but once the heart is committed to Him, after each brief excursion away from Him the attention will return again and rest upon Him like a wandering bird coming back to its window.

I would emphasize this one committal, this one great volitional act which establishes the heart's intention to gaze forever upon Jesus. God takes this intention for our choice and makes what allowances He must for the thousand distractions which beset us in this evil world. He knows that we have set the direction of our hearts toward Jesus, and we can know it too, and comfort ourselves with the knowledge that a habit of soul is forming which will become after a while a sort of spiritual reflex requiring no more conscious effort on our part.

Faith is the least self-regarding of the virtues. It is by its very nature scarcely conscious of its own existence. Like the eye which sees everything in front of it and never sees itself, faith is occupied with the Object upon which it rests and pays no attention to itself at all. While we are looking at God we do not see ourselves—blessed riddance. The man who has struggled to purify himself and has had nothing but repeated failures will experience real relief when he stops tinkering with his soul and looks away to the perfect One. While he looks at Christ the very things he has so long been trying to do will be getting done within him. It will be God working in him to will and to do.

A. W. Tozer, in *The Pursuit of God*

Praying in the Spirit

The Spirit himself intercedes for us with groanings too deep for words. And . . . the Spirit intercedes for the saints according to the will of God.

(Romans 8:26-27, esv)

Praying and reading your Bible are inextricably connected. The Spirit of God often uses the Word of God when you pray. When I pray about something, Scripture often comes to mind, and I immediately open my Bible to the passage I believe the Spirit of God brought to my attention. I see this as God guiding me by His Word. As I pray about a particular matter, the Spirit of God takes the Word of God and applies it to my heart and mind to reveal the truth of the situation for which I am praying.

God's Word tells us that we have a divine intercessor — the Holy Spirit (see Romans 8:26-27). The Spirit has an advantage over us — He already knows God's will — and when He intercedes for us, He is in absolute agreement with God's will and helps us know the will of God as we pray.

The Holy Spirit "will not speak on His own, but He will speak whatever He hears. He will also declare to you what is to come" (John 16:13, hcsb). When you pray, anticipate that the Holy Spirit already knows what God has prepared for you. The Spirit does not guide you on His own initiative; He tells you what He hears from the Father and guides you to pray for what He knows the Father wants to do in your life.

When I review what I've journaled that God is saying to me when I pray and read His Word, I begin to see what God is telling me about Himself, His purposes, and His ways. I often see a pattern develop. As I watch the direction the Spirit is leading me to pray, I get an indication of what God is saying to me.

When the Holy Spirit reveals a truth to you in prayer, He is present and actively working in your life. This kind of prayer is a divine encounter.

Henry Blackaby and Richard Blackaby, in *Experiencing God*

NEVER FAILING, DAY BY DAY

Steadfast love surrounds the one who trusts in the LORD.
(PSALM 32:10, ESV)

God's love cannot fail. It is steadfast, constant and fixed. In all the adversities we go through, God's love is unfailing. As He says to us in Isaiah 54:10, "The mountains may depart and the hills be removed, but my steadfast love shall not depart from you, and my covenant of peace shall not be removed" (ESV).

Because His love cannot fail, He will allow into our lives only the pain and heartache that is for our ultimate good. Even the grief that He Himself brings into our lives is tempered with His compassion. "Though he cause grief, he will have compassion according to the abundance of his steadfast love" (Lamentations 3:32, ESV). Even the fires of affliction will be tempered by His compassion, which arises out of His unfailing love.

God brought grief into Paul's life for his good, but he also showed compassion and said to him, "My grace is sufficient for you" (2 Corinthians 12:9, ESV). He provided Paul with the divine resources to meet the trials.

I think of a physician whose son was born with an incurable birth defect, leaving him crippled for life. I asked the father how he felt when he, who had dedicated his life to treating the illnesses of other people, was confronted with an incurable condition in his own son. He told me his biggest problem was his tendency to capsule the next twenty years of his son's life into that initial moment when he learned of his son's condition. Viewed that way, the adversity was overwhelming. God does not give twenty years of grace today. Rather, He gives it day by day. As the song says, "Day by day, and with each passing moment, strength I find to meet my trials here."[28]

JERRY BRIDGES, IN *TRUSTING GOD*

God Never Fully Explains

God . . . does great things that we cannot comprehend.

(Job 37:5, esv)

Usually when we're being trained by someone in a skill, such as in athletics or music, our teacher or coach will explain the purpose of the particular drills he puts us through. Though these drills may at times be tedious and even painful, we can endure them because we know their purpose and the intended end result.

But God never explains to us all that He's doing, or why. There's no indication that God ever explained to Job the reasons for all of his terrible sufferings. As readers, we're taken behind the scenes to observe the spiritual warfare between God and Satan, but as far as we can tell from Scripture, God never told Job about that.

The fact is, God hasn't really told us, even in Scripture, why He allowed Satan to so afflict Job as he did. On the basis of the truth of Romans 8:28 (which was just as valid for Job as it is for us), we must conclude that God had a much higher purpose in allowing Satan's onslaughts against Job than merely using Job as a pawn in a "wager" between Himself and Satan. Satan's part in the drama seems to slip into oblivion; he's never again mentioned after his two challenges of God in Job 1–2. The story doesn't conclude with a conversation with Satan in which God claims "victory" over him.

Rather, the story concludes with a conversation between God and Job in which Job acknowledges that through his trials he has come into a new and deeper relationship with God. "I had heard of you by the hearing of the ear," Job says, "but now my eye sees you" (42:5, esv). We may conclude that this deeper relationship was one (but probably not all) of the results God had in mind all along.

Sometimes afterward we can see some of the beneficial results of adversity in our lives, but we seldom can see it during the time of the adversity.

Jerry Bridges, in *Trusting God*

Lovingly Enfolded

The word is near you, in your mouth and in your heart (that is, the word of faith that we proclaim).
(Romans 10:8, esv)

Faith is not in itself a meritorious act; the merit is in the One toward Whom it is directed. Faith is a redirecting of our sight, a getting out of the focus of our own vision and getting God into focus.

Sin has twisted our vision inward and made it self-regarding. Unbelief has put self where God should be, and is perilously close to the sin of Lucifer, who said he would set his throne above the throne of God. Faith looks *out* instead of *in* and the whole life falls into line.

All this may seem too simple. But we have no apology to make. To those who would seek to climb into heaven after help or descend into hell God says, "The word is nigh thee, even in . . . the word of faith" (Romans 10:8, kjv). The word induces us to lift up our eyes unto the Lord, and the blessed work of faith begins.

When we lift our inward eyes to gaze upon God we are sure to meet friendly eyes gazing back at us, for it is written that the eyes of the Lord run to and fro throughout all the earth. The sweet language of experience is "Thou God seest me" (Genesis 16:13, kjv). When the eyes of the soul looking out meet the eyes of God looking in, heaven has begun right here on this earth.

"When all my endeavor is turned toward Thee because all Thy endeavor is turned toward me; when I look unto Thee alone with all my attention, nor ever turn aside the eyes of my mind, because Thou dost enfold me with Thy constant regard; when I direct my love toward Thee alone because Thou, who are Love's self hast turned Thee toward me alone. And what, Lord, is my life, save that embrace wherein Thy delightsome sweetness doth so lovingly enfold me?" So wrote Nicholas of Cusa four hundred years ago.[29]

A. W. Tozer, in *The Pursuit of God*

WITH US

Fear not, for I am with you . . . I will strengthen you,
I will help you, I will uphold you.
(ISAIAH 41:10, ESV)

God is *with us* in our troubles. He does not merely send grace from heaven to meet our trials. He Himself comes to help us. "Fear not," He says to us; "I am the one who helps you" (Isaiah 41:14, ESV). He promises, "When you pass through the waters, *I will be with you*; and through the rivers, they shall not overwhelm you; when you walk through fire you shall not be burned, and the flame shall not consume you" (43:2, ESV, emphasis added). He will not spare us from the waters of sorrow and the fires of adversity; but He will go through them with us, regardless of their nature or cause.

It's often in the very midst of our adversities that we experience the most delightful manifestations of His love. "For as we share abundantly in Christ's sufferings, so through Christ we share abundantly in comfort too" (2 Corinthians 1:5, ESV).

Christ identifies with us in our distresses. When He confronted Saul on the road to Damascus, He said, "Saul, Saul, why are you persecuting me?" And in answer to Saul's question, "Who are you, Lord?" He replied, "I am Jesus, whom you are persecuting" (Acts 9:4-5, ESV). Because His people were in union with Him, to persecute them was to persecute Him. This truth is no different today. You're in union with Christ, just as surely as the disciples were in the time of the book of Acts. And because of this union, Christ shares your adversities.

In whatever way we view our adversities, we find God's grace is sufficient, His love adequate. God's unfailing love for us is an objective fact affirmed over and over in the Scriptures. It is true whether we believe it or not. Our doubts do not destroy God's love, nor does our faith create it. It originates in the very nature of God, who is love, and it flows to us through our union with His beloved Son.

JERRY BRIDGES, IN *TRUSTING GOD*

FAITH IS EASY

So that the promise by faith in Jesus Christ might be given to those who believe.
(GALATIANS 3:22, ESV)

If faith is the gaze of the heart at God, and if this gaze is but the raising of the inward eyes to meet the all-seeing eyes of God, it follows that it is one of the easiest things possible to do. It would be like God to make the most vital thing easy and place it within the range of possibility for the weakest and poorest of us.

Because believing is looking, it can be done without special equipment or religious paraphernalia. God has seen to it that the one life-and-death essential can never be subject to the caprice of accident. Equipment can break down or get lost, water can leak away, records can be destroyed by fire, the minister can be delayed or the church burn down. All these are external to the soul and subject to accident or mechanical failure: but *looking* is of the heart and can be done successfully by any man standing up or kneeling down or lying in his last agony a thousand miles from any church.

Because believing is looking it can be done any time. No season is superior to another for this sweetest of all acts. A man is not nearer to Christ on Easter Sunday than he is, say, on Saturday, August 3, or Monday, October 4. As long as Christ sits on the mediatorial throne, every day is a good day and all days are days of salvation.

Neither does place matter in this blessed work of believing God. Lift your heart and let it rest upon Jesus and you are instantly in a sanctuary, though it be a Pullman berth or a factory or a kitchen. You can see God from anywhere if your mind is set to love and obey Him. This heart-gaze is, in fact, happily practiced every day by many, and is beyond the reach of none.

A. W. TOZER, IN *THE PURSUIT OF GOD*

LIKE A BEE WITH NECTAR

The eyes of those who see will not be closed,
and the ears of those who hear will give attention.
(ISAIAH 32:3, ESV)

When we come to the Scriptures as a part of our conscious strategy to cooperate with God for the full redemption of our life, *desire that His revealed will should be true for us.* Next, we should *begin with those parts of Scripture with which we have some familiarity.* You may think that this is not a big beginning. But keep in mind that your aim is not to become a scholar or to impress others with your knowledge of the Bible — a dreadful trap. That aim will only cultivate pride and lay a foundation for the petty, quarrelsome spirit so regrettably, yet so commonly, observed in those outwardly identified as the most serious students of the Scriptures.

Your aim must be only to nourish your soul on God's Word to you. Go first to those parts of the Bible you already know, therefore, and count on your later growth and study to lead you to other parts that will be useful.

Do not try to read a great deal at once. As Madame Guyon wisely counsels, "You must become as the bee who penetrates into the depths of the flower. You plunge deeply within to remove its deepest nectar."[30] It is better in one year to have ten good verses transferred *into the substance of our lives* than to have every word of the Bible flash before our eyes. Remember that "the letter kills, but the Spirit gives life" (2 Corinthians 3:6, ESV). We read to open ourselves to the Spirit.

Come to your chosen passages as to a place where you will have a holy meeting with God. Read a small part of the passage and dwell on it, praying for the assistance of God's Spirit in bringing *fully* before your mind and into your life the realities expressed. Always ask, "What is my life like because this is true, and how shall I speak and act because of this?"

DALLAS WILLARD, IN *HEARING GOD*

When We Doubt

How long, O Lord? Will you hide yourself forever?
(Psalm 89:46, ESV)

We will almost always struggle with doubts about God's love during our times of adversity. If we never had to struggle, our faith would not grow. But we must engage in the struggle with our doubts; we must not let them overwhelm us. During seemingly intolerable times, we may feel like David, who said at a time of great distress: "How long, O Lord? Will you forget me forever? How long will you hide your face from me?" (Psalm 13:1, ESV).

David had his doubts; he struggled with them. In fact, in the next verse he continues his struggle as he asks, "How long must I take counsel in my soul and have sorrow in my heart all the day?" (verse 2, ESV). He felt God had, at least for a time, forgotten him. But by the enabling power of God, David won his struggle. He overcame his doubts. He could then say, "I have trusted in your steadfast love; my heart shall rejoice in your salvation. I will sing to the Lord, because he has dealt bountifully with me" (Psalm 13:5-6, ESV).

You and I, like David, must wrestle with our thoughts. With God's help we, too, can come to the place, even in the midst of our adversities, where we will be able to say, "I trust in Your unfailing love."

It is true that we are just as dependent upon the Holy Spirit to enable us to trust in God's love as we are dependent upon Him to enable us to obey His commands. But just as we are responsible to obey in confidence that He is at work in us, so we are responsible to trust Him in that same attitude of dependence and confidence. Many times in our distress we may have to do as one man did before Jesus when he "cried out and said, 'I believe; help my unbelief!'" (Mark 9:24, ESV).

Jerry Bridges, in *Trusting God*

Waiting and Working

From of old no one has heard or perceived by the ear, no eye has seen a God besides you, who acts for those who wait for him.

(Isaiah 64:4, esv)

Waiting on God has its value in this: it makes us strong in work for God. Our waiting on God secures the working of God for us and in us, out of which our work must spring. As waiting on God lies at the root of all true working for God, so working for God must be the fruit of all true waiting on Him. Our great need is to hold the two sides of the truth in perfect conjunction and harmony.

It is as we elevate working for God to its true place, as the highest exercise of spiritual privilege and power, that the absolute need and the divine blessing of waiting on God can be fully known.

But there are many who work for God yet know little of what it is to wait on Him. They do not know that *God's work can be done only in God's strength, by God Himself working in us.* They do not understand that it is only as in utter weakness we depend upon Him, His power can rest on us. And so they have no conception of a continual waiting on God as being one of the first and essential conditions of successful work. Christ's Church and the world are sufferers today — oh, so terribly! — not only because so many of its members are not working for God, but because so much working for God is done without waiting on God.

God will work for His Church that waits on Him. Let us pray that the Holy Spirit may show us how sacred and how urgent our calling is to work, how absolute our dependence is upon God's strength to work in us, how sure it is that those who wait on Him shall renew their strength, and how we shall find waiting on God and working for God to be indeed inseparably one.

Andrew Murray, in *Working for God*

Trusting God for Who You Are

Who has made man's mouth? Who makes him mute, or deaf, or seeing, or blind? Is it not I, the Lord?

(Exodus 4:11, ESV)

If we have physical or mental disabilities or impairments, it is because God in His wisdom and love created us that way. We may not understand why God chose to do that, but that is where our trusting Him has to begin.

This truth is admittedly difficult to accept, especially if you or a loved one is the object of such disability. But Jesus affirmed God's hand in disabilities. When the disciples asked Him why a certain man was born blind, He replied, "That the works of God might be displayed in him" (John 9:3, ESV).

That hardly seems fair, does it? Why should that man suffer blindness all those years merely to be available to display God's work on a certain day? Is God's glory worth a man's being born blind? And what about our own physical disabilities or inadequacies? Is God's glory worthy of those also? Are we willing to take our physical limitations, our learning disabilities, and even our appearance problems to God and say, "Father, You are worthy of this infirmity in my life. I believe You created me just the way I am because You love me and You want to glorify Yourself through me. *I will trust You for who I am.*"

This is the path to self-acceptance. And we must continually keep in mind that the God who created us the way we are is wise enough to know what's best for us, and loving enough to bring it about. Certainly we'll sometimes struggle with who we are. Our disabilities and infirmities are always with us, so we have to learn to trust God in this area continually. We have to learn to say with David, "You formed my inward parts; you knitted me together in my mother's womb" (Psalm 139:13, ESV).

Jerry Bridges, in *Trusting God*

So That Others Glorify God

Let your light shine before others, so that they may see your good works and give glory to your Father who is in heaven.

(Matthew 5:16, ESV)

The aim of our good works is that God may be glorified. You remember how our Lord said to the Father: "I have glorified thee on the earth: I have finished the work which thou gavest me to do" (John 17:4, KJV). We read more than once of His miracles, that the people glorified God. It was because what He had wrought was manifestly by a Divine power. It is when our good works thus too are something more than the ordinary virtues of refined men, and bear the impress of God upon them, that men will glorify God. They must be the good works of which the Sermon on the Mount is the embodiment—a life of God's children doing more than others, seeking to be perfect as their Father in heaven is perfect. This glorifying of God by men may not mean conversion, but it is a preparation for it when an impression favorable to God has been made. The works prepare the way for the words, and are an evidence to the reality of the Divine truth that is taught, while without them the world is powerless.

The whole world was made for the glory of God. Christ came to redeem us from sin and bring us back to serve and glorify Him. Believers are placed in the world with this one object, that they may let their light shine in good works, so as to win men to God. As truly as the light of the sun is meant to lighten the world, the good works of God's children are meant to be the light of those who know and love not God. What need that we form a right conception of what good works are, as bearing the mark of something heavenly and divine, and having a power to compel the admission that God is in them.

Andrew Murray, in *Working for God*

Pleasure in Giving

Each one must give as he has decided in his heart, not reluctantly or under compulsion, for God loves a cheerful giver.

(2 Corinthians 9:7, esv)

In 2 Corinthians 9:6-7, Paul motivates the Corinthians to be generous. I take this passage to mean that God is not pleased when people act benevolently but don't do it gladly. When people don't find pleasure (Paul's word is *cheer*) in their acts of service, God doesn't find pleasure in them. He loves cheerful givers, cheerful servants. What sort of cheer? Surely the safest way to answer that question is to remember what sort of cheer moved the Macedonians to be generous. It was the overflow of joy in the grace of God. Therefore, the giver God loves is the one whose joy in Him overflows "cheerfully" in generosity to others.

If you try to abandon the pursuit of your full and lasting joy, you cannot love people or please God. If love is the overflow of joy in God that gladly meets the needs of others, then to abandon the pursuit of *this* joy is to abandon the pursuit of love. And if God is pleased by cheerful givers, then to abandon the pursuit of *this* cheerfulness sets you on a course in which God takes no delight. If we are indifferent to whether we do a good deed cheerfully, we are indifferent to what pleases God. For God loves a cheerful giver.

Therefore, it is essential that we be Christian Hedonists on the horizontal level in our relationships with other people, and not just on the vertical axis in our relationship with God.

If love is the overflow of joy in God that gladly meets the needs of other people, and if God loves such joyful givers, then this joy in giving is a Christian duty, and the effort not to pursue it is sin.

John Piper, in *Desiring God*

PERSONAL, BUT NOT PRIVATE

For building up the body of Christ, until we all attain . . . to mature manhood, to the measure of the stature of the fullness of Christ.

(EPHESIANS 4:12-13, ESV)

Many Christians today feel that their walk with God is private and independent. They see no need for joining a church or making themselves accountable to other believers. Some view the church in terms of how it can help them accomplish the ministry God has given them personally, rather than seeking how their lives fit into the larger work the Lord is doing in the congregation. The Bible teaches that our walk with God is personal, but it is not private. Sin makes people independent. Salvation makes us interdependent on one another. Scripture teaches that the church is a body in which each member is vitally important to the others.

While Christians have personal access to God through Christ as their one Mediator (see 1 Timothy 2:5), God created the church as His redemptive agent in the world. He is at work accomplishing His purposes, and He places every member in a church to accomplish His purpose through each congregation. Members are enabled and equipped by the Holy Spirit to function where the Father has placed them in the body. Then the body functions as Christ leads, until every member becomes spiritually mature.

What God is doing in and through the body is essential to my knowing how to respond to Him. Where I see Him working in the body, I make the necessary adjustments and put my life there too. In the church, I let God use me in any way He chooses to complete His work. This was Paul's goal when he said, "We proclaim Him, warning and teaching everyone with all wisdom, so that we may present everyone mature in Christ" (Colossians 1:28, HCSB). Paul constantly urged believers to become vitally involved with his life and ministry. The effectiveness of Paul's ministry rested on them (see Colossians 4:3; 2 Thessalonians 3:1-2; Ephesians 6:19).

HENRY BLACKABY AND RICHARD BLACKABY, IN *EXPERIENCING GOD*

Everything Planned

In your book were written, every one of them, the days that were formed for me, when as yet there was none of them.
(Psalm 139:16, esv)

In Psalm 139:16, what David seems to express is that all the experiences of his life, day by day, were written down in God's book before he was even born. For all of us, this truth refers not simply to God's prior knowledge of what will occur in our lives but to His plan for our lives.

God created each of us uniquely to fulfill the plan He has ordained for us. His plan for you and His creation of you were consistent. He equipped you to fulfill His purpose for you. God's plan embraces the family and social setting into which you were born. It also includes all the seemingly chance or random happenings in your life and all the sudden and unexpected turns of events, both "good" and "bad."

God's plan for us also embraces that which He wants us to *be* and to *do.* God sovereignly determines our respective functions in the body of Christ and gives us the corresponding spiritual gifts with which to perform those functions (see Romans 12:4-6; 1 Corinthians 12:7-11). Moreover, our spiritual gifts are generally consistent with the physical and mental abilities as well as the temperaments with which God created us.

God has planned our days before even one of them came to be. He said to Jeremiah, "*Before I formed you in the womb* I knew you, and *before you were born* I consecrated you" (Jeremiah 1:5, esv, emphasis added). Paul viewed his apostolic call in the same manner; he speaks of how God "set me apart before I was born, and . . . called me by his grace" (Galatians 1:15, esv).

Just as we must trust God for who we are, we must also trust Him for *what* we are — an engineer or a missionary, a homemaker or a nurse.

Jerry Bridges, in *Trusting God*

THE SOURCE OF OUR GOOD WORKS

Let your light shine before others, so that they may see your good works and give glory to your Father who is in heaven.

(MATTHEW 5:16, ESV)

Of Christ it is written: "In him was life; and the life was the light of men" (John 1:4, KJV). The Divine life gave out a Divine light.

Of His disciples, Christ said: "He that followeth me shall not walk in darkness, but shall have the *light of life*" (John 8:12, KJV, emphasis added).

Christ is our life and light. When it is said to us, "Let your light shine," the deepest meaning is, *Let Christ, who dwells in you, shine.* As you do your good works in the power of His life, your light shines out to all who see you. And because Christ in you is your light, your works — however humble and feeble they be — can carry with them a power of Divine conviction. The measure of the Divine power which works them in you will be the measure of the power working in those who see them.

Give way, O child of God, to the life and light of Christ dwelling in you, and men will see in your good works that for which they will glorify your Father which is in heaven.

As needful as that the sun shines every day — yea, more so — is it that every believer lets his light shine before men. For this we have been created anew in Christ, to hold forth the Word of Life, as lights in the world. Christ needs you urgently to let His light shine through you. Perishing men around you need your light, if they are to find their way to God. God needs you to let His glory be seen through you.

As wholly as a lamp is given up to lighting a room, every believer ought to give himself up to be the light of a dark world.

ANDREW MURRAY, IN *WORKING FOR GOD*

Week 40 / Tuesday

Nonconformity, for His Sake

What will it profit a man if he gains the whole world and forfeits his soul? Or what shall a man give in return for his soul?

(Matthew 16:26, esv)

The world places little value on the soul. A body in the hand is worth two souls in the bush, according to the *zeitgeist* of our generation. The world spirit invites us to play now and pay later, though the emphasis is on the now. This is the popular way to go.

For the Christian to resist the seduction of this world, he must risk going against the tide. He must be willing to risk the loss of pleasing men to gain pleasing God. Hence Jesus said, "Blessed are you when they revile and persecute you, and say all kinds of evil against you falsely for My sake. Rejoice and be exceedingly glad, for great is your reward in heaven, for so they persecuted the prophets who were before you" (Matthew 5:11-12, nkjv). The key words in this beatitude are "for My sake." The nonconformity we are called to is not simply nonconformity for nonconformity's sake. Anyone can call attention to himself by being a maverick. It is the "for My sake" that separates cheap nonconformity from the genuine article. There is no virtue in being "out of it" indiscriminately. Our nonconformity must be *selective.* It must be at the points that matter.

The apostle Paul said, "Do not be conformed to this world, but be transformed by the renewal of your mind" (Romans 12:2, esv). The call to transformation does not mean withdrawal from the world. We need no more monasteries. We neither surrender to the world nor flee from the world. We are to penetrate the world with a new and different spirit.

We should not flee this world. But, oh, how many Christians try to do so. And in doing so, they may actually be displeasing the God who wants the world to be redeemed, not escaped.

R. C. Sproul, in *Pleasing God*

The High Honor of Working for God

For it will be like a man going on a journey,
who called his servants and entrusted to them his property.
(Matthew 25:14, esv)

In the parable of the talents we have a most instructive summary of our Lord's teaching regarding the work He has given His servants to do.

He "called his own servants, and delivered unto them his goods," and went on his journey (Matthew 25:14, kjv, emphasis added). Our Lord went to heaven, leaving His work, with all His goods, to the care of His church. His goods were the riches of His grace, spiritual blessings in heavenly places, His Word and Spirit, with all the power of His life on the throne of God—all these He gave in trust to His servants to be used in carrying out His work on earth. Here we have the true root-principle of Christian service: *Christ has made Himself dependent for the extension of His kingdom on the faithfulness of His people.*

"Unto one he gave five talents, to another two, and to another one; to [each] man according to his several ability" (Matthew 25:15, kjv, emphasis added). Though there was a difference in the measure, every one received a portion of the master's goods. It is in connection with the service we are to render to each other that we read of the grace given to each of us according to the measure of the gift of Christ (see Ephesians 4:7). This truth has almost been lost sight of: *Every believer, without exception, has been set apart to take an active part in the work of winning the world for Christ.* Christ was first a son, then a servant; every believer is first a child of God, then a servant. It is the highest honor of a son to be a servant, to have the father's work entrusted to him. The work of the Church will never be done right until *every believer feels that the one object of his being in the world* is to work for the kingdom. The first duty of the servants in the parable was to spend their life in caring for their master's interests.

Andrew Murray, in *Working for God*

GREAT CONTENTMENT IN GOD

Since we have been justified by faith, we have peace with God through our Lord Jesus Christ.
(ROMANS 5:1, ESV)

Those who know God have great contentment in God.

There is no peace like the peace of those whose minds are possessed with full assurance that they have known God, and God has known them, and that this relationship guarantees God's favor to them in life, through death, and on forever.

This is the peace whose substance he analyzes in full in Romans 8. "There is therefore now no condemnation for those who are in Christ Jesus. . . . The Spirit himself bears witness with our spirit that we are children of God, and if children, then heirs. . . . We know that for those who love God all things work together for good. . . . And those whom he justified he also glorified. . . . If God is for us, who can be against us? . . . Who shall bring any charge against God's elect? It is God who justifies. . . . Who shall separate us from the love of Christ? . . . For I am sure that neither death nor life . . . nor things present nor things to come . . . nor anything else in all creation, will be able to separate us from the love of God in Christ Jesus our Lord" (verses 1,16-17,28,30-31,33,35, 38-39, ESV).

This is the peace which Shadrach, Meshach, and Abednego knew; hence the calm contentment with which they stood their ground in the face of Nebuchadnezzar's ultimatum. Their reply is classic: "O Nebuchadnezzar, we have no need to answer you in this matter. [No panic!] If this be so, our God whom we serve is able to deliver us from the burning fiery furnace, and he will deliver us out of your hand, O king. [Courteous, but unanswerable—they knew their God!) But if not [if no deliverance comes], be it known to you, O king, that we will not serve your gods" (Daniel 3:16-18, ESV). Live or die, they are content.

The comprehensiveness of our contentment is another measure whereby we may judge whether we really know God.

J. I. PACKER, IN *KNOWING GOD*

NEW EYES, NEW UNITY

And I, when I am lifted up from the earth,
will draw all people to myself.
(JOHN 12:32, ESV)

Without giving much thought to what is going on within them, many constantly practice the habit of inwardly gazing upon God. They know that something inside their hearts sees God. Even when they are compelled to withdraw their conscious attention in order to engage in earthly affairs, there is within them a secret communion always going on. Let their attention but be released for a moment from necessary business, and it flies at once to God again.

I do not want to leave the impression that the ordinary means of grace have no value. They most assuredly have. Private prayer should be practiced by every Christian. Long periods of Bible meditation will purify our gaze and direct it; church attendance will enlarge our outlook and increase our love for others. Service and work and activity — all are good and should be engaged in by every Christian. But at the bottom of all these things, giving meaning to them, will be the inward habit of beholding God. A new set of eyes (so to speak) will develop within us enabling us to be looking at God while our outward eyes are seeing the scenes of this passing world.

Someone may fear that we are magnifying private religion out of all proportion, that the "us" of the New Testament is being displaced by a selfish "I." Has it ever occurred to you that one hundred pianos all tuned to the same fork are automatically tuned to each other? They are of one accord by being tuned, not to each other, but to another standard to which each one must individually bow. So one hundred worshippers met together, each one looking away to Christ, are in heart nearer to each other than they could possibly be were they to become "unity" conscious and turn their eyes away from God to strive for closer fellowship.

A. W. TOZER, IN *THE PURSUIT OF GOD*

God Takes the Initiative

He leads me beside still waters. . . . He leads me in paths of righteousness for his name's sake.
(Psalm 23:2-3, esv)

The realization that God has ordained our days for us leads logically to the thought, "Can I trust God to guide me in that plan? What if I make a mistake and miss the way?" In answering such questions, I find it helpful to distinguish between God's guidance and that which has come to be called by such terms as "finding the will of God." We think so much about our responsibility to discover God's will in a situation or to make wise decisions in life's choices, but the biblical emphasis seems to be on God's guiding us.

Consider the book of Acts. The only reference to the disciples seeking to determine the will of God occurs in the choosing of Matthias to succeed Judas. From that point onward, it is a record of God's guiding His people. In Acts 16, for example, Paul and his companions were moving ahead in their missionary journey in a logical progression. Twice, however, they were stopped by the Holy Spirit and then, as a result of Paul's vision, they concluded God was calling them to Macedonia. As they moved ahead, the Spirit guided them, stopping them in two places and calling them to another. The account doesn't tell us how the Spirit guided; it simply says that He did.

God did have a plan for Paul and his team that was more specific than the Great Commission to make disciples of all nations. The provinces of Asia and Bithynia that Paul was prevented from entering were just as needy as Macedonia. But it was God's plan that Paul should take the gospel to Macedonia and then to the entire Grecian peninsula. God did not leave it to Paul to seek His will. Rather, as Paul moved along, God took the initiative to guide him.

Jerry Bridges, in *Trusting God*

Trusting His Way

His way is in whirlwind and storm, and the clouds are the dust of his feet.

(Nahum 1:3, esv)

In the later chapters of Genesis, after Joseph had become prime minister of Egypt, he could surely see some of the results of the affliction God had allowed in his life—but he certainly could not see them while going through it. To him the whole painful process (as narrated in Genesis 37–40) must have seemed devoid of any meaning and very contrary to his expectations of the future, as given to him through his dreams.

But whether we see beneficial results in this life or not, we're still called upon to trust God that in His love He wills what is best for us and in His wisdom He knows how to bring it about.

I think of a dear friend who for more than thirty years has passed through one adversity after another—incredible physical problems in the family, numerous financial difficulties, and family heartaches. As far as I can tell, no apparent "good" has come out of any of these adversities. There has been no happy ending as in the case of Joseph. Yet, in a recent letter received from her, this friend said, "I know God makes no mistakes: 'As for God, His way is perfect.'"

So we should never demand that God explain or justify His actions or what He permits in our lives. Margaret Clarkson said, "We may not demand of a sovereign Creator that He explain Himself to His creatures. . . . God had good and sufficient reasons for His actions; we trust His sovereign wisdom and love."[31]

When I say we should never ask God why, I'm not talking about the reactive and spontaneous cry of anguish when calamity first befalls us or one we love. Rather, I'm speaking of the persistent and demanding why that has an accusatory tone toward God in it. The former is a natural human reaction; the latter is a sinful human reaction.

Jerry Bridges, in *Trusting God*

The Master's Reward for Our Work

Now after a long time the master of those servants came and settled accounts with them.
(Matthew 25:19, esv)

Christ keeps watch over the work He has left to be done on earth; His kingdom and glory depend upon it. He will not only hold reckoning when He comes again to judge, but comes unceasingly to inquire of His servants as to their welfare and work. He comes to approve and encourage, to correct and warn. By His word and Spirit He asks us to say whether we are using our talents diligently and living only and entirely for His work.

Some He finds laboring diligently, and to them He frequently says: "Enter into the joy of thy Lord." Others He sees discouraged, and them He inspires with new hope. Some He finds working in their own strength; these He reproves. Still others He finds sleeping or hiding their talent; to such His voice speaks in solemn warning: "From him that hath not shall be taken away even that he hath" (Matthew 25:29, kjv).

Christ's heart is in His work every day. He watches over it with the most intense interest; let us not disappoint Him nor deceive ourselves.

That the man of the one talent should have been the one to fail, and to be so severely punished, is a lesson of deep solemnity. It calls the church to beware lest, by neglecting to teach the feebler ones, she allow them to let their gifts lie unused.

In teaching the great truth that every branch is to bear fruit, special stress must be laid on the danger of thinking this can be expected only of the strong and advanced Christian. Care must be taken that the feeblest Christians receive special training, so that they, too, may joyfully have their share in the service of their Lord and all the blessedness it brings. If Christ's work is to be done, not one can be missed.

Andrew Murray, in *Working for God*

The Unchanging Center

I will arise and go to my father, and I will say to him, "Father, I have sinned against heaven and before you."

(Luke 15:18, esv)

The cause of all our human miseries is a radical moral dislocation, an upset in our relation to God and to each other. For whatever else the Fall may have been, it was most certainly a sharp change in man's relation to his Creator. He adopted toward God an altered attitude, and by so doing destroyed the proper Creator-creature relation in which, unknown to him, his true happiness lay. Essentially salvation is the restoration of a right relation between man and his Creator, a bringing back to normal of the Creator-creature relation.

A satisfactory spiritual life will begin with a complete change in relation between God and the sinner; not a judicial change merely, but a conscious and experienced change affecting the sinner's whole nature. The atonement in Jesus' blood makes such a change judicially possible, and the working of the Holy Spirit makes it emotionally satisfying.

The story of the prodigal son perfectly illustrates this latter phase. He had brought a world of trouble upon himself by forsaking the position which he had properly held as son of his father. At bottom his restoration was nothing more than a reestablishing of the father-son relation which had existed from his birth and had been altered temporarily by his act of sinful rebellion. This story overlooks the legal aspects of redemption, but it makes beautifully clear the experiential aspects of salvation.

In determining relationships, there must be somewhere a fixed center against which everything else is measured. Such a center is God. When God would make His Name known to mankind He could find no better word than "I am." When He speaks in the first person He says, "I am"; when we speak of Him we say "He is"; when we speak to Him we say, "Thou art." Everyone and everything else measures from that fixed point. "I am that I am," says God; "I change not."

A. W. Tozer, in *The Pursuit of God*

Certain Guidance

I am the Lord your God . . .
who leads you in the way you should go.
(Isaiah 48:17, esv)

We do have a responsibility to make wise decisions or to discover the will of God, whichever term we may prefer to use. But God's plan for us is not contingent upon our decisions. God's plan is not contingent at all. God's plan is sovereign. It includes our foolish decisions as well as our wise ones.

God's means of guidance are infinite. As I look back over the decades of my Christian life, I am amazed at the many and diverse ways by which God has guided me. God is at work guiding all the details of my life.

Like most Christians, I've struggled over the right choice at some of those "fork in the road" decision points which we encounter from time to time. I may have made some wrong decisions; I don't know. But God in His sovereignty has faithfully guided me in His paths through right decisions and wrong ones. I'm where I am today not because I've always made wise decisions or correctly discovered the will of God at particular points along the way, but because God has faithfully led me and guided me along the path of His will for me.

God does guide. He does not play games with us. He does not look down from heaven at our struggles to know His will and say, "I hope you make the right decision." Rather, in His time and in His way He will lead us in His path for us.

We can trust God to guide us. He will lead us all the way. And when we stand before His throne we will not be singing about successfully discovering the will of God; rather we'll be rejoicing in how He led us all the way.

Jerry Bridges, in *Trusting God*

Life and Work

My food is to do the will of him who sent me and to accomplish his work.
(John 4:34, esv)

The highest manifestation of the Divine Being is in His work. In His work, Christ showed forth His own glory and that of the Father. It was because of the work He had done — and because in it He had glorified the Father — that He claimed to share the glory of the Father in heaven. The greater works He was *to do* in answer to the prayer of the disciples was that the Father might be glorified in the Son. Work is indeed the highest form of existence, the highest manifestation of the Divine glory in the Father and in His Son.

What is true of God is true of His creature. Life is movement, life is action, and life reveals itself in what it accomplishes. The bodily life, the intellectual, the moral, the spiritual life — individual, social, national life — each of these is judged of by its work. The character and quality of the work depends on the life: as the life, so the work. And, on the other hand the life depends on the work; without this there can be no full development and manifestation and perfecting of the life: as the work, so the life.

This is especially true of the spiritual life — the life of the Spirit in us. There may be a great deal of religious work with its external activities, the outcome of human will and effort, with but little true worth and power, because the Divine life is feeble. When the believer does not know that Christ is living in him, does not know the Spirit and power of God working in him, there may be much earnestness and diligence, with little that lasts for eternity. There may, on the contrary, be much external weakness and apparent failure, and yet results that prove that the life is indeed of God.

The work depends upon the life. And the life depends on the work for its growth and perfection.

Andrew Murray, in *Working for God*

Feeling and Sharing Grace's Power

Stephen, full of grace and power, was doing great wonders and signs among the people.
(Acts 6:8, esv)

We don't want to just *see* the grace of God in all its beauty, saving sinners and sanctifying saints. We want to share the power of that grace. We want to feel it saving. We want to feel it conquer temptation in *our* lives. We want to feel it using *us* to save others. But why? Because our joy in God is insatiably greedy. The more we have, the more we want. The more we see, the more we want to see. The more we feel, the more we want to feel.

This means that the holy greed for joy in God that wants to see and feel more and more manifestations of His glory will push a person into love. My desire to feel the power of God's grace conquering the pride and selfishness in my life inclines me to behavior that demonstrates the victory of grace, namely, love. Genuine love is so contrary to human nature that its presence bears witness to an extraordinary power. The Christian Hedonist pursues love because he is addicted to the experience of that power. He wants to feel more and more of the grace of God reigning in his life.

Virtually all people outside Christ are possessed by the desire to find happiness by overcoming some limitation in their lives and having the sensation of power. The all-important difference between the non-Christian and the Christian Hedonist in this pursuit of joy is that the Christian Hedonist has discovered that self-confidence will never satisfy the longing of his heart to overcome finitude. He has learned that what we are really made for is not the thrill of feeling our own power increase, but the thrill of feeling God's power increase, conquering the precipices of un-love in our sinful hearts.

The joy of experiencing the power of God's grace defeating selfishness is an insatiable addiction.

John Piper, in *Desiring God*

WORTHY OF ALL OUR HONOR

Worthy are you, our Lord and God, to receive glory and honor and power, for you created all things, and by your will they existed and were created.

(REVELATION 4:11, ESV)

As the sailor locates his position on the sea by "shooting" the sun, so we may get our moral bearings by looking at God. We must begin with God. We are right when and only when we stand in a right position relative to God, and we are wrong so far and so long as we stand in any other position.

Much of our difficulty as seeking Christians stems from our unwillingness to take God as He is and adjust our lives accordingly. We insist upon trying to modify Him and to bring Him nearer to our own image. The flesh whimpers against the rigor of God's inexorable sentence and begs like Agag for a little mercy, a little indulgence of its carnal ways. It is no use.

We can get a right start only by accepting God as He is and learning to love Him for what He is. As we go on to know Him better we shall find it a source of unspeakable joy that God is just what He is. Some of the most rapturous moments we know will be those we spend in reverent admiration of the Godhead. In those holy moments the very thought of change in Him will be too painful to endure.

So let us begin with God.

As the self-existent One, He gave being to all things, and all things exist out of and for Him. Every soul belongs to God and exists by His pleasure.

God being who and what He is, and we being who and what we are, the only thinkable relation between us is one of full lordship on His part and complete submission on ours. We owe Him every honor that it is in our power to give Him. Our everlasting grief lies in giving Him anything less.

A. W. TOZER, IN *THE PURSUIT OF GOD*

The Crisis of Belief

With man it is impossible, but not with God.
For all things are possible with God.
(Mark 10:27, esv)

We face the same crisis of belief the people in the Bible experienced. Anytime God leads you to do something that has God-sized dimensions, you'll face a crisis of belief. What you do next reveals what you really believe about God.

When God invites you to join Him in His work, He presents a God-sized assignment He wants to accomplish. It will be obvious you can't do it on your own. If God doesn't help, you will fail. This is the crisis point at which many people decide not to follow what they sense God is leading them to do. Then they wonder why they do not experience God's presence, power, and activity the way some Christians do.

The word *crisis* comes from a Greek word that means "decision." The same word is often translated "judgment." We aren't talking about a calamity in your life such as an accident or death. This crisis is not a disaster or a bad thing. *It is a turning point or a fork in the road that calls for a decision. You must decide what you believe about God.* How you respond when you reach this turning point will determine whether or not you proceed with God in something only He can do or whether you can continue on your own way and miss what God has purposed for your life. This is not a one-time experience. How you live your life daily is a testimony of what you believe about God.

We forget that when God speaks, He always reveals what *He* is going to do—not what He wants us to do for Him. We join Him so He works through us. We are not called upon to accomplish the task by our ingenuity, ability, or limited resources. With faith, we can proceed confidently because we know He is going to bring to pass what He purposes.

Henry Blackaby and Richard Blackaby, in *Experiencing God*

GOOD REASON TO REJOICE

Count it all joy, my brothers, when you meet trials of various kinds.

(JAMES 1:2-4, ESV)

We can be sure that the development of a beautiful Christlike character will not occur in our lives without adversity. Think of those lovely graces Paul calls the fruit of the Spirit in Galatians 5:22-23. The first four traits he mentions — love, joy, peace, and patience — can be developed only in the womb of adversity.

We may think we have true Christian love until someone offends us or treats us unjustly. Then we begin to see anger and resentment well up within us. We may conclude we have learned about genuine Christian joy until our lives are shattered by an unexpected calamity or grievous disappointment. Adversities spoil our peace and sorely try our patience. God uses those difficulties to reveal our need to grow so that we'll reach out to Him to change us more and more into the likeness of His Son.

Both Paul and James speak of rejoicing in our sufferings (see Romans 5:3-4; James 1:2-4). Most of us, if we're honest with ourselves, have difficulty with that idea. Endure them, perhaps, but rejoice? That often seems like an unreasonable expectation. We are not masochistic; we don't enjoy pain.

But Paul and James both say that we should rejoice in our trials because of their beneficial results. It's not the adversity considered in itself that is to be the ground of our joy. Rather, it is the expectation of the results, the development of our character, that should cause us to rejoice in adversity. God does not ask us to rejoice because we have lost our job or a loved one has been stricken with cancer or a child has been born with an incurable birth defect. But He does tell us to rejoice because we believe He's in control of those circumstances and is at work through them for our ultimate good.

JERRY BRIDGES, IN *TRUSTING GOD*

Life's Destiny

I glorified you on earth, having accomplished the work that you gave me to do.
(John 17:4, esv)

All life has a destiny; it cannot accomplish its purpose without work; life is perfected by work. The highest manifestation of its hidden nature and power comes out in its work. And so work is the great factor by which the hidden beauty and the Divine possibilities of the Christian life are brought out.

In the child of God, work must take the same place it has in God Himself. As in the Father and the Son, so with the Holy Spirit dwelling in us, work is the highest manifestation of life.

Work must be restored to its right place in God's scheme of the Christian life as in very deed the highest form of existence. To be the intelligent, willing channel of the power of God, to be capable of working the very work of God, to be animated by the Divine Spirit of love, and in that to be allowed to work life and blessing to men — it is this that gives nobility to life, because it is for this we are created in the image of God. As God never for a moment ceases to work His work of love and blessing in us and through us, so our working out what He works in us is our highest proof of being created anew in His likeness.

If God's purpose is to be carried out — with the perfection of the individual believer, and with the appointment of His Church as the body of Christ to carry on His work of winning back a rebellious world to His allegiance and love — working for God must have much greater prominence given to it as the true glory of our Christian calling. Every believer must be taught that, as work is the only perfect manifestation, and therefore the perfection of life in God and throughout the world, so our work is to be our highest glory.

Shall it be so in our lives?

Andrew Murray, in *Working for God*

WHO IS HIGHEST?

Be exalted, O God, above the heavens!
Let your glory be over all the earth!
(PSALM 57:5, ESV)

The pursuit of God will embrace the labor of bringing our total personality into conformity to His. And this not judicially, but actually. I do not here refer to the act of justification by faith in Christ. I speak of a voluntary exalting of God to His proper station over us and a willing surrender of our whole being to the place of worshipful submission which the Creator-creature circumstance makes proper.

The moment we make up our minds that we are going on with this determination to exalt God over all, we step out of the world's parade. We shall find ourselves out of adjustment to the ways of the world, and increasingly so as we make progress in the holy way. We shall acquire a new viewpoint; a new and different psychology will be formed within us; a new power will begin to surprise us by its upsurgings and its outgoings.

Our break with the world will be the direct outcome of our changed relation to God. For the world of fallen men does not honor God.

Millions call themselves by His Name, it is true, and pay some token respect to Him, but a simple test will show how little He is really honored among them. Let the average man be put to the proof on the question of who is *above*, and his true position will be exposed. Let him be forced into making a choice between God and money, between God and men, between God and personal ambition, God and self, God and human love, and God will take second place every time. Those other things will be exalted above. However the man may protest, the proof is in the choices he makes day after day throughout his life.

A. W. TOZER, IN *THE PURSUIT OF GOD*

A WORK THAT WILL BE COMPLETED

Blessed is the man whom you discipline, O LORD,
and whom you teach out of your law.
(PSALM 94:12, ESV)

Fortunately, God doesn't ask us how or when we want to grow. He's the Master Teacher, training His pupils when and how He deems best. He is, in the words of Jesus, the Gardener who prunes the branches of His vineyard. The healthy vine requires both nourishment and pruning. Through the Word of God we're nourished (see Psalm 1:2-3), but through adversity we're pruned. Both the Hebrew and Greek languages express *discipline* and *teaching* by the same word. God intends that we grow through the disciplines of adversity as well as through instruction from His Word.

One of the most encouraging passages in the Bible is Philippians 1:6: "I am sure of this, that he who began a good work in you will bring it to completion at the day of Jesus Christ" (ESV). He will not fail to finish the work He has begun in us. He's committed to "working in us that which is pleasing in his sight" (Hebrews 13:21, ESV). As Horatius Bonar wrote, "God's treatment must succeed. It cannot miscarry or be frustrated even in its most arduous efforts, even in reference to its minutest objects. It is the mighty power of God that is at work within us and upon us, and this is our consolation. . . . All is love, all is wisdom, and all is faithfulness, yet all is also power."[32]

That God cannot fail in His purpose for adversity in our lives, that He will accomplish that which He intends, is a great encouragement to me. Sometimes I do fail to respond to difficulties in a God-honoring way. But my failure does not mean God has failed. Even my painfully sharp awareness of failure may be used of God, for example, to help me grow in humility. And perhaps that was God's intention all along.

JERRY BRIDGES, IN *TRUSTING GOD*

ABIDING IN THE FATHER'S WORK

The Son can do nothing of his own accord,
but only what he sees the Father doing.
(JOHN 5:19, ESV)

Jesus Christ became man that He might show us what a true man is, how God meant to live and work in man, and how man may find his life and do his work in God.

Christ's work was the fruit, the earthly reflection of the heavenly Father working. And it was not as if Christ merely saw and copied what the Father willed or did: "The Father *that dwelleth in me,* he doeth the works" (John 14:10, KJV, emphasis added). Christ did all His work in the power of the Father dwelling and working in Him. So complete and real was His dependence on the Father that He used these strong expressions: "The Son can do *nothing* of himself, but what he seeth the Father do"; "I can of mine own self do *nothing*" (John 5:19,30, KJV, emphasis added). As literally as what He said is true of us, "Apart from me you can do nothing" (John 15:5, ESV), is it true of Him too: "The Father that dwelleth in me . . . doeth the works" (John 14:10, KJV).

Come and learn from our Lord Jesus the secret of true work for God. "My Father worketh . . . and I work" (John 5:17, KJV). Divine Fatherhood means that God is all, and gives all, and works all. Divine Sonship means continual dependence on the Father, and the reception, moment by moment, of all the strength needed for His Work.

Your one need is to wait for and to trust in His working, in deep humility and weakness. Learn from this that God can only work in us as He dwells in us. Cultivate the holy sense of God's continual nearness and presence, of your being His temple, and of His dwelling in you. Offer yourself for Him to work in you all His good pleasure. You will find that work, instead of being a hindrance, can become your greatest incentive to a life of fellowship and childlike dependence.

ANDREW MURRAY, IN *WORKING FOR GOD*

Free to Honor God

Be exalted, O God, above the heavens!
Let your glory be over all the earth!
(Psalm 108:5, esv)

"Be thou exalted" (kjv) is the language of victorious spiritual experience. It is a little key to unlock the door to great treasures of grace. It is central in the life of God in the soul. Let the seeking man reach a place where life and lips join to say continually, "Be thou exalted," and a thousand minor problems will be solved at once. His Christian life ceases to be the complicated thing it had been before and becomes the very essence of simplicity. By the exercise of his will he has set his course, and on that course he will stay as if guided by an automatic pilot. The hidden motions of the Spirit are working in his favor, and "the stars in their courses" fight for him. He has met his life problem at its center, and everything else must follow along.

Let no one imagine he will lose anything of human dignity by this voluntary sell-out of his all to his God. Rather, he finds his right place of high honor as one made in the image of his Creator. His deep disgrace lay in his moral derangement, his unnatural usurpation of the place of God. His honor will be proved by restoring again that stolen throne. In exalting God over all, he finds his own highest honor upheld.

Anyone who might feel reluctant to surrender his will to the will of another should remember Jesus' words, "Whosoever committeth sin is the servant of sin" (John 8:34, kjv). We must of necessity be servant to someone, either to God or to sin. The sinner prides himself on his independence, completely overlooking the fact that he is the weak slave of the sins that rule his members. The man who surrenders to Christ exchanges a cruel slave driver for a kind and gentle Master whose yoke is easy and whose burden is light.

A. W. Tozer, in *The Pursuit of God*

Submitting to His Training

Humble yourselves, therefore, under the mighty hand of God.
(1 Peter 5:6, ESV)

If any adversity coming across our path were not beneficial, God would not allow it or send it, "For he does not willingly afflict or grieve the children of men" (Lamentations 3:33, ESV). God does not delight in our sufferings. He brings only that which is necessary, but He does not shrink from that which will help us grow.

Because He's at work in our lives through adversity, we must learn to respond to what He's doing. His sovereign work never negates our responsibility. Just as God teaches us through adversity, we must seek to learn from it.

To learn from adversity and receive the beneficial effects God intends, we can first submit to it — not reluctantly, as the defeated warrior submits to his conqueror, but voluntarily, as the patient on the operating table submits to the skilled hand of the surgeon. Don't try to frustrate the gracious purpose of God by resisting His providence in your life. Rather, insofar as you're able to see what God is doing, make His purpose your purpose.

This doesn't mean we shouldn't use all legitimate means at our disposal to minimize adversity's effects. It means we should accept from God's hand the success or failure of those means as He wills, and at all times seek to learn whatever He might be teaching us.

Sometimes we'll perceive quite clearly what God is doing, and in those instances we should respond to God's teaching in humble obedience. At other times we may not be able to see at all what He's doing. At those times, we should respond in humble faith, trusting Him to work out in our lives that which we need to learn. Both attitudes are important, and God wants one at one time and the other at another time.

Jerry Bridges, in *Trusting God*

True Nobility

As the living Father sent me, and I live because of the Father, so whoever feeds on me, he also will live because of me.

(John 6:57, ESV)

Jesus Christ became man that He might show us what true man is — the true relation between man and God, the true way of serving God and doing His work. When we are made new creatures in Christ Jesus, the life we receive is the very life that was and is in Christ, and it is only by studying His life on earth that we know how we are to live. His dependence on the Father is the law of our dependence on Him and on the Father through Him.

Christ counted it no humiliation to be able to do nothing of Himself, to be always and absolutely dependent on the Father. He counted it His highest glory, because all His works were the works of the all-glorious God in Him.

When shall we understand that to wait on God — to bow before Him in perfect helplessness, and let Him work all in us — is our true nobility, and the secret of the highest activity? This alone is the true Son-life, the true life of every child of God. As this life is known and maintained, the power for work will grow, because the soul is in the attitude in which God can work in us, as the God who worketh for him that waiteth on Him (see Isaiah 64:4).

It is the ignorance or neglect of the great truths — that there can be no true work for God *but as God works it in us,* and that God cannot work in us fully *but as we live in absolute dependence on Him* — that is the explanation of the universal complaint of so much Christian activity with so little real result. The revival which many are longing and praying for must begin with this: the return of Christians to their true place before God — in Christ and like Christ, one of complete dependence and continual waiting on God to work in them.

Andrew Murray, in *Working for God*

HONORING GOD, HONORED BY GOD

If anyone serves me, the Father will honor him.
(JOHN 12:26, ESV)

There is a logic behind God's claim to preeminence. That place is His by every right in earth or heaven. While we take to ourselves the place that is His the whole course of our lives is out of joint. Nothing will or can restore order till our hearts make the great decision: God shall be exalted above.

"Them that honour me I will honour," said God once to a priest of Israel (1 Samuel 2:30, KJV), and that ancient law of the kingdom stands today unchanged by the passing of time or the changes of dispensation. The whole Bible and every page of history proclaim the perpetuation of that law.

Sometimes the best way to see a thing is to look at its opposite. Eli and his sons are placed in the priesthood with the stipulation that they honor God in their lives and ministrations. This they fail to do, and God sends Samuel to announce the consequences. Unknown to Eli this law of reciprocal honor has been all the while secretly working, and now the time has come for judgment to fall. Hophni and Phineas, the degenerate priests, fall in battle, the wife of Hophni dies in childbirth, Israel flees before her enemies, the ark of God is captured by the Philistines and the old man Eli falls backward and dies of a broken neck. Thus stark tragedy followed upon Eli's failure to honor God.

Set over against this almost any Bible character who honestly tried to glorify God in his earthly walk. See how God winked at weaknesses and overlooked failures as He poured upon His servants grace and blessing untold. Let it be Abraham, Jacob, David, Daniel, Elijah, or whom you will; honor followed honor as harvest the seed. The man of God set his heart to exalt God above all; God accepted his intention as fact and acted accordingly. Not perfection, but holy intention made the difference.

A. W. TOZER, IN *THE PURSUIT OF GOD*

God's Word in Our Adversities

For the commandment is a lamp and the teaching a light,
and the reproofs of discipline are the way of life.
(Proverbs 6:23, esv)

To profit most from adversity, we should bring the Word of God to bear upon our situation. We should ask God to bring to our attention pertinent passages of Scripture, and then look for those passages.

My first great lesson on the sovereignty of God is still stamped indelibly on my mind after many years. It came as I was desperately searching the Scriptures to find some kind of an answer to a severe time of testing.

As we do this, we'll find we not only profit from the circumstances themselves, but we gain new insight into the Scriptures. Martin Luther reportedly said, "Were it not for tribulation I should not understand the Scriptures." Although we may be going to the Scriptures to learn how to respond to our adversities, we find those adversities in turn help us to understand the Scriptures. It is not that we will learn from adversity something different from what we can learn from the Scriptures. Rather, adversity enhances the teaching of God's Word and makes it more profitable to us. In some instances it clarifies our understanding or causes us to see truths we had passed over before. At other times it will transform "head knowledge" into "heart knowledge" as theological theory becomes a reality to us.

The Puritan Daniel Dyke said, "Look not for any new diverse doctrine to be taught thee by affliction, which is not in the word. For in truth, herein stands our teaching by affliction, that it fits and prepares us for the word, by breaking and sub-dividing the stubbornness of our hearts, and making them pliable, and capable of the impression of the word."

We might say, then, that the Word of God and adversity have a synergistic effect as God uses both of them together to bring about growth in our lives that neither the Word nor adversity would accomplish by itself.

Jerry Bridges, in *Trusting God*

Sharing Christ's Work

Whoever believes in me will also do the works that I do.

(John 14:12, esv)

Christ revealed the secret of His and of all Divine service — man yielding himself for God to dwell and to work in him.

When Christ now promises, "He that believeth on me, the works that I do shall he do also" (John 14:12, KJV), the law of the Divine inworking remains unchanged. In us, as much as in Him — one might even say a thousand times more than with Him — it must still ever be: *The Father in me doeth the works.* With Christ and with us, it is "the same God which worketh all in all" (1 Corinthians 12:6, KJV).

How this is to be, is taught us in the words, "He that believeth on me." That does not only mean, *for salvation,* as a Savior from sin. But much more. Christ had just said, "*Believe me that I am in the Father, and the Father in me. . . .* The Father *that dwelleth in me, he* doeth the works" (John 14:10-11, KJV, emphasis added). We need to believe in Christ as *the One in and through whom the Father unceasingly works.* To believe in Christ is to receive Him into the heart. When we see the Father's working inseparably connected with Christ, we know that to believe in Christ, and receive Him into the heart, is to receive the Father dwelling in Him and working through Him.

The works His disciples are to do cannot possibly be done in any other way than His own are done.

The law of the Divine working is unchangeable: God's work can be done only by God Himself. It is as we see this in Christ, and receive Him in this capacity, as the One in and through whom God works all, and so yield ourselves wholly to the Father working in Him and in us, that we shall do greater works than He did.

Andrew Murray, in *Working for God*

Sought and Found

You will seek me and find me, when you seek me with all your heart.
(Jeremiah 29:13, esv)

The question is not whether we are good at theology, or "balanced" (horrible, self-conscious word!) in our approach to problems of Christian living; the question is, can we say — simply, honestly, not because we feel that as evangelicals we ought to, but because it is plain matter of fact — that we have known God?

Do we desire such knowledge of God? Then —

First, we must recognize how much we lack knowledge of God. We must learn to measure ourselves not by our knowledge about God, not by our gifts and responsibilities in the church, but by how we pray and what goes on in our hearts. Many of us, I suspect, have no idea how impoverished we are at this level. Let us ask the Lord to show us.

Second, we must seek the Savior. When He was on earth, He invited men to company with Him; thus they came to know Him, and in knowing Him to know His Father. The Old Testament records preincarnate manifestations of the Lord Jesus doing the same thing — companying with men, in character as the angel of the Lord, in order that men might know Him. The book of Daniel tells us of what appear to be two such instances — for who was the fourth man, "like a son of the gods" (3:25, esv), who walked with Daniel's three friends in the furnace? And who was the angel whom God sent to shut the lions' mouths when Daniel was in their den (see 6:22)? The Lord Jesus Christ is now absent from us in body, but spiritually it makes no difference; still we may find and know God through seeking and finding His company.

It is those who have sought the Lord Jesus till they have found Him who can stand before the world to testify that they have known God.

J. I. Packer, in *Knowing God*

Finding True Freedom

Truly, truly, I say to you, everyone who commits sin is a slave to sin.

(John 8:34, esv)

Freedom is an essential element of joy. None of us would be happy if we were not free from what we hate and free for what we love. And where do we find true freedom? Psalm 119:45 says, "I shall walk in freedom, for I sought your precepts" (author's translation). The picture is one of open spaces. The Word frees us from smallness of mind (see 1 Kings 4:29) and from threatening confinements (see Psalm 18:19).

Jesus says, "You will know the truth, and the truth will set you *free*" (John 8:32, esv, emphasis added). The freedom He has in mind is freedom from the slavery of sin (see 8:34). Or, to put it positively, it is freedom for holiness. The promises of God's grace provide the power that makes the demands of God's holiness an experience of freedom rather than fear. Peter described the freeing power of God's promises like this: "Through [his precious and very great promises] you may become partakers of the divine nature, having escaped from the corruption that is in the world because of sinful desire" (2 Peter 1:4, esv). In other words, when we trust the promises of God, we sever the root of corruption by the power of a superior promise.

Therefore we should pray for each other the way Jesus prays for us in John 17:17: "Sanctify them in the truth; your word is truth" (esv). There is no abiding joy without holiness, for the Scripture says, "Strive . . . for the holiness without which no one will see the Lord" (Hebrews 12:14, esv). How important, then, is the truth that sanctifies! How crucial is the Word that breaks the power of counterfeit pleasures! And how vigilant we should be to light our paths and load our hearts with the Word of God! "Your word is a lamp to my feet and a light to my path" (Psalm 119:105, esv). "I have stored up your word in my heart, that I might not sin against you" (verse 11, esv).

John Piper, in *Desiring God*

Honoring God, Pleasing God

I honor my Father. . . . I do not seek my own glory.
(John 8:49-50, esv)

In His lowly manhood, Jesus humbled Himself and gladly gave all glory to His Father in heaven. He sought not His own honor, but the honor of God who sent Him. "If I honour myself," He said on one occasion, "my honour is nothing: it is my Father that honoureth me" (John 8:54, kjv).

Another saying of Jesus, and a most disturbing one, was put in the form of a question: "How can ye believe, which receive honour one of another, and seek not the honour that cometh from God only?" (John 5:44, kjv). If I understand this correctly, Christ taught here the alarming doctrine that the desire for honor among men made belief impossible.

Is this sin at the root of religious unbelief? Could it be that those "intellectual difficulties" which men blame for their inability to believe are but smoke screens to conceal the real cause that lies behind them? Is this the secret back of religious self-righteousness and empty worship? I believe it may be. The whole course of the life is upset by failure to put God where He belongs. We exalt ourselves instead of God and the curse follows.

In our desire after God let us keep always in mind that God also hath desire, and His desire is toward the sons of men, and more particularly toward those sons of men who will make the once-for-all decision to exalt Him over all. Such are these precious to God above all treasures of earth or sea.

In them God finds a theater where He can display His exceeding kindness toward us in Christ Jesus. With them God can walk unhindered, toward them He can act like the God He is.

A. W. Tozer, in *The Pursuit of God*

ADJUSTMENTS REQUIRED

Though he was rich, yet for your sake he became poor,
so that you by his poverty might become rich.
(2 CORINTHIANS 8:9, ESV)

When God speaks, revealing what He is about to do, that revelation is your invitation to adjust your life to Him. As you adjust your heart and mind to Him and to His purposes and ways, you are in a position to obey. You can't continue business as usual or stay where you are and go with God at the same time.

This truth is clearly evident in the Scriptures. Enormous changes and adjustments were required whenever God's people determined to obey His calling. Some had to leave family and country. Others had to abandon long-held prejudices and reorient their thinking. Men and women were willing to leave behind life goals, ideals, and desires. Everything had to be yielded to God, and their entire life adjusted to Him. The moment the necessary adjustments were made, however, God began to accomplish His purposes through them. Each one learned that adjusting one's life to God is always well worth the cost.

His own Son gave up more than anyone. Jesus emptied Himself of position and glory in heaven to join the Father in providing salvation through His death on the cross. Jesus couldn't stay where He was in heaven and be a part of the Father's plan to redeem humanity on earth.

If you want to be a disciple of Jesus, you have no choice. You will have to make significant alterations in your life. Following your Master means going where He goes. Until you are ready to make *any* change necessary to follow and obey what God has said, you will be of little use to God. Your greatest difficulty in following God may come at this point.

The only way to follow Him is to align our thinking and our actions with His ways. Before we can follow Jesus, we must be willing to make whatever adjustment is necessary.

HENRY BLACKABY AND RICHARD BLACKABY, IN *EXPERIENCING GOD*

Remember

And you shall remember the whole way that the Lord your God has led you.
(Deuteronomy 8:2, esv)

To profit most from our adversities, we must *remember* them and the lessons we learned from them. God wants us to do more than simply endure our trials, even more than merely find comfort in them. He wants us to remember them, not just as trials or sorrows, but as His disciplines — His means of bringing about growth in our lives.

In Deuteronomy 8:3, Moses reminded the Israelites of how God "humbled you and let you hunger and fed you with manna . . . that he might make you know that man does not live by bread alone, but man lives by every word that comes from the mouth of the Lord" (esv). (The "word . . . from the mouth of the Lord" in this passage is not the Word of Scripture but the word of God's providence; see Psalm 33:6,9 and 148:5 for similar usage.) God wanted to teach the Israelites that they were dependent upon Him for their daily bread. He did this by bringing adversity in the form of hunger into their lives. But in order to profit from this lesson, they were commanded to "remember" it (see Deuteronomy 8:2). We, too, if we are to profit from the painful lessons God teaches us, must remember them.

I once learned a rather painful lesson after trying to subtly usurp some of God's glory for my own reputation. God holds me responsible to remember that lesson. Every time I come across God's words in Isaiah 42:8, "My glory I give to no other" (esv), in either my Bible reading or my Scripture memory review, I should remember that painful circumstance and let the lesson sink more deeply into my heart. Every time I stand up to teach God's Word I should remember that lesson and purge my heart of any desire to enhance my own reputation. This is the way adversity becomes profitable to us.

Jerry Bridges, in *Trusting God*

Determination to Remember

Remember the wondrous works that he has done,
his miracles and the judgments he uttered.
(1 Chronicles 16:12, esv)

Somewhere along the line, the idea of being a *decisive* and *determined* Christian has lost out in the fashion stakes. We have let the world squeeze us into its mold. For there, in the world, the idea of *permanent* commitment is rare indeed, even in areas like employment or marriage. Nowadays we cannot promise anything.

The tragedy is that the spirit of the age has infected the people of God's new age, in the church. Sometimes we cover our failure over with theology (of all things!) — we know ourselves too well to promise very much to God! But that is bad theology. It is also bad spirituality. For God calls us to promise ourselves to Him in a lifelong commitment of faithfulness and obedience. He does not regard our failure here as a becoming modesty, or an understandable reticence. He has other names for it: *disobedience, disloyalty, backsliding, faithlessness.*

Our spiritual forefathers recognized this disposition in their own hearts, but determined to have "hearts for God"; they made every effort to overcome and conquer it. That is why their diaries would sometimes contain the *vows* or *covenants* they made to the Lord. In His presence they would commit themselves, by His grace, to remember Him and to live the whole of their lives before Him.

Do you have the resolution to vow to the Lord that, in a new way, you will remember Him? If the knowledge of God is to be anything more to you than an intellectual pastime, you need to do this. It is part of your *worship* of God. The praise we are to give Him includes the praise of a life that fulfills the vow to serve Him (see Psalm 65:1). Yielding yourself — deliberately, intelligently — to the Lord is part of your worship (see Romans 12:1-2).

Sinclair Ferguson, in *A Heart for God*

Honoring God by Trusting Him

Such knowledge is too wonderful for me; it is high; I cannot attain it.
(Psalm 139:6, esv)

"Providence is wonderfully intricate," C. H. Spurgeon proclaimed in a sermon on divine providence. He continued: "Ah! you want always to see through Providence, do you not? You never will, I assure you. You have not eyes good enough. You want to see what good that affliction was to you; you must believe it. You want to see how it can bring good to the soul; you may be enabled in a little time; but you can not see it now; you must believe it. Honor God by trusting him."[33]

In Job's final response to God, he humbly acknowledges God's unfathomable ways. After repeating a piercing question from God — "Who is this that obscures my counsel without knowledge?" — Job then says, "Surely I spoke of things I did not understand, things too wonderful for me to know" (Job 42:3, niv).

God's ways, Job realized, were too wonderful for him to know or understand. When he saw God in His great majesty and sovereignty, he repented in "dust and ashes" of his previous arrogant questioning (verse 6, niv). Job stopped asking and simply trusted.

David, in a similar manner, bowed to the sovereign purposes and infinite wisdom of God. "O Lord," he said, "my heart is not lifted up; my eyes are not raised too high; I do not occupy myself with things too great and too marvelous for me" (Psalm 131:1, esv).

These "great" and "marvelous" things referred to are the secret purposes of God and His infinite means for accomplishing them. David did not exercise his heart in seeking to understand them. Instead he stilled and quieted his soul in submission and trust toward God.

If we're to honor God by trusting Him, and if we're to find peace for ourselves, we must come to the place where we can honestly say, "God, I do not have to understand. I will just trust You."

Jerry Bridges, in *Trusting God*

Greater Works

Whoever believes in me will also do the works that I do; and greater works than these will he do, because I am going to the Father.

(John 14:12, esv)

The "greater works" (John 14:12) are an ingathering of souls—accomplished by the disciples at Pentecost with three thousand baptized and multitudes added to the Lord; and by Philip at Samaria, with the whole city filled with joy; and by the men of Cyprus and Cyrene, and, later on, Barnabas at Antioch, with much people added to the Lord; and by Paul in his travels; and by a countless host of Christ's servants down to our day. All have done what the Master calls "greater works" than His own.

The reason is plain: "Because I am going to the Father." When He entered the glory of the Father, all power in heaven and on earth was given Him as our Redeemer. In a way more glorious than ever, the Father was to work through Him, and He was then to work through His disciples. Even as His own work on earth "in the days of the weakness of the flesh" had been in a power received from the Father in heaven, so His people, in their weakness, would do works like His—and greater works—in the same way, through a power received from heaven.

Christ connects these greater works with this promise: the Father will do whatever the believer asks (see John 14:13-14). Prayer in the name of Jesus will be the expression of that dependence that waits on Him for His working.

Let every believer strive to learn the blessed lesson: I am to do the works I have seen Christ doing; I may even do greater works, as I yield myself to Christ exalted on the throne, in a power He had not on earth; I may count on Him working in me according to that power. My one need is the spirit of dependence and waiting, and prayer and faith, that Christ abiding in me will do the works, even whatsoever I ask.

Andrew Murray, in *Working for God*

For Greater Fruitfulness

Every branch that does bear fruit he prunes,
that it may bear more fruit.
(John 15:2, esv)

Jesus speaks in John 15 of how God prunes every fruit-bearing branch so that it will be even more fruitful. In the natural realm, pruning is important for fruit bearing. An unpruned vine will produce a great deal of unproductive growth but little fruit. Cutting away unwanted and useless growth forces the plant to use its life to produce fruit.

In the spiritual realm, God must prune us. Because even as believers we still have a sinful nature, we tend to pour our spiritual energies into that which is not true fruit. We tend to seek position, success, and reputation even in the body of Christ. We tend to depend upon natural talents and human wisdom. And then we are easily distracted and pulled by the things of the world — its pleasures and possessions.

God uses adversity to loosen our grip on those things that are not true fruit. A severe illness, the death of someone dear to us, the loss of material substance, the tarnishing of our reputation, the turning aside of friends, or the dashing of our cherished dreams on the rocks of failure — any of those things can cause us to reassess what is really important in our life. After experiencing such difficulties, position or possessions or even reputation no longer seems so important. We begin to relinquish our desires and expectations — even good ones — to the sovereign will of God. We come more and more to depend on God and to desire only that which will count for eternity. God is pruning us so that we will be more fruitful.

We often resist this work of God in our lives. But as we look to God, we may be sure to see how in due time His discipline "yields the peaceful fruit of righteousness to those who have been trained by it" (Hebrews 12:11, esv).

Jerry Bridges, in *Trusting God*

GOD-CENTERED VICTORY

How can we who died to sin still live in it?
(ROMANS 6:2, ESV)

One of the most troublesome areas for many Christians relates to Romans 6:11-12, where Paul on one hand says we're dead to sin and in the next verse exhorts us not to let sin reign in our mortal bodies. Why should we turn away from sin that's already dead?

The answer to this seeming contradiction underscores the joint responsibility for sanctification. We're dead to sin because Christ died to sin for us. He settled the ultimate victory. But as we live day by day, sin still remains a constant reality. Though God gives us the will to be holy, the daily fight requires our continuing effort.

Holy living demands constant examination of our actions and motives. But in doing so we must guard against the tendency to focus totally on self, which is easy to do — especially as the culture's egocentric values invade the church. In fact, this self-indulgent character of our times is a major reason the topic of true holiness is so neglected today by Christian teachers, leaders, writers, and speakers. We have, perhaps unconsciously, substituted a secularized self-centered message in its place. For when we speak of "victory" in the Christian life, we all too often mean personal victory — how God will conquer sin *for us* (at least those sins we'd like to be rid of — those extra ten pounds, that annoying habit, maybe a quick temper). This reflects not only egocentricity but an incorrect view of sin.

Sin is not simply the wrong we do our neighbor when we cheat him, or the wrong we do ourselves when we abuse our bodies. Sin, all sin, is a root rebellion and offense against God — what R. C. Sproul calls "cosmic treason."

Our goal as believers is to seek to please God, not what He can do for us. Personal victories may come, but they're a result, not the object. True Christian maturity — holiness, sanctification — is God-centered.

CHARLES COLSON, IN *LOVING GOD*

The True Worth of Our Good Works

We are his workmanship, created in Christ Jesus for good works, which God prepared beforehand, that we should walk in them.

(Ephesians 2:10, esv)

We have been "saved through faith; . . . *not of works.* . . . For we are his workmanship, created in Christ Jesus *unto good works,* which God hath before ordained that we should walk in them" (Ephesians 2:8-10, kjv, emphasis added).

We have been saved, not *of works,* but *for good works.* How vast the difference! How essential the apprehension of that difference to the health of the Christian life! Not *of* works which we have done, as the source whence salvation comes . . . and yet *for* good works, as the fruit and outcome of salvation, as part of God's work in us—the one thing for which we have been created anew. As worthless as are our works in procuring salvation, so infinite is their worth as that for which God has created and prepared us. Let us seek to hold these two truths in their fullness of spiritual meaning. The deeper our conviction that we have been saved, not of works, but of grace, the stronger the proof we should give that we have indeed been saved for good works.

If works could have saved us, there was no need for our redemption. Because our works were all sinful and vain, God undertook to make us anew—we are now His workmanship, and all the good works we do are His workmanship too.

So complete was sin's ruin that God had to do the work of creation over again in Christ Jesus. In Him, and especially in His resurrection from the dead, He created us anew, after His own image, into the likeness of Christ.

In the power of that life and resurrection, we are able, we are perfectly fitted, for doing good works. We may rest assured that a Divine capacity for good works is the very law of our being. If we but know and believe in this our destiny—we can, we will, be fruitful unto every good work.

Andrew Murray, in *Working for God*

For Greater Holiness

He disciplines us for our good, that we may share his holiness.

(Hebrews 12:10, esv)

What exactly is the connection between adversity and holiness?

For one thing, adversity reveals the corruption of our sinful nature. We don't know ourselves or the depths of sin remaining in us. We agree with Scripture's teachings and assume that agreement means obedience. At least we intend to obey.

Who of us doesn't read that list of Christian virtues called "the fruit of the Spirit"—"love, joy, peace, patience, kindness, goodness, faithfulness, gentleness, self-control" (Galatians 5:22-23, esv)—and agree we want all those traits in our lives? We even begin to think we are making good progress in growing in them.

But then adversity comes. We find we're unable to love, from the depths of our hearts, the person who's the instrument of the adversity. We're not disposed to trust God; unbelief and resentment surge within us. We're dismayed at the scene. Our growth in Christian character seems to vanish like a vapor. We feel as if we're back in spiritual kindergarten. But through this experience, God has revealed to us some of the remaining corruption within us.

"Blessed," Jesus said, "are the poor in spirit . . . those who mourn . . . those who hunger and thirst for righteousness" (Matthew 5:3-4,6, esv). These descriptions refer to the believer who has been humbled over his sinfulness, who mourns because of it, and yearns with all his heart for God to change him. But no one adopts this attitude without being exposed to the evil and corruption of his own heart. God uses adversity to do this.

In making us holy, God wants to get at the root corruption of our sinful nature. He uses adversity to enlighten our minds about our own needs as well as the teachings of Scripture. He uses adversity to rein in our affections that have been drawn out to unholy desires and to subdue our stubborn and rebellious wills.

Jerry Bridges, in *Trusting God*

Work, for God Works in You

Work out your own salvation with fear and trembling, for it is God who works in you, both to will and to work for his good pleasure.
(Philippians 2:12-13, esv)

Work out your own salvation, such as God has meant it to be — a walk in all the good works which God has prepared for you (see Ephesians 2:10). Study to know exactly what the salvation is God has prepared for you, all that He has meant and made it possible for you to be, and work it out with fear and trembling. Let the greatness of this Divine and most holy life, hidden in Christ, your own absolute impotence, and the terrible dangers and temptations besetting you, make you work in fear and trembling. And yet, that fear need never become unbelief, nor that trembling discouragement, *for* — it is God which worketh in you.

Here is the secret of a power that is absolutely sufficient for everything we have to do, of a perfect assurance that we can do all that God really means us to do. God works in us both to will and to work.

First, *to will* He gives the insight into what is to be done, the desire that makes the work pleasure, the firm purpose of the will that masters the whole being, and makes it ready and eager for action.

And then *to work*. He does not work to will, and then leave us unaided to work it out ourselves. The will may have seen and accepted the work, and yet the power be lacking to perform. The renewed will of Romans 7 delighted in God's law, and yet the man was impotent *to do*, until in Romans 8:2-4, by the law of the Spirit of life in Christ Jesus, he was set free from the law of sin and death; then could the righteousness of the law be fulfilled in him, as one who walked not after the flesh but after the Spirit.

Andrew Murray, in *Working for God*

A Pleasing Trust

I am not ashamed, for I know whom I have believed.
(2 Timothy 1:12, ESV)

Why is unbelief a sin? To refuse to believe God is to be guilty of slandering His righteous character. It is to assume that either God does not know what He is talking about or that what He says is in fact evil. Either way we assault His divine integrity. Either His omniscience or His righteousness is brought into question.

But isn't blind faith a weakness? Indeed it is. There is a great difference between faith and credulity. Credulity is gullibility, naiveté. It is based on superstition and irrational prejudice. To believe something with no reason for believing is not a virtue. But God does not require that. He asks us to believe in that which He utters in the fullness of light and with consummate evidence. He does not ask us to believe in a Resurrection without first bringing Jesus forth from the grave. He does ask us to trust Him for the future, but such trust is not blind. It rests upon God's perfect track record. He has demonstrated over and over that His promises are certain.

If Satan can destroy our implicit trust in God, then his goal of seduction is achieved. We fall to the temptation of unbelief. Adam fell. He did not believe God. Jesus, the second Adam, lived by the Word of God. His trust in the Father could not be shaken. He did not yield to the tempter.

Before Jesus' temptation, He had heard the voice of the Father, who declared His approval of the Son: "I am well pleased" (Matthew 3:17, KJV). We can feel certain that God was also well pleased at Jesus' victory in the temptation. Jesus chose well between the word of Satan the liar and the Word of God. He cast His lot with trust and belief instead of selfish doubt and skepticism. Both then and now, God takes pleasure in His children when they trust.

R. C. Sproul, in *Pleasing God*

For Greater Dependence

I am the vine; you are the branches. Whoever abides in me and I in him, he it is that bears much fruit, for apart from me you can do nothing.

(John 15:5, esv)

God must continually be at work on our tendency to rely on ourselves instead of on Him. Apart from our union with Christ and a total reliance upon Him, we can do nothing that glorifies God. We live in a world that worships independence and self-reliance, and because of our own sinful nature, we can easily fall into the world's pattern of thinking. God has to teach us through adversity to rely on Him instead of own business acumen, our ministry experience, and even our goodness and morality.

The apostle Paul described a time when he and his band of men were "utterly burdened beyond our strength"; he saw, however, the higher purpose in this: "to make us rely not on ourselves but on God who raises the dead" (2 Corinthians 1:8-9, esv). They had no place to turn except to God.

Paul had to learn dependence on God in the spiritual as well as the physical realm. His "thorn in the flesh" (2 Corinthians 12:7, kjv) was an adversity he desperately wanted to be rid of. But God let it remain, not only to curb any tendency for pride in Paul's heart, but also to teach him to rely on God's strength. Paul had to learn that it was not his strength but God's grace — God's enabling power — that he must depend on.

Paul was one of the most brilliant men in history, with an abundance of natural intellect. God also gave him divine revelations, some so glorious that Paul wasn't permitted to tell about them. But God never allowed Paul to depend on either his intellect or his revelations. He had to depend on God's grace, just as you and I do. And he learned this through severe adversity.

If God is going to use you and me, He will bring adversity into our lives so that we, too, may learn experientially our dependence on Him.

Jerry Bridges, in *Trusting God*

ALL THINGS ARE POSSIBLE

The Father who dwells in me does his works.

(JOHN 14:10, ESV)

The working of the Father in him was the source of all the man Christ Jesus did. For us — in our new man, created in Christ Jesus — the unceasing dependence on the Father is indeed our fellowship with God: God Himself working in us to will and to do (see Philippians 2:12-13).

Let us seek to learn the true secret of working for God. It is not that we do our best and leave God to do the rest. It is this: We know that God working His salvation *in* us is the secret of our working it *out*. That salvation includes every work we have to do. *Our trusting God to work in us is the measure of our fitness to work effectively.*

The promises in the Gospels — "All things are possible to him that believeth" (Mark 9:23, KJV) and "According to your faith be it unto you" (Matthew 9:29, KJV) — have their full application here. The deeper our faith in God's working in us, the more freely will the power of God work in us, the more true and fruitful will our work be.

Have you really believed that your only power to do God's work is as one created in Christ Jesus for good works, as one in whom God Himself works to will and to work? Have you yielded yourself to wait for that working? Do you work because you know God works in you?

Say not that these thoughts are too high. The work of leading young souls to Christ is too high for us indeed, but if we live as little children, believing that God will work everything in us, we shall do His work in His strength.

Work, for God worketh in you. Beseech God to show you that in all our service, our first care must be the daily renewing of the Holy Spirit.

ANDREW MURRAY, IN *WORKING FOR GOD*

God-Centered, Self-Centered Prayer

Call upon me in the day of trouble;
I will deliver you, and you shall glorify me.
(Psalm 50:15, esv)

Prayer is the very heart of Christian Hedonism. God gets the glory precisely because He shows Himself full and strong to deliver us into joy. And we attain fullness of joy precisely because He is the all-glorious source and goal of life.

We do not glorify God by providing His needs, but by praying that He would provide ours — and trusting Him to answer. Someone may say that this is self-centered. But what does *self-centered* mean? If it means I passionately desire to be happy, then yes, prayer is self-centered. But is this a bad thing, if what I cry for is that God's name be hallowed in my life? If my cry is for His reign to hold sway in my heart? If my cry is for His will to be done in my life as it is done by angels in heaven? If I crave the happiness of seeing and experiencing these things in my life, is that bad?

How is the will of God done in heaven? Sadly? Burdensomely? Begrudgingly? No! It is done gladly! If I then pray, *Thy will be done on earth as it is in heaven,* how can I not be motivated by a desire to be glad? It is a contradiction to pray for the will of God to be done in my life the way it is in heaven, and then to say that I am indifferent to whether I am glad or not. When the earth *rejoices* to do His will and does it perfectly, His will shall be done on earth as it is in heaven.

This pursuit of happiness in prayer is radically God-centered. In my craving to be happy, I acknowledge that at the center of my life there is a gaping hole of emptiness without God. This hole constitutes my need and my rebellion at the same time. I want it filled, but I rebel at God's filling it with Himself. By grace I awake to the folly of my rebellion and see that if it is filled with God, my joy will be full.

John Piper, in *Desiring God*

PERSEVERANCE AND FAITH

For you have need of endurance, so that when you have done the will of God you may receive what is promised.

(HEBREWS 10:36, ESV)

Perseverance is the quality of character that enables one to pursue a goal in spite of obstacles and difficulties. It's one thing to simply bear up under adversity. This in itself is commendable. But the Christian life is meant to be active, not passive. The Christian is called to pursue with diligence the will of God. He calls us to do more than simply bear the load of adversity; He calls us to persevere (to press forward) in the face of it. He wants all Christians to finish well. He wants us to "run with endurance" (Hebrews 12:1, ESV).

Each of us has been given a race to run, a will of God to do. Along the way, all of us encounter innumerable obstacles and occasions for discouragement. God wants us to persist in doing His will whatever those obstacles might be. How can we do it?

Both Paul and James give us the same answer. Paul says, "Suffering produces perseverance" (Romans 5:3, NIV); James adds, "The testing of your faith produces steadfastness" (James 1:3, ESV). We see here a mutually enhancing effect. Adversity produces perseverance, and perseverance enables us to meet adversity. A good analogy is found in weight training. Lifting weights develops muscle, and the more one's muscles are developed, the heavier the weight one can lift.

Though perseverance is developed in the crucible of adversity, it is energized by *faith*. Again, consider the analogy of weight training. Although the weights on a bar provide the resistance needed to develop muscle, they do not provide the energy. That must come from within the athlete's body. In the case of adversity, the energy must come from God through faith. It is God's strength, not ours, that enables us to persevere—and we lay hold of His strength through faith.

JERRY BRIDGES, IN *TRUSTING GOD*

FAITH WORKING THROUGH LOVE

For in Christ Jesus neither circumcision nor uncircumcision counts for anything, but only faith working through love.
(GALATIANS 5:6, ESV)

Faith working through love — what a perfect description of the new life!

The power for work is love. It was love that moved God to all His work in creation and redemption. It was love that enabled Christ as man to work and to suffer as He did. It is love that can inspire us with the power of a self-sacrifice that seeks not its own, but is ready to live and die for others. It is love that gives us the patience that refuses to give up the unthankful or the hardened. It is love that reaches and overcomes the most hopeless. Both in ourselves and those for whom we labor, love is the power for work. Let us love as Christ loved us.

The power for love is faith. Faith roots its life in the life of Christ Jesus, which is all love. Faith knows, even when we cannot realize fully, the wonderful gift that has been given into our heart in the Holy Spirit shedding abroad God's love there. Faith knows that there is a fountain of love within that can spring up into eternal life, that can flow out as rivers of living waters. It assures us that we can love, that we have a Divine power to love within us, as an unalienable endowment of our new nature.

The power to exercise and show love is work. It is only by doing that you know you have; a grace must be acted out before we can rejoice in its possession. This is the unspeakable blessedness of work, and makes it so essential to a healthy Christian life that it wakens up and strengthens love, and makes us partakers of its joy.

Faith working through love — in Christ Jesus nothing avails but this.

ANDREW MURRAY, IN *WORKING FOR GOD*

Wise Listening

Blessed are the meek, for they shall inherit the earth.
(Matthew 5:5, esv)

A fairly accurate description of the human race might be furnished one unacquainted with it by taking the Beatitudes, turning them wrong side out and saying, "Here is your human race." For the exact opposite of the virtues in the Beatitudes are the very qualities which distinguish human life and conduct.

In the world of men we find nothing approaching the virtues of which Jesus spoke in the opening words of the famous Sermon on the Mount. Instead of poverty of spirit we find the rankest kind of pride; instead of mourners we find pleasure seekers; instead of meekness, arrogance; instead of hunger after righteousness we hear men saying, "I am rich and increased with goods and have need of nothing"; instead of mercy we find cruelty; instead of purity of heart, corrupt imaginings; instead of peacemakers we find men quarrelsome and resentful; instead of rejoicing in mistreatment we find them fighting back with every weapon at their command.

Into a world like this the sound of Jesus' words comes wonderful and strange, a visitation from above. It is well that He spoke, for no one else could have done it as well; and it is good that we listen. His words are the essence of truth. He is not offering an opinion; Jesus never uttered opinions.

He never guessed; He knew, and He knows. His words are not as Solomon's were, the sum of sound wisdom or the results of keen observation. He spoke out of the fullness of His Godhead, and His words are very Truth itself. He is the only one who could say "blessed" with complete authority, for He is the Blessed One come from the world above to confer blessedness upon mankind. And His words were supported by deeds mightier than any performed on this earth by any other man.

It is wisdom for us to listen.

A. W. Tozer, in *The Pursuit of God*

Helping Us Serve

You, Lord, have helped me and comforted me.
(Psalm 86:17, esv)

Another reason God brings adversity into our lives is to equip us for more effective service. All that we have considered so far — pruning, holiness, dependence, and perseverance — contributes to making us useful instruments in God's service.

Paul writes of how God "comforts us in all our affliction, so that we may be able to comfort those who are in any affliction, with the comfort with which we ourselves are comforted by God" (2 Corinthians 1:4, esv). Everyone faces times of adversity, and everyone needs a compassionate and caring friend who'll come alongside and offer comfort and encouragement during those times. As we experience God's comfort and encouragement in our adversities, we're equipped to be His instrument of comfort and encouragement to others. We pass on to others what we've received from God ourselves. To the extent we're able to lay hold of the great truths of God's sovereignty, wisdom, and love and find comfort and encouragement from them in our adversities, we'll be able to minister to others in their times of distress.

To do that, we must first of all show compassion, the deep feeling of sharing in the suffering of another and the desire to relieve that suffering. If we're to really help others in their time of adversity, we must also bring encouragement — to fortify them with the spiritual and emotional strength to persevere in times of adversity. We do this by pointing them to the trustworthiness of God as revealed to us in Scripture. Only to the extent that we ourselves have been comforted and encouraged by the Holy Spirit through His Word will we be able to comfort and encourage others.

Adversity in our own lives, rightly responded to, enables us to be instruments of comfort and encouragement to others.

Jerry Bridges, in *Trusting God*

Fruit-Bearing and Working

Walk in a manner worthy of the Lord, fully pleasing to him, bearing fruit in every good work.

(Colossians 1:10, esv)

There is a difference between fruit and work. Fruit is that which comes spontaneously, without thought or will, the natural and necessary outcome of a healthy life. Work, on the contrary, is the product of effort guided by intelligent thought and will. In the Christian life we have the two elements in combination. In the words "bearing fruit in every good work" we have the practical summing up of this truth.

Because God works by His life in us, the work we do is fruit. Because, in the faith of His working, we have to will and to work, the fruit we bear is work. In the harmony between the perfect spontaneity that comes from God's life and Spirit animating us, and our cooperation with Him as His intelligent fellow-laborers, lies the secret of all true work.

The words "bearing fruit in every good work" suggest that as an apple-tree or a vine is planted solely for its fruit, so the great purpose of our redemption is that God may have us for His work and service. In the parable of the vine, our Lord insisted on this: "He that abideth in me, and I in him, the same bringeth forth *much fruit*. . . . Herein is my Father glorified, that ye bear *much fruit*" (John 15: 5,8, kjv, emphasis added). Nothing is more to the honor of a husbandman than to succeed in raising an abundant crop — much fruit is glory to God.

The call to be fruitful in every good work is for every Christian without exception. The grace that fits for it, of which the prayer, in which our words are found, speaks, is for everyone.

Every branch fruitful in every good work — this is an essential part of God's gospel. As we grasp this, we shall boldly give ourselves to the diligence, sacrifice, and effort needed for a life that bears fruit in every good work.

Andrew Murray, in *Working for God*

He Knows His Own

I know my own and my own know me. . . .
I know them, and they follow me.
(John 10:14.27, esv)

God's knowledge of those who are His implies personal affection, redeeming action, covenant faithfulness, and providential watchfulness, toward those whom God knows. It implies, in other words, salvation, now and forever.

What matters supremely, therefore, is not, in the last analysis, the fact that I know God, but the larger fact which underlies it — that *He knows me.* I am graven on the palms of His hands. I am never out of His mind. All my knowledge of Him depends on His sustained initiative in knowing me. I know Him, because He first knew me, and continues to know me. He knows me as a friend; and there is no moment when His eye is off me, or His attention distracted from me, and no moment, therefore, when His care falters.

This is momentous knowledge. There is unspeakable comfort — the comfort that energizes, be it said, not enervates — in knowing that God is constantly taking knowledge of me in love and watching over me for my good. There is tremendous relief in knowing that His love to me is utterly realistic, based at every point on prior knowledge of the worst about me, so that no discovery now can disillusion him about me, in the way I am so often disillusioned about myself, and quench His determination to bless me. There is, certainly, great cause for humility in the thought that He sees all the twisted things about me that my fellow men do not see (and am I glad!), and that He sees more corruption in me than that which I see in myself (which, in all conscience, is enough). There is, however, equally great incentive to worship and love God in the thought that, for some unfathomable reason, He wants me as His friend, and desires to be my friend, and has given His Son to die for me in order to realize this purpose.

J. I. Packer, in *Knowing God*

The Rest of Meekness

Come to me, all who labor and are heavy laden,
and I will give you rest.
(Matthew 11:28, ESV)

The burden borne by mankind is a heavy and a crushing thing. It attacks the heart and mind and reaches the body only from within.

First, there is the burden of *pride*. The labor of self-love is a heavy one indeed. Think for yourself whether much of your sorrow has not arisen from someone speaking slightingly of you. As long as you set yourself up as a little god to which you must be loyal there will be those who will delight to offer affront to your idol. How then can you hope to have inward peace?

There is also the burden of *pretense*. By this I mean not hypocrisy, but the common human desire to put the best foot forward and hide from the world our real inward poverty. For sin has played many evil tricks upon us, and one has been infusing into us a false sense of shame. There is hardly a man or woman who dares to be just what he or she is without doctoring up the impression. The fear of being found out gnaws like rodents within their hearts.

Another source of burden is *artificiality*. I am sure that most people live in secret fear that some day they will be careless and by chance an enemy or friend will be allowed to peep into their poor empty souls. So they are never relaxed.

The heart of the world is breaking under this load. There is no release from our burden apart from the meekness of Christ. Good keen reasoning may help slightly, but so strong is this vice that if we push it down one place it will come up somewhere else. To men and women everywhere Jesus says, "Come unto me . . . and I will give you rest" (Matthew 11:28, KJV). The rest He offers is the rest of meekness, the blessed relief which comes when we accept ourselves for what we are and cease to pretend.

A. W. Tozer, in *The Pursuit of God*

Never Misled

I glorified you on earth, having accomplished the work that you gave me to do.

(John 17:4, esv)

The Holy Spirit will never mislead you about the Father's will. In order that you not miss the purpose God has for you, He has given His Spirit to guide you according to His will. The Spirit also *enables* you to do God's will. You are completely dependent on God for the knowledge and for the ability to achieve His purposes. You must be patient and wait until you hear a word from God about His will and His ways.

Jesus is our model. He never failed to know and do His Father's will. Everything the Father proposed to do through His life, the Lord Jesus did. Thus, Jesus could claim at the end of His life that He had completed everything His Father had given Him to do.

What was the key to Jesus' perfect obedience? He was always rightly related to the Father. If you walk in a consistent relationship with God, then you should never come to a time that you do not know His will. There should never be a situation in which you are not enabled by the Holy Spirit to carry out God's will.

In Jesus, we have the picture of a perfect love relationship with the Father. Jesus consistently lived out that relationship. You and I quickly conclude that we are a long way from that, but Christ is fully present in us to help us know and do God's will (see Galatians 2:20). We need to adjust our lives to God and faithfully live out that relationship with absolute dependence on Him. He will never fail to draw us into the middle of His purpose and enable us to do it — as He did for people throughout Scripture.

You, too, will be blessed when God does a special, God-sized work through you. You will come to know Him in a way that brings joy to your life.

Henry Blackaby and Richard Blackaby, in *Experiencing God*

Deeper with God

I had heard of you by the hearing of the ear, but now my eye sees you.
(Job 42:5, esv)

Perhaps the most valuable way we profit from adversity is in the deepening of our relationship with God. Through adversity we learn to bow before His sovereignty, to trust His wisdom, and to experience the consolations of His love. We begin to pass from knowing about God to knowing God Himself in a personal and intimate way.

In Philippians 3:10, Paul speaks of the fellowship of sharing in the sufferings of Jesus Christ, that is, of believers sharing with our Lord in His sufferings. Paul's goal, he declares, is this: "that I may know him and the power of his resurrection, and may share his sufferings, becoming like him in his death" (esv). This verse has given expression to the deepest heart cry of believers down through the centuries: the desire to know Christ in an ever-increasing intimate, personal way.

I can remember as a young Christian being challenged to "know Christ and to make Him known," and I can remember praying, because of Philippians 3:10, that God would enable me to know Christ more and more. I have to confess, though, that deep inside it always bothered me a bit that Paul not only wanted to know Christ Himself but also wanted to experience the fellowship of His sufferings. To know Christ in a more intimate way and to experience the power of His resurrection in my life appealed to me, but not the suffering. I shrank from that. But I've come to see that the message of Philippians 3:10 is a "package deal." Part of coming to know Christ in a more intimate way is through the fellowship of His sufferings. If we're to truly grow in knowing Christ, and to experience the power of His resurrection, we can be sure we'll experience the fellowship of His sufferings to some degree.

Jerry Bridges, in *Trusting God*

Easy Forgetfulness

They forgot his works and the wonders that he had shown them.
(Psalm 78:11, ESV)

Reflect, for a moment, on your past. Did it once fill you with a sense of excitement and thanksgiving that God had brought you to Himself, had set you free to serve and love Him? Did you once gratefully trace the steps by which you came to Christ, the different ways in which God taught you, the people He brought your way and through whom He molded you into what you are now?

Do you still reflect on God's grace in your life? Are you still conscious that being a Christian means experiencing the living touch of God on your daily life? Or have you, like the Israelites, failed to profit from the Lord's activity? Now life simply "happens," events and experiences come and go, almost indistinguishably. You no longer see the Lord's hand at work. You no longer sense yourself to be the child of a Father who is always teaching you, always disciplining you for His own glory.

The forgetfulness of the Hebrews is apparently a recurring syndrome for Christians as well. In the New Testament we come across the same symptoms, and the Christians need to be told, "In your struggle against sin you have not yet resisted to the point of shedding your blood. And have you forgotten the exhortation that addresses you as sons? 'My son, do not regard lightly the discipline of the Lord, nor be weary when reproved by him. For the Lord disciplines the one he loves, and chastises every son whom he receives.'" (Hebrews 12:4-6, ESV, quoting Proverbs 3:11-12). Here Old Testament and New Testament experience are the same. The writer recognized a diminishing level of commitment to holiness on the one hand, coupled with a forgetfulness of God's Word and a blindness to God's activity on the other.

Is that dismal plane of experience where you and I are?

Sinclair Ferguson, in *A Heart for God*

DON'T INTERPRET, BUT LEARN

Blessed is the man whom you discipline,
O LORD, and whom you teach out of your law.
(PSALM 94:12, ESV)

Because God's wisdom is infinite and His ways inscrutable to us, we should be very careful in seeking to interpret the ways of God in His providence, especially in particular events. Additionally, we need to be cautious of others who offer themselves as interpreters about the why and wherefore of all that is happening.

Be wary of those who say, "God let this happen so that you might learn such and such a lesson." The fact is we do not know what God is doing through a particular set of circumstances or events.

This doesn't mean we shouldn't seek to learn from God's providence. Quite the contrary. The psalmist learned God's decrees experientially through affliction (see Psalm 119:71). The people of Israel also learned through God's adverse providence in their lives, as Moses pointed out: "He humbled you and let you hunger and fed you with manna, which you did not know, nor did your fathers know, that he might make you know that man does not live by bread alone, but man lives by every word that comes from the mouth of the LORD" (Deuteronomy 8:3, ESV).

By putting His people in a situation where they could not simply go to the cupboard for their daily bread, God taught them that they were utterly dependent upon Him. God was leading the nation into a land where material provision would be "naturally" plentiful (see Deuteronomy 8:7-9). He knew they would be tempted by the pride of their own hearts to say, "My power and the might of my hand have gotten me this wealth" (verse 17, ESV). So before they entered the land, God taught them of their dependence through His divine providence.

Embracing such dependence ourselves, we'll often be able to say with the psalmist, "It is good for me that I was afflicted, that I might learn your statutes" (Psalm 119:71, ESV).

JERRY BRIDGES, IN *TRUSTING GOD*

From Resurrection to Work

Be steadfast, immovable, always abounding in the work of the Lord, knowing that in the Lord your labor is not in vain.

(1 Corinthians 15:58, esv)

The fifteenth chapter of 1 Corinthians, in its Divine revelation of the meaning of Christ's resurrection, gives us a living Savior who revealed Himself to His disciples on earth and to Paul from heaven. It secures to us the complete deliverance from all sin. It is the pledge of His final victory over every enemy, when He gives up the kingdom to the Father, and God is all in all. It assures us of the resurrection of the body, and our entrance on the heavenly life.

Paul had closed his argument with his triumphant appeal to Death and Sin and the Law: "O death, where is thy sting? O grave, where is thy victory? The sting of death is sin; and the strength of sin is the law. But thanks be to God, which giveth us the victory through our Lord Jesus Christ" (verses 55-57, kjv). And then follows, after fifty-seven verses of exultant teaching concerning the mystery and the glory of the resurrection life in our Lord and His people, just one verse of practical application: "*Therefore,* my beloved brethren, be ye steadfast, unmoveable, always abounding in the work of the Lord" (verse 58, kjv, emphasis added).

The faith in a risen, living Christ, and in all that His resurrection is to us in time and eternity, is to fit us for — to prove itself in — *abounding work for our Lord!*

It cannot be otherwise. Christ's resurrection was His final victory over sin, and death, and Satan, and His entrance upon His work of giving the Spirit from heaven and extending His kingdom throughout the earth. And those who shared the resurrection joy at once received the commission to make known the joyful news. The resurrection is the beginning and the pledge of Christ's victory over all the earth. The faith and joy of the resurrection life are the inspiration and the power for the work of doing it.

Andrew Murray, in *Working for God*

The Meek Man Knows

Take my yoke upon you, and learn from me, for I am gentle and lowly in heart, and you will find rest for your souls.
(Matthew 11:29, esv)

Rest is not something we do; it is what comes to us when we cease to do. Jesus calls us to His rest, and meekness is His method. The meek man cares not at all who is greater than he, for he has long ago decided the esteem of the world is not worth the effort. He develops toward himself a kindly sense of humor and learns to say, "Oh, so you have been overlooked? And now you feel hurt because the world is saying about you the very things you have been saying about yourself? Only yesterday you were telling God you were nothing, a mere worm of the dust. Where is your consistency? Come on, humble yourself, and cease to care what men think."

The meek man is not a human mouse afflicted with a sense of his own inferiority. Rather he may be in his moral life as bold as a lion and as strong as Samson; but he has stopped being fooled about himself. He has accepted God's estimate of his own life. He knows he is as weak and helpless as God has declared him to be, but paradoxically, he knows at the same time that he is in the sight of God of more importance than angels. *In himself, nothing; in God, everything*—that is his motto. He knows the world will never see him as God sees him, and he has stopped caring. He will be patient to wait for the day when everything will get its own price tag, and real worth will come into its own. "Then shall the righteous shine forth as the sun in the kingdom of their Father" (Matthew 13:43, kjv). He is willing to wait for that day. In the meantime he will have attained a place of soul rest. As he walks on in meekness he will be happy to let God defend him. The old struggle to defend himself is over. He has found the peace which meekness brings.

A. W. Tozer, in *The Pursuit of God*

How He Seeks Us

You have tried my heart, you have visited me by night,
you have tested me.
(Psalm 17:3, ESV)

Repeatedly in the Bible, we see men and women of God drawn into a deeper relationship with God through adversity. There's no doubt that all the circumstances in the long delay of the birth of Isaac and then the experience of taking his only son up to the mountain to offer as a sacrifice brought Abraham into a much deeper relationship with God. The psalms are replete with expressions of ever-deepening knowledge of God as the psalmists seek Him in times of adversity (see, for example, Psalm 23; 42; 61; 62).

You and I obviously do not seek out adversity just so we can develop a deeper relationship with God. Rather God, through adversity, seeks us out. It is God who draws us more and more into a deeper relationship with Him. If we're seeking Him, it's because He's seeking us. One of the strong cords with which He draws us into a more intimate, personal relationship with Him is adversity. If we'll seek to cooperate with God, we'll find that we'll be drawn into a deeper relationship with Him. We'll come to know Him as Abraham and Job and David and Paul came to know Him.

As we experience God's seeking of us through adversity, sometimes we'll be able to see how we are profiting from it, while at other times we'll wonder what God is doing. One thing we may be sure of, however: For the believer, all pain has meaning; all adversity is profitable.

There's no question that adversity is difficult. It usually takes us by surprise and seems to strike where we're most vulnerable. It often appears completely senseless and irrational; but to God, none of it is either senseless or irrational. He has a purpose in every pain He brings or allows in our lives. We can be sure that in some way He intends it for our profit and His glory.

Jerry Bridges, in *Trusting God*

ABOUNDING GRACE FOR ABOUNDING WORK

God is able to make all grace abound to you,
so that . . . you may abound in every good work.
(2 CORINTHIANS 9:8, ESV)

Every thought of abounding grace is to be connected with the abounding in good works for which it is given. And every thought of abounding work is to be connected with the abounding grace that fits for it.

Abounding grace has *abounding work for its aim.* Grace and good works are not at variance with each other. What Scripture calls *the works of the law, our own works, the works of righteousness which we have done, dead works* — works by which we seek to merit God's favor — these are indeed the opposite of grace. But they are also the opposite of the good works which spring from grace, and for which alone grace is bestowed. As irreconcilable as are the works of the law with the freedom of grace, so essential and indispensable are the works of faith — good works — to the true Christian life. God makes grace to abound that good works may abound. The measure of true grace is tested and proved by the measure of good works. God's grace abounds in us that we may abound in good works. We need to have the truth deeply rooted in us: Abounding grace has *abounding work for its aim.*

And abounding work needs abounding grace as its source and strength. Men may be diligent in doing religious work in their own strength, with little thought of that grace which alone can accomplish true, spiritual, effective work. For all work that is to be really acceptable to God, and truly fruitful — not only for some visible result here on earth, but for eternity — the grace of God is indispensable. Paul continually speaks of his own work as owing everything to the grace of God working in him: "I laboured more abundantly than they all: yet not I, but the grace of God which was with me" (1 Corinthians 15:10, KJV).

ANDREW MURRAY, IN *WORKING FOR GOD*

SICK AND SERVING

Those who are well have no need of a physician, but those who are sick. I came not to call the righteous, but sinners.

(MARK 2:17, ESV)

The difference between Uncle Sam and Jesus Christ is that Uncle Sam won't enlist you in his service unless you are healthy and Jesus won't enlist you unless you are sick. Christianity is fundamentally convalescence ("Pray without ceasing" [1 Thessalonians 5:17, KJV] = Keep buzzing the nurse). Patients do not serve their physicians. They trust them for good prescriptions. The commands of the Bible are more like a doctor's health prescription than an employee's job description.

Therefore, our very lives hang on not working for God. "To the one who works, his wages are not counted as a gift but as his due. And to the one who does not work but believes in him who justifies the ungodly, his faith is counted as righteousness" (Romans 4:4-5, ESV). Workmen get no gifts. They get their due. If we would have the gift of justification, we dare not work. God is the Workman in this affair. And what He gets is the trust of His client and the glory of being the benefactor of grace, not the beneficiary of service.

Nor should we think that after justification our labor for God's wages begins: "Did you receive the Spirit by works of the law or by hearing with faith? Are you so foolish? Having begun by the Spirit, are you now being perfected by the flesh?" (Galatians 3:2-3, ESV). God was the Workman in our justification, and He will be the Workman in our sanctification.

Religious "flesh" always wants to work for God (rather than humbling itself to realize that God must work for it in free grace). But "if you live according to the flesh you will die" (Romans 8:13, ESV). That is why our very lives hang on not working for God. Then shall we not serve Christ? It is commanded: "Serve the Lord" (Romans 12:11, ESV). Those who do not serve Christ are rebuked (see Romans 16:18). Yes, we must serve Him. But we will beware of serving in a way that implies a deficiency on His part or exalts our indispensability.

JOHN PIPER, IN *DESIRING GOD*

The Sacrament of Living

So, whether you eat or drink, or whatever you do,
do all to the glory of God.
(1 Corinthians 10:31, esv)

Paul's exhortation to "do all to the glory of God" is more than pious idealism. It is an integral part of the sacred revelation and is to be accepted as the very Word of Truth. It opens before us the possibility of making every act of our lives contribute to the glory of God. Lest we should be too timid to include everything, Paul mentions specifically eating and drinking. This humble privilege we share with the beasts that perish. If these lowly animal acts can be so performed as to honor God, then it becomes difficult to conceive of one that cannot.

Think of a Christian believer in whose life the twin wonders of repentance and the new birth have been wrought. He is now living according to the will of God as he understands it from the written Word. Of such a one it may be said that every act of his life is or can be as truly sacred as prayer, or baptism, or the Lord's Supper. To say this is not to bring all acts down to one dead level; it is rather to lift every act up into a living kingdom and turn the whole life into a sacrament. If a sacrament is an external expression of an inward grace, then we need not hesitate to accept the above thesis. By one act of consecration of our total selves to God, we can make every subsequent act express that consecration.

That we see this truth is not enough. We must practice living to the glory of God, actually and determinedly. By meditation upon this truth, by talking it over with God often in our prayers, by recalling it to our minds frequently as we move about among men, a sense of its wondrous meaning will begin to take hold of us. The old painful duality will go down before a restful unity of life. The knowledge that we are all God's, that He has received all and rejected nothing, will unify our inner lives and make everything sacred to us.

A. W. Tozer, in *The Pursuit of God*

Constant Care

He has said, "I will never leave you nor forsake you."
(Hebrews 13:5, ESV)

God wants us to firmly grasp the truth that whatever circumstances may indicate, we must believe, on the basis of His promise, that He has not forsaken us or left us to the mercy of those circumstances.

We never lose God's presence and help, but we may sometimes lose the sense of them. Job, in his distress, could not find God. He said, "Behold, I go forward, but he is not there, and backward, but I do not perceive him; on the left hand when he is working, I do not behold him; he turns to the right hand, but I do not see him." Then he added: "But he knows the way that I take; when he has tried me, I shall come out as gold" (Job 23:8-10, ESV). Job apparently wavered, as we do, between trust and doubt. Here he says he couldn't find God anywhere; God had completely withdrawn the comforting sense of His presence. But though he couldn't see Him, Job believed God was watching over him and would bring him through that trial as purified gold.

You and I will sometimes have the same experience as Job—perhaps not in the same kind or intensity of sufferings, but in the seeming inability to find God anywhere. God will seem to hide Himself from us. Even the prophet Isaiah said to God on one occasion, "Truly, you are a God who hides himself, O God of Israel, the Savior" (Isaiah 45:15, ESV).

We should learn from Job and Isaiah so that we are not totally surprised and dismayed when, in the time of our distress, we can't seem to find God. At these times we must cling to His bare but inviolate promise, "I will never leave you nor forsake you." God may hide Himself from our sense of His presence, but He never allows our adversities to hide us from Him.

Jerry Bridges, in *Trusting God*

Always a Test

You shall remember the Lord your God,
for it is he who gives you power to get wealth.
(Deuteronomy 8:18, esv)

Those who know their own hearts recognize how easily each of us may fall into the sin of pride and self-sufficiency, when God intends us to be humble and learn that our sufficiency depends upon Him.

Have affluence and prosperity proved to be a snare in your life? Jesus spoke of this danger in His parable of the sower and the soils. Some soil failed to produce fruit because of the presence of thorns, which Jesus interpreted to be "the cares of the world and the deceitfulness of riches and the desires for other things," which "enter in and choke the word, and it proves unfruitful" (Mark 4:19, esv).

God provides all we need, but we become obsessed by the gift rather than the Giver, and soon we think of His "gifts" as our "rights," as though we had earned them or deserved them. More and more we secretly desire to write across our lives, "I did it my way." And as a consequence we distance ourselves from the Lord, become insensitive to Him, and forget His grace.

Prosperity is a gift. It can be a blessing; *it is always a test.* That was what Moses urged the people to realize. Both adversity and prosperity have that function in our Christian lives. They test whether or not we have a commitment to the Lord that will help us see both those experiences in relation to Him. All Christians encounter one or the other. Most of us have regularly experienced both. Did you pass the test? Did your experience draw you closer to the Lord as you committed your way to Him? Or did you, like the Israelites, forget Him and become wrapped up in yourself—in either your problems or your achievements?

Will you face up to these issues, and make a fresh vow to the Lord that, with His help, through His grace, you will not go on forgetting Him?

Sinclair Ferguson, in *A Heart for God*

God's Wisdom Overrules Our Adversaries

Many are the plans in the mind of a man,
but it is the purpose of the Lord that will stand.
(Proverbs 19:21, esv)

God's wisdom is higher than the cunning of our adversaries. This should bring great comfort to us. We often find adversity from contrary circumstances easier to bear than that which comes from the hands of other people. David apparently felt this way; in 2 Samuel 24:14, he says, "I am in great distress. Let us fall into the hand of the Lord, for his mercy is great; but let me not fall into the hand of man" (esv).

People may scheme to treat us unjustly, take advantage of us, or "use" us for their own selfish ends. But Proverbs 21:30 says, "No wisdom, no understanding, no counsel can avail against the Lord" (esv). Therefore we can say in Paul's words, "If God is for us, who can be against us?" (Romans 8:31, esv). Even the most nefarious schemes of our adversaries can accomplish only what God has sovereignly ordained for us and in His infinite wisdom skillfully brings to pass.

When Saul sought to kill David, and David went into hiding, God used those months and years to build into David the character that made him a great king and a man after God's own heart. Many of his most meaningful psalms were apparently written during this time. One of my favorites, Psalm 34, was written when David was reduced to acting as an insane man for fear of a heathen king. Yet that's the psalm I most frequently turn to when I struggle with discouragement. What Saul meant for evil, God meant for good.

God's wisdom is greater than the wisdom of any of our adversaries, whether they be other people or the devil himself. Therefore we should not fear what they seek to do, or even succeed in doing to us. God is just as much at work in those things as He is in the adversities of sickness, death, financial reversal, and ravages of nature.

Jerry Bridges, in *Trusting God*

PREPARED FOR EVERY GOOD WORK

If anyone cleanses himself from what is dishonorable, he will be a vessel for honorable use, set apart as holy, useful to the master . . . ready for every good work.

(2 TIMOTHY 2:21, ESV)

Paul gives us four steps in the path in which a man can become a vessel unto honor in the great household of God. These are: cleansing (an intense desire to be cleansed from every sin lies at the root of fitness for true service); being sanctified (the refilling and being possessed of the spirit of holiness, through whom the soul becomes God-possessed, and so partakes of His holiness); the meetness for the Master to use as He will; and the spirit of preparedness for every good work.

We are vessels for our Lord to use. In every work we do, it is to be Christ using us and working through us. The sense of being a servant, dependent on the Master's guidance, working under the Master's eye — instruments used by Him and His mighty power — lies at the root of effectual service. It maintains that unbroken dependence, that quiet faith, through which the Lord can do His work. It keeps up that blessed consciousness of the work being all His, which leads the worker to become the humbler the more he is used. His one desire is to be meet for the Master's use.

It is not enough that we desire or attempt to do good works. We need training and care to be prepared. The word *prepared* means not only equipment, fitness, but also the disposition, the alacrity which keeps a man on the outlook and makes him earnestly desire and joyfully avail himself of every opportunity of doing his Master's work. As he lives in touch with his Lord Jesus, and holds himself as a cleansed and sanctified vessel, ready for Him to use, and he sees how good works are what he was redeemed for, and what his fellowship with his Lord is to be proved in, they become the one thing he is to live for. He is prepared unto every good work.

ANDREW MURRAY, IN *WORKING FOR GOD*

Sacred or Secular?

Whatever you do, in word or deed, do everything in the name of the Lord Jesus, giving thanks to God the Father through him.

(Colossians 3:17, esv)

One of the greatest hindrances to internal peace which the Christian encounters is the common habit of dividing our lives into two areas, the sacred and the secular. As these areas are conceived to exist apart from each other and to be morally and spiritually incompatible, and as we are compelled by the necessities of living to be always crossing back and forth from the one to the other, our inner lives tend to break up so that we live a divided instead of a unified life. Most Christians are caught in its trap. They cannot get a satisfactory adjustment between the claims of the two worlds. They try to walk the tight rope between two kingdoms and they find no peace in either. Their strength is reduced, their outlook confused and their joy taken from them.

I believe this state of affairs to be wholly unnecessary. We have gotten ourselves on the horns of a dilemma, true enough, but the dilemma is not real. It is a creature of misunderstanding. The sacred-secular antithesis has no foundation in the New Testament. Without doubt a more perfect understanding of Christian truth will deliver us from it.

The Lord Jesus Christ Himself is our perfect example, and He knew no divided life. In the Presence of His Father He lived on earth without strain from babyhood to His death on the cross. God accepted the offering of His total life, and made no distinction between act and act. "I do always those things that please him" (John 8:29, kjv) was His brief summary of His own life as it related to the Father. As He moved among men He was poised and restful. What pressure and suffering He endured grew out of His position as the world's sin-bearer; they were never the result of moral uncertainty or spiritual maladjustment.

This truth must "run in our blood" and condition the complexion of our thoughts, if we would escape from the toils of the sacred-secular dilemma.

A. W. Tozer, in *The Pursuit of God*

The Work of Casting Our Cares

Casting all your anxieties on him, because he cares for you.
(1 Peter 5:7, esv)

First Peter 5:7 is a very familiar passage of Scripture to many of us; in fact it seems too familiar. Let's go back then, and take a deeper look.

God cares for you! Not only will He never leave you — that's the negative side of the promise — but *He cares for you*. He is not just there with you, *He cares for you.*

His care is constant — not occasional or sporadic. His care is total — even the very hairs of your head are numbered. His care is sovereign — nothing can touch you that He does not allow. His care is infinitely wise and good so that again in the words of John Newton, "If it were possible for me to alter any part of his plan, I could only spoil it."[34]

We must learn to cast our anxieties on Him. Dr. John Brown says of this verse, "The figurative expression 'cast,' not lay, seems to intimate that the duty enjoined is one that requires an effort; and experience tells us it is no easy matter to throw off the burden of carefulness."[35] So we're back to the matter of choice. We must — by an act of the will, in dependence on the Holy Spirit — say something such as, "Lord, I choose to cast off this anxiety onto You, but I cannot do this of myself. I will trust You by Your Spirit to enable me to, having cast my anxiety on You, not to take it back upon myself."

Trust is not a passive state of mind. It is a vigorous act of the soul by which we choose to lay hold on the promises of God and cling to them despite the adversity that at times seeks to overwhelm us.

Jerry Bridges, in *Trusting God*

To God, as One Approved

Do your best to present yourself to God as one approved, a worker who has no need to be ashamed, rightly handling the word of truth.

(2 Timothy 2:15, esv)

A workman that needeth not to be ashamed is one who is not afraid to have the master come and inspect his work. In hearty devotion to it, in thoroughness and skill, he presents himself approved to him who employs him. God's workers are to give diligence to present themselves approved to Him to have their work worthy of Him unto all well-pleasing.

A workman is one who knows his work, who gives himself wholly to it, who is known as a working man, who takes delight in doing his work well. Such every Christian worker is to be — a workman who makes a study of it to invite and expect the Master's approval.

"Handling aright the word of truth." The word is a seed, a fire, a hammer, a sword; it is bread; it is light. Workmen in any of these spheres can be our example. In work for God everything depends upon handling the word aright. Therefore it is that the personal subjection to the word, and the experience of its power, is spoken of as the one means of our being completely furnished to every good work.

As one yields himself wholly and heartily to all this, and the true Spirit-filled word gets mastery of his whole being, he becomes a man of God, complete and furnished completely to every good work. He becomes a workman approved of God, who needs not to be ashamed, rightly handling the word of God.

And so the man of God has the double mark — his own life wholly molded by the Spirit-breathed word — and his whole work directed by his rightly handling that word.

Andrew Murray, in *Working for God*

THE LORD'S NEED OF OUR BODY

May your whole spirit and soul and body be kept blameless at the coming of our Lord Jesus Christ.
(1 THESSALONIANS 5:23, ESV)

That monkish hatred of the body which figures so prominently in the works of certain early devotional writers is wholly without support in the Word of God. Common modesty is found in the Sacred Scriptures, it is true, but never prudery or a false sense of shame. The New Testament accepts as a matter of course that in His incarnation our Lord took upon Him a real human body, and no effort is made to steer around the downright implications of such a fact. He lived in that body here among men and never once performed a nonsacred act. His presence in human flesh sweeps away forever the evil notion that there is about the human body something innately offensive to the Deity.

God created our bodies, and we do not offend Him by placing the responsibility where it belongs. He is not ashamed of the work of His own hands.

Perversion, misuse, and abuse of our human powers should give us cause enough to be ashamed. Bodily acts done in sin and contrary to nature can never honor God. Wherever the human will introduces moral evil we have no longer our innocent and harmless powers as God made them; we have instead an abused and twisted thing which can never bring glory to its Creator.

We need no more be ashamed of our body—the fleshly servant that carries us through life—than Jesus was of the humble beast upon which He rode into Jerusalem. "The Lord hath need of him" may well apply to our mortal bodies (Mark 11:3, KJV). If Christ dwells in us we may bear about the Lord of glory as the little beast did of old and give occasion to the multitudes to cry, "Hosanna in the highest" (Mark 11:10, KJV).

A. W. TOZER, IN *THE PURSUIT OF GOD*

Christ's Faith, My Faith

I have been crucified with Christ.
It is no longer I who live, but Christ who lives in me.
(Galatians 2:20, esv)

The faith by which Jesus Christ lived, His faith in God and His kingdom, is expressed in the gospel He preached — the good news that the kingdom rule of God is available to humankind here and now. His followers did not have this faith within themselves, and they long regarded it only as *His* faith, not theirs. Even after they came to have faith *in Him,* they did not share His faith.

Once, in the middle of the Sea of Galilee, the disciples' boat was almost beaten under by the waves while Jesus slept calmly. His disciples woke Him crying, "Save us, Lord; we are perishing" (Matthew 8:25, esv). Jesus reproachfully replied, "Why are you afraid, O you of little faith?" (8:26, esv). Now the disciples obviously had great faith in Jesus. They called upon Him, counting on Him to save them. But *they did not have His great faith in God.* It was because they did not have *His* faith that He spoke of how little faith they had.

Some Christians too commonly demonstrate that the notions of "faith *in* Christ" and "love *for* Christ" leave Christ *outside* the personality of the believer. One wonders whether the modern translations of the Bible are not being governed by the need to turn our weakened practice into the norms of faith.

Such exterior notions cannot provide the mutual abiding (see John 15:5) that causes us branches to bring forth much fruit and without which we can do nothing. It is as such abiding branches that we "we were reconciled to God by the death of his Son"; so that, "much more, now that we are reconciled, shall we be saved by his life" (Romans 5:10, esv).

Our additional life, though it is still our life, is also God's life in us: His thoughts, His faith, His love, all *literally* imparted to us, shared with us, by His word and Spirit.

Dallas Willard, in *Hearing God*

Giving Thanks Always

Give thanks in all circumstances;
for this is the will of God in Christ Jesus for you.
(1 Thessalonians 5:18, esv)

We're to be thankful in bad times and good times, for adversities as well as for blessings. All circumstances — whether favorable or unfavorable to our desires — are to be occasions for thanksgiving.

Thanksgiving is not a natural virtue; it is a fruit of the Spirit, given by Him. The unbeliever isn't inclined to give thanks. He may welcome circumstances that are in accord with his wishes and complain about those that are not, but it never occurs to him in either case to give thanks. If he sees life as anything beyond chance, he may congratulate himself for his successes and blame others for his failures, but he never sees the hand of God in his life. One of the most indicting statements in the Bible about natural man is Paul's charge that "although they knew God, they did not honor him as God or *give thanks to him*" (Romans 1:21, esv, emphasis added).

In his gospel, Luke tells the story of ten lepers who were healed by Christ (see Luke 17:11-19). All ten cried out to be healed, all ten actually experienced Christ's healing power, but only one came back to Jesus to thank Him. How prone we are to be as the other nine, quick to ask for God's help but forgetful to give Him thanks. In fact, our problem is far deeper than mere forgetfulness. We are imbued with a spirit of ingratitude because of our sinful nature. We must cultivate a new spirit, the spirit of gratitude, which the Holy Spirit has implanted within us at our salvation.

Thanksgiving is an admission of dependence. Through it we recognize that in the physical realm God "gives to all mankind life and breath and everything" (Acts 17:25, esv); while in the spiritual realm, it is God who, "when we were dead in our trespasses, made us alive together with Christ" (Ephesians 2:5, esv).

Jerry Bridges, in *Trusting God*

Trained for the Work of God

All Scripture is breathed out by God and profitable . . .
that the man of God may be competent, equipped for every good work.
(2 Timothy 3:16-17, esv)

Inspired is Spirit-breathed — the life in a seed, God's Holy Spirit is in the word. The Spirit in the word and the Spirit in our heart is One. As by the power of the Spirit within us we take the Spirit-filled word, we become spiritual men.

This word is given *for teaching,* the revelation of the thoughts of God *for reproof,* the discovery of our sins and mistakes *for correction,* the removal of what is defective to be replaced by what is right and good *for instruction which is in righteousness,* the communication of all the knowledge needed to walk before God in His ways.

It is the man of God who allows God's word to do its work of reproving and correcting and instructing in his own life who will be *complete, completely furnished unto every good work.* Complete equipment and readiness for every good work — that is what every worker for God must aim at.

You may feel as if you know not how or what to work aright. Fear not — all learning begins with ignorance and mistakes. Be of good courage. He who has endowed human nature with the wonderful power that has filled the world with such skilled and cunning workmen, will He not much more give His children the grace they need to be His fellow workers? Let the necessity that is laid upon you — the necessity that you should glorify God, that you should bless the world, that you should through work ennoble and perfect your life and blessedness, urge you to give immediate and continual diligence to be a workman completely furnished unto every good work.

It is only in doing we learn to do aright. Begin working under Christ's training. He will perfect His work in you, and so fit you for your work for Him.

Andrew Murray, in *Working for God*

Expect to Be Humbled

Humble yourselves, therefore, under the mighty hand of God . . . casting all your anxieties on him, because he cares for you.

(1 Peter 5:6-7, esv)

The immediate connection of the thoughts in 1 Peter 5:6-7 should be encouraging to us in times of adversity. On the one hand we're to humble ourselves under God's mighty hand — submitting with a spirit of humility to His sovereign dealings with us. On the other, we're to cast our anxieties on Him, convinced of His care.

The anxieties, of course, arise out of the adversities that God's mighty hand brings into our lives. We're to accept the adversities but not the anxieties. Our tendency is just opposite.

The way to cast our anxieties on the Lord is through humbling ourselves under His sovereignty, then trusting Him in His wisdom and love. Humility should be both a response to adversity and a fruit of it. Paul was clear that the primary purpose of his thorn in the flesh was to curb his tendency toward pride (see 2 Corinthians 12:7). If Paul had this tendency to pride, surely we do also. Therefore, we can put it down as a principle: Whenever God blesses us in any way that might engender pride in us, He'll also give us a "thorn in the flesh" to oppose and undermine that pride. We'll be made weak in some way through one or more adversities in order that we might recognize that our strength is in Him, not in ourselves.

We can choose how we'll respond to such a thorn in the flesh. We can chafe under it, often for months or even years, or we can accept it from God, humbling ourselves under His mighty hand. When we truly humble ourselves before Him, we'll in due time experience the sufficiency of His grace, for "God opposes the proud, but gives grace to the humble" (James 4:6, esv).

Jerry Bridges, in *Trusting God*

The Work of Grace

And I am sure of this, that he who began a good work in you will bring it to completion at the day of Jesus Christ.

(Philippians 1:6, ESV)

The New Testament knows both a *will* of grace and a *work* of grace. The former is God's eternal plan to save; the latter is God's "good work in you" (Philippians 1:6, ESV), whereby He calls men into living fellowship with Christ (see 1 Corinthians 1:9), raises them from death to life (see Ephesians 2:1-6), seals them as His own by the gift of His Spirit (see Ephesians 1:13-14), transforms them into Christ's image (see 2 Corinthians 3:18), and will finally raise their bodies in glory (see Romans 8:30; 1 Corinthians 15:47-54). It was fashionable among Protestant scholars some years ago to say that grace means God's loving attitude as distinct from His loving work, but that is an unscriptural distinction. For instance, in 1 Corinthians 15:10—"by the *grace* of God I am what I am, and his *grace* toward me was not in vain. On the contrary, I worked harder than any of them, though it was not I, but the *grace* of God that is with me" (ESV, emphasis added)—the word *grace* clearly denotes God's loving work in Paul, whereby He made him first a Christian and then a minister.

What is the *purpose* of grace? Primarily, to restore man's relationship with God. When God lays the foundation of this restored relationship, by forgiving our sins as we trust His Son, He does so in order that henceforth we and He may live in fellowship, and what He does in renewing our nature is intended to make us capable of, and actually to lead us into, the exercise of love, trust, delight, hope, and obedience Godward—those acts which, from our side, made up the reality of fellowship with God, who is constantly making Himself known to us. This is what all the work of grace aims at—an ever deeper knowledge of God, and an ever closer fellowship with Him. Grace is God drawing us sinners closer and closer to Himself.

J. I. Packer, in *Knowing God*

The Nerve Center

And this is the confidence that we have toward him,
that if we ask anything according to his will he hears us.
(1 John 5:14, ESV)

Separation from Jesus means sadness. Restoration of fellowship means joy. Therefore, we learn that no Christian can have fullness of joy without a vital fellowship with Jesus Christ. Knowledge about Him will not do. Work for Him will not do. We must have personal, vital fellowship with Him; otherwise, Christianity becomes a joyless burden.

In his first letter, John wrote, "Our fellowship is with the Father and with his Son Jesus Christ. And we are writing these things so that our joy may be complete" (1 John 1:3-4, ESV). Fellowship with Jesus shared with others is essential to fullness of joy.

The first reason, then, why prayer leads to fullness of joy is that prayer is the nerve center of our fellowship with Jesus. He is not here physically to see. But in prayer we speak to Him just as though He were. And in the stillness of those sacred times, we listen to His Word and we pour out to Him our longings.

Perhaps John 15:7 is the best summary of this two-sided fellowship of prayer: "If you abide in me, and my words abide in you, ask whatever you wish, and it will be done for you" (ESV). When the biblical words of Jesus abide in our mind, we hear the very thoughts of the living Christ, for He is the same yesterday, today, and forever. And out of that deep listening of the heart comes the language of prayer, which is a sweet incense before God's throne. The life of prayer leads to fullness of joy because prayer is the nerve center of our vital fellowship with Jesus.

Prayer is God's appointed way to fullness of joy because it is the vent of the inward burnings of our heart for Christ. If we had no vent, if we could not commune with Him in response to His Word, we would be miserable indeed.

John Piper, in *Desiring God*

Pray for Deliverance from Adversity

My Father, if it be possible, let this cup pass from me; nevertheless, not as I will, but as you will.
(Matthew 26:39, esv)

A spirit of humble acceptance toward God or forgiveness toward others does not mean we should not pray for deliverance from the adversities that come upon us. Scripture teaches just the opposite. A number of the psalms, for example, contain fervent prayers for deliverance from trouble. Most of all, we have the example of the Lord Jesus Himself and His prayer of deliverance in Gethsemane.

As long as the ultimate outcome of an adversity is in doubt (for example, in the case of sickness or a spiritually rebellious child), we should continue to pray, asking God to change the situation. But we should pray this in the same spirit as Jesus did—not as we will, but as God wills. We certainly must never demand of God that He change the situation.

We should also pray for deliverance from the attacks of Satan. Those attacks, like the injuries of other people or the calamitous events of nature, are under the sovereign control of God. Without God's permission, Satan cannot attack us or go beyond limits God has set (see Job 1:12; 2:6; Luke 22:31). We don't know why, in a specific instance, God allows Satan to attack us. But sometimes the reason is that we may engage in spiritual warfare—that we may "resist the devil" (James 4:7, esv).

We should pray for deliverance, and we should learn to resist the attacks of Satan in the power of Jesus Christ. But we should always pray in an attitude of humble acceptance of that which is God's will. Sometimes God's will is deliverance from the adversity; sometimes it's the provision of grace to accept the adversity. Trusting God for the grace to accept adversity is as much an act of faith as is trusting Him for deliverance from it.

Jerry Bridges, in *Trusting God*

What You Get

They remembered that God was their rock,
the Most High God their redeemer.
(Psalm 78:35, esv)

The solemn truth of the gospel is that, in spiritual things, you get what you set your heart on. Set your heart on knowing God and He will reveal Himself through His Word; set your heart on serving Him and you will not lack the opportunity to do so. But set your heart on nothing of spiritual consequence, and that is precisely what you will receive — *nothing of spiritual consequence.* Set your heart on your own ambitions, and they will, very likely, be fulfilled. God may give you your heart's desire. He did exactly that for his people in the wilderness. He saved them for His own sake and glory, and led them through the desert, yet "they soon forgot his works; they did not wait for his counsel. But they had a wanton craving in the wilderness, and put God to the test in the desert; *he gave them what they asked*, but sent a wasting disease among them" (Psalm 106:13-15, esv, emphasis added).

All that, despite Moses' warning to them: "And if you forget the Lord your God and go after other gods and serve them and worship them, I solemnly warn you today that you shall surely perish. Like the nations that the Lord makes to perish before you, so shall you perish, because you would not obey the voice of the Lord your God" (Deuteronomy 8:19-20, esv).

Think for a moment about where your life has led you thus far? What ambitions and aspirations have been fulfilled? Has the Lord given you many of the things you longed for — materially, personally, socially, professionally? But now, meditate on this: *Do you have the Lord Himself with these things, or do you have them without Him?* Have you forgotten the Lord?

The man or woman who has a heart for God will be someone who is determined to remember the Lord.

Sinclair Ferguson, in *A Heart for God*

A SWEET PAIN

Who shall bring any charge against God's elect? It is God who justifies. Who is to condemn? Christ Jesus . . . indeed is interceding for us.

(ROMANS 8:33-34, ESV)

Paul's questions in Romans 8:33-34 are rhetorical. When he asks who shall bring a charge against God's elect, he is saying, "Nobody dare!"

Our defense against the accusation of Satan is the gospel. He despises the gospel. He denies the gospel. He wants us to seek our justification somewhere other than in our Christ, who clothes us with His perfect righteousness. Satan will lay charges against us. He will condemn us. He will shout into our ears that our garments are filthy, that we are too sinful to ever be pleasing to a righteous God. But in Christ we say, "Begone, slanderer—who shall bring a charge against God's elect? My Savior has covered me. He has taken away my iniquity. He prays for me at this very moment. Cover your ears, devil, lest you hear the intercession of Christ for me. Christ is my righteousness. His merit is mine. Nothing can separate me from His love."

We please God when we resist temptation and do not sin. Certainly part of our maturing in the Lord is to do this more and more. But we do sin, and again and again, and as we grow in the Lord we become even more conscious of how many ways we can find to sin against God and others. But part of our growth is becoming more and more sure of God's acceptance of us. He does not save us because of our spotless lives, but because we are clothed in Christ's righteous garments. Our awareness of our sin is painful indeed, but it is a sweet pain that drives us into the arms of the loving Father. We please Him when we return to Him, something Satan the accuser does his best to prevent. When Satan whispers to the believer, "You, with all your sin, can't be pleasing to God," the believer replies, "Ah, but I am. To God be the glory."

R. C. SPROUL, IN *PLEASING GOD*

ZEALOUS FOR GOOD WORKS

Jesus Christ . . . gave himself for us . . . to purify for himself a people for his own possession who are zealous for good works.

(TITUS 2:13-14, ESV)

Christ *gave Himself for us,* He redeemed us *from all iniquity,* He cleansed *us for Himself,* He took us for a people, *for His own possession.* And all with the one object, that we should be a people *zealous for good works.* Christ expects us to be zealots for good works — ardently, enthusiastically devoted to their performance.

One thing that wakens zeal in work is a great and urgent sense of need. A great need stirs the heart and the will, rouses all the energies of our being. Christ needs urgently our good works. We are His servants, the members of His body, without whom He cannot possibly carry on His work on earth. The work is so great — with hundreds of millions unsaved — that not one worker can be spared. There are thousands of Christians today who feel their own business is urgent and must be attended to, and have no conception of the urgency of Christ's work committed to them. The Church must waken up to teach each believer this.

A second great element of zeal in work is delight in it. Once we give our hearts to it, and seek for the training that makes us in some degree skilled workmen, there is no greater joy than that of sharing in Christ's work of mercy and beneficence.

Then comes the highest motive, the personal one of attachment to Christ our Redeemer: "The love of Christ constraineth us" (2 Corinthians 5:14, KJV). This love, renewed in us by the renewing of the Holy Ghost day by day, becomes a zeal for Christ that shows itself as a zeal for good works.

"Zealous of good works!" Let us accept it as our calling. Let us be sure it is the very nature of the new life within us. Let us in faith claim it as an integral part of our redemption — Christ Himself will make it true in us.

ANDREW MURRAY, IN *WORKING FOR GOD*

Living in a God-Governed World

From the rising of the sun to its setting,
the name of the Lord is to be praised!
(Psalm 113:3, esv)

Going beyond our own personal circumstances, God's infinite wisdom —directing His sovereign power—governs the world.

As we look around us, it seems that much of the world is outside God's control and much of what happens makes no sense. But if we accept that God is sovereign, we must conclude that He's in control of all circumstances and is guiding them with His infinite wisdom to their appointed purpose. They're not just an assortment of uncontrolled and unrelated events. Rather, they're all part of God's perfect pattern and plan, which will one day be shown to be for both His glory and the good of His church.

We must learn to quiet our hearts in regard to God's government of the universe. We must come to the place where we can say, in the words of David, "I have calmed and quieted my soul" (Psalm 131:2, esv) about all the tragedies that come on mankind around the world.

This doesn't mean we're to become indifferent and callous to the tremendous amount of suffering that goes on around the world. We should pray for the victims of tragedies and, where opportunity permits, respond tangibly to the relief of their sufferings. But we can be compassionate without questioning God about His government of the world.

It is not only an irreverent act to question God's wisdom, it is also spiritually debilitating. We not only besmirch God's glory, but we also deprive ourselves of the comfort and peace that come by simply trusting Him without requiring an explanation. An unreserved trust of God, when we don't understand what is happening or why, is the only road to peace and comfort and joy. God wants us to honor Him by trusting Him, but He also desires that we experience the peace and joy that come as a result.

Jerry Bridges, in *Trusting God*

Sources

Blackaby, Henry, and Richard Blackaby. *Experiencing God.* Nashville: B&H Publishing, 1990, 2008. Used by permission.

Bridges, Jerry. *Trusting God.* Colorado Springs, CO: NavPress, 1988, 2008. Used by permission.

Colson, Charles. *Loving God.* Grand Rapids, MI: Zondervan, 1987, 1996. Used by permission.

Ferguson, Sinclair. *A Heart for God.* Carlisle, PA: Banner of Truth, 1987. Used by permission.

Murray, Andrew. *Waiting on God* and *Working for God.* Public domain.

Packer, J. I. *Knowing God.* Downers Grove, IL: InterVarsity, 1973, 1993. Used by permission.

Piper, John. *Desiring God.* Colorado Springs, CO: Multnomah, 1986, 2003. Used by permission.

Sproul, R. C. *Pleasing God.* Peabody, MA: Hendrickson Publishers, 1988. Used by permission.

Tozer, A. W. *The Pursuit of God.* Public domain.

Willard, Dallas. *Hearing God.* Downers Grove, IL: InterVarsity, 1984, 1999. Used by permission.

NOTES

1. A. H. Strong, quoted in Dallas Willard, *In Search of Guidance* (Ventura, CA: Regal, 1984), 91.
2. Richard Trench, *Synonyms of the New Testament*, Part Two (London: Macmillan, 1863), 85.
3. J. Edwin Orr, "The First Word of the Gospel" (unpublished essay), 1980.
4. Dietrich Bonhoeffer, *Cost of Discipleship* (New York: Macmillan, 1963), 45–46.
5. William Saroyan, *Rock Wagram* (New York: Seabury, 1951).
6. Augustine, quoted in John Blanchard, *Gathered Gold* (Welwyn, England: Evangelical Press, 1984), 332.
7. Philip E. Hughes, *Hope for a Despairing World* (Grand Rapids, MI: Baker, 1977), 40–41.
8. Charles H. Spurgeon, sermon at New Park Street Chapel, Southwark, London, January 7, 1855.
9. Charles Bridges, *An Exposition of the Book of Proverbs* (Evansville, IN: Sovereign Grace Book Club, 1959), 364.
10. Frederick B. Meyer, *The Secret of Guidance* (Chicago: Moody, 1997), 12.
11. Alexander Carson, *Confidence in God in Times of Danger* (Swengel, PA: Reiner, 1975), 55.
12. Philip E. Hughes, *Hope for a Despairing World* (Grand Rapids, MI: Baker, 1977), 18.
13. George MacDonald, quoted in J. R. Miller, "Finding One's Mission" (Swengel, PA: Reiner Publications, n.d.), 2.
14. John Calvin, *Institutes of the Christian Religion*, ed. John T. McNeill, trans. Ford Lewis Battles (Philadelphia: Westminster, 1960), 3.25.10.
15. William Wilberforce, *Real Christianity*, James H. Houston, ed. (Portland, OR: Multnomah, 1982), 87.
16. These words by Boris Kornfeld, a Russian Jew and doctor who converted to Christianity, were included in Kornfeld's story as related by Charles Colson in *Loving God* (Grand Rapids, MI: Zondervan, 1996), 27–36.
17. Thomas Lye, "How Are We to Live by Faith on Divine Providence?" *Puritan Sermons* 1659–1689 (Wheaton, IL: Richard Owen Roberts, Publisher, 1981), 1:374.
18. Lye, 1:374.

19. Carson.
20. Basil Manly Sr., *Southern Baptist Sermons on Sovereignty and Responsibility* (Harrisonburg, VA: Sprinkle Publications, 1984), 15–16.
21. Don Baker, *Pain's Hidden Purpose* (Portland, OR: Multnomah, 1984), 103.
22. Baker, 103.
23. G. C. Berkouwer, *The Providence of God* (Grand Rapids, MI: Eerdmans, 1983), 23.
24. Edward J. Young, *The Book of Isaiah* (Grand Rapids, MI: Eerdmans, 1984), 3:383.
25. William Hendriksen, *New Testament Commentary: Exposition of Ephesians* (Grand Rapids, MI: Baker, 1967), 102–103.
26. John Brown, *Expository Discourses on 1 Peter* (1848; reprint edition, Edinburgh: Banner of Truth Trust, 1975), 1:106.
27. Mother Teresa, quoted in Malcolm Muggeridge, *Something Beautiful for God* (New York: Harper and Row, 1971), 66.
28. Lina Sandell Berg, "Day by Day," 1865; translated by Andrew L. Skoog.
29. Nicholas of Cusa, *The Vision of God* (New York: E. P. Dutton, 1928), 17.
30. Madame Guyon, *Experiencing the Depths of Jesus Christ* (Goleta, CA: Christian Books, 1975), 16.
31. Margaret Clarkson, *Destined for Glory* (Grand Rapids, MI: Eerdmans, 1983), 19.
32. Horatius Bonar, *When God's Children Suffer* (New Canaan, CT: Keats Publishing, 1981; originally published as *Night of Weeping*), 31.
33. C. H. Spurgeon, *God's Providence* (Choteau, MT: Gospel Mission, n.d.), 19.
34. John Newton, *The Works of John Newton* (Edinburgh: Banner of Truth, 1985), 5:624.
35. John Brown, *Expository Discourses on 1 Peter* (1848; rpr. Edinburgh: Banner of Truth, 1975), 2:539.

Scripture Index

Topical Index

About the Authors

Henry Blackaby and his oldest son, **Richard Blackaby**, serve together in Blackaby Ministries International, traveling worldwide as Bible teachers. They wrote *Experiencing God* (with Claude King) in 1990. Henry Blackaby formerly pastored churches in California and his native Canada. Richard Blackaby pastored a church in Canada and served as president of the Canadian Southern Baptist Seminary. The Blackabys have also written *Spiritual Leadership* (2001) and a number of other books.

Jerry Bridges is a longtime staff member and former financial vice president of The Navigators. Besides *Trusting God* (1988), his many books include *The Pursuit of Holiness* (1978), *Transforming Grace* (1991), and *Respectable Sins* (2007).

Charles Colson served as President Richard Nixon's "hatchet man" before becoming a Christian in 1973. He served a seven-month prison sentence for obstruction of justice in 1974 and went on to found Prison Fellowship Ministries. He told the story of his conversion in *Born Again* (1976). He wrote *Loving God* in 1987.

Sinclair Ferguson is the senior minister of First Presbyterian Church in Columbia, South Carolina. He also teaches systematic theology at Westminster Theological Seminary in Dallas. He wrote *A Heart for God* in 1987.

Andrew Murray was a pastor and.Bible teacher in South Africa in the late nineteenth and early twentieth centuries. He wrote scores of devotional volumes; besides *Waiting on God* and *Working for God*, these also included *Abide in Christ*, *Absolute Surrender*, *The Deeper Christian Life*, and *The Spirit-Filled Life*. He died in 1917.

J. I. Packer taught theology in his native England before becoming a professor of theology at Regent College in Canada in 1979. He wrote *Knowing God* in 1973; his dozens of other books include *Evangelism and the Sovereignty of God* (1961), *Keep in Step with the Spirit* (1984), *Rediscovering Holiness* (1992), and *A Quest for Godliness* (1994). He also served as general editor of the English Standard Version of the Bible (2001).

John Piper is the pastor for preaching at Bethlehem Baptist Church in Minneapolis. He earlier taught biblical studies at Bethel University and Seminary in St. Paul. He has written more than forty books in addition to *Desiring God* (1986). These include *The Supremacy of God in Preaching* (1990), *The Pleasures of God* (1991), and *Don't Waste Your Life* (2003).

R. C. Sproul, theologian and pastor, is the founder and president of Ligonier Ministries. He has written expositional commentaries on John, Romans, and 1 and 2 Peter. Besides *Pleasing God* (1988), his numerous books include *Knowing Scripture* (1977), *The Holiness of God* (1985), *Chosen by God* (1986), and *What Is Reformed Theology?* (1997). He also served as general editor of the *Reformation Study Bible* (2005).

A. W. Tozer was a twentieth-century pastor, serving churches in the United States and Canada. Besides *The Pursuit of God* (1948), his books include *The Divine Conquest* (1950) and *The Knowledge of the Holy* (1961). He died in 1963.

Dallas Willard is a professor in the School of Philosophy at the University of Southern California. Besides *Hearing God* (1984), he also wrote *The Divine Conspiracy* (1998), *Renovation of the Heart* (2002), and numerous others.